And God Created the French

"A critical book, full of caustic observation and
irony. The author has succeeded in shaking us
up, gently but without complacence ... This
time, we have ourselves become the subject of
the anthropologist's curiosity."
　　　　　—Pierre Assouline, editor-in-chief of
　　　　　Lire Magazine, on the RTL radio network.

"... this book has been penned by a serious observer with a clairvoyant and judicious eye for
the truth. Reading Louis-Bernard Robitaille's
prose can sometimes make us squirm, but this
is also a very funny book, rich in stories and
anecdotes, and a faithful portrait of the French."
　　　　　—Jean-Marc Stricker, on the
　　　　　France-Inter radio network.

By the same author:

Erreurs de parcours, Boréal, 1982 (Montréal)
Paris, France, Boréal, 1989 (Montréal)
La République de Monte-Carlo, roman, Denoël 1990 (Paris)
Le Testament du Gouverneur, Boréal Compact, 1992 (Montréal)
Et Dieu créa les Français, Robert Davies, 1995 (Montréal-Paris)
Et Dieu créa les Français II - l'autre planète, Robert Davies, 1999
Le Zoo de Berlin, roman, Boréal 2000 (Montréal)
Planet France, Robert Davies, fall 2000, (Montréal-Paris)

Canadian Cataloguing in Publication Data

Robitaille, Louis-Bernard

And God Created the French
Translation of: Et Dieu créa les Français

ISBN 1-55207-028-X

1. French. 2. France–Civilization–1945-   . 3. Quebeckers. I.
Title

DC34.R6213 2000   944.083   C00-940033-8

*Interested readers may consult our permanent
and ever-evolving catalogue on the Internet at:*
http://www.rdppub.com

And God Created the French

by Louis-Bernard Robitaille

Translated by Donald Winkler

ROBERT DAVIES

MONTREAL–TORONTO–PARIS

ISBN 1-55207-028-X

Ordering information

USA/Canada
General Distribution Services
1-800-387-0141 / 387-0172 (Canada)
1-800-805-1083 (USA)

France/Belgium
CED-Dilisco
122, rue Marcel Hartmann
94400 Ivry
Tel. (01)49-59-50-50 Fax (01)46-71-05-06

Switzerland
Diffulivre
41, rue des Jordils
1050 Saint-Sulpice
Tel. 21-691-5331 Fax 691-5330

or from the publisher
Robert Davies Multimedia Publishing Inc.
330-4999, St. Catherine Street
Westmount, Qc H3Z 1T3 Canada
Tel. 514-481-2440 Fax 514-481-9973
mail@rdppub.com

The publisher wishes to thank the SODEC (Québec)
and the Canada Council for the Arts
for their generous support of its publishing program.

Table of Contents

Preface xiii
Foreword 7

I. The Uncertainty Principle

The Uncertainty Principle 13

II. Getting One's Bearings

1. Literary Overtures 31
2. Some Crucial Data 36
3. Good Manners 40
4. The "de" is Not For Burning 46
5. Louis XVI, The Discomfiting Ghost 51
6. The Spectre of the Count of Falloux 55
7. The War of Words 61
8. French Women, Try a Little Harder! 68
9. The De Gaulle Monument 73

III. Unease in "La Bonne Société"

1. The Serene Comfort of the "Bonne Société" 83
2. The Abolition of Money 90
   ARISTOCRATIC NOSTALGIA 90
   PHARAONIC 90
   AFFAIRS TO REMEMBER 107
3. The Demon of Literature 115
4. Cathodic Death Threats 123
5. In Mickey's Shadow 130
   THE MAGIC KINGDOM DRAWS NIGH: APRIL, 1991 130
   EURODISNEY, THE NEW CITY: APRIL, 1992 134
   THE HOUR OF GLORY: APRIL 12, 1992, 9:30 AM 138
   SCROOGE MCDUCK LAYS HIS CARDS ON THE TABLE:
   MARCH 20, 1994 141
6. Tomorrow We'll Dream in American 145

IV. The Portrait Gallery

1. The Devils 155
   THE DIVINE MARQUIS AND THE PATRON SAINT OF THE LUBERON 155
   CELINE, THE EVIL GENIUS 160
2. The Bizarre 165
   THE UNTOUCHABLE MONSIEUR BOULET 165
   LORD OF THE ANTS 170
   A MERCENARY IN BOSNIA 175
3. Irregulars 179
   VISIONS OF ADJANI 179
4. The Illustrious Nomads 186
   MICHEL LEGRAND: UMBRELLAS AND OSCARS 186
   LOUIS MALLE, GENTLEMAN TRAVELLER 194
5. Serene Perfection 202
   DENEUVE THE IMMACULATE 202
   ECHENOZ, A MODERN CLASSIC 209
   GIROUD, GRANDE DAME AND HONEST MAN 214

V. The Canucks and the Yanks

Discovering the Other Solitude 223
The Complete Exile 227
France and Voltaire's "Acres of Snow" 238
Céline Dion: The Cinderella of Show-Biz 246
The La Fayette Syndrome 250

VI. Enduring Enigmas

Enduring Enigmas 259
When the South Takes Over the North 267
Pockets of Resistance — Schifres' Law — 273

Preface

I have always dreamed of reading, for example, an anthropological study by an African professor concerning Belgian tribal feuds between the Walloons and the Flemish. My friend Louis-Bernard Robitaille, while no African himself, is undeniably closer to us culturally than I sometimes think we are to ourselves . . . and yet this "American cousin" of ours doesn't need to particularly torture his brain to cast on the enclosure we strangely call the "Hexagon" the eye of the famous Persian who was in a sense the "African" of Montesquieu in his famous *Letters*.

Because when all is said and done, one can never really do without a "Persian observer," in this case, a Canadian. And the Walloon from Liège would never have a true vision of the incomprehensible rituals of his own tribe until he caught its glimpse in the distant and knowingly hilarious appreciation of the African, who, alas! becomes anew the austere sociologist that he remains at heart when analyzing the criss-crossed customs and morality of the Bakongos and the Balubas.

We French must thank Robitaille for giving us this demystified image of ourselves as seen through his accurate personal lens, an image brimming with the irony born of well-deserved complicity. Thanks to him, our collective "us" has become, if only for a moment, a collective "them," inhabiting a space where rational complexity has been transformed into exquisite perplexity, revealing an "otherness" which is, and more than just a little, a highly accurate family portrait.

"Who am I? Where am I going, to what end do I err, in what state do I roam?" asks the humorist. Difficult to answer, except perhaps in the manner of Pierre Dac, who has been quoted as saying: "I am me. I emerge from my home and when my travels are done, back there I go!" Robitaille, in fact, describes us as a nation, a vast French tribal entity composed of thousands of clans grouped together into hundreds of hordes which, above and beyond the tribulations which mimic its constant metamorphoses, remains true unto itself, emerging from its own place in the world, and when its travels are done, thence returns.

So here we are, this curious people at once enslaved by its rituals and liberated by them, roped in by a super-hierarchical class identity, haunted by the daily rage to rend the straightjacket asunder and yet seduced by the indescribable pleasure of returning to its comfortable embrace in the evening, at battle's end. A slightly banal community, hirsute cavemen in its mind, stuffed shirts in reality, attached to its shrines as if they were lifebuoys, especially when the buoys take the form of the zinc counter of a bistro. France, which has never completely gotten over the fears and agitation of the Revolution, nor its cowardliness and the bitterness of the 1940 occupation by Hitler, regularly discards its Constitutions because it is incapable of reforming even its grammar, decapitates individually what it adores as a nation, calls for social democracy in order to better reinvent its hierarchically initiate but well-promoted evolution, believes itself to be and describes itself as extremist republican all the better to savor the most archaically sophisticated rules of social convention, conjures up a revolt or a revolution every so often only to find itself, once the dust has settled, again shackled with a French Academy in morning suits that knits together a dictionary as ridiculous as it is useless, with prefects who dress in navy officers' caps and ministerial cabinets rife with particle bureaucrats. Paradoxical France, whose clannish intelligentsia spat on the best television the world had to offer and settled, in the end, for the most idiotic, who waged war against Mickey Mouse and got Al Capone in his place, who showered the world with the most universal literature ever conceived, and then decided, as a consequence of the unpleasantness which this cultural imperialism brought home, to only talk through its navel, the better to ensure that what it had to say would no longer be of interest to anyone.

It is this France that our American cousin shows us in a brilliant looking-glass whose telling lens has been carved straight out of the far-off, the frozen, the mighty St. Lawrence River.

Jean-François Kahn

Foreword

If we are to believe the longstanding legend, France has been resented ever since its birth. All its European neighbors, to the north, to the east, even to the south, when they saw this new country in their midst, joined forces at once to pool their indignation and send emissaries before God to voice their complaints. To this single land, they said, God had granted everything: the Mediterranean Sea and the Atlantic Ocean, the fertile plain and the proud mountains, the sun of the south and the melancholy mists of the north, cooking with butter and cooking with oil, the inexhaustible subtleties of the most wondrous vineyards in the world and the conviviality of a land where beer flows freely. Was this his idea of divine justice?

God gave ear to this torrent of arguments, and in his heart of hearts admitted that on this occasion, yes, he had been overly prodigal. So to make up for those unfair benefits and bounties... God created the French.

And so the other Europeans went home, mollified. Justice had been done.

* * *

The anecdote may not be historically accurate. Some would call it a cheap joke that you can find just as easily on other continents - in Latin America its butt is the "arrogant" Argentinians. But it does reveal a certain cast of mind. Besides, the French readily own up to being "intolerable." Or rather, as a Parisian colleague told me recently, "they insist on denigrating themselves, whether in their own company or in front of foreigners, and declare themselves guilty of every fault in the book... even if deep down they don't believe it for a moment, and are convinced, in fact, that they're better than anyone else."

The French, who one must agree are the wittiest people in society (a bit like the Italians, but in a different, more *universal* way), spend an inordinate amount of time making fun of their own (supposed) shortcomings, their obsession with past grandeur, their congenital incapacity to succeed in business, their weakness in industry compared to the Germans, their historical fecklessness compared to the British, their sexual braggadocio, their preoccupation with food, their political and financial scandals, and their "shortfall in military grandeur since 1815," (to quote François Furet). When you have spent enough time with them, you come to appreciate that journalists of a certain repute, political figures, diplomats, can be extremely amusing company in a vein that is rather wicked, always intelligent, and never petty. And they are endowed with a virtue they derive, perhaps, from the historic and geographic centrality of France: an overall level of culture that largely exceeds the European norm.

Even if the French would be the first to say - without believing it - that they are impossible, the fact is that that's what other Europeans most often accuse them of. What Scandinavians, Italians, Germans and Spaniards tend to hold against them is their presumed *pretentiousness*. Seen from outside the French, as portrayed in the media or as casually encountered, seem like exalted emissaries of Louis XV, rather than ordinary citizens in the modern world. Of course, the same Europeans would probably say much the same thing about the British, whose national pride also seems out of proportion to their current status.

Both France and Great Britain were once great European nation states, each in turn dominated Europe for long periods during the eighteenth and nineteenth centuries, and (pending Berlin's rejoining the ranks), they boast the two major capitals on the continent. All of which makes it easy for their populations to behave atrociously toward each other, toward the "small" European countries, and even the "heavyweight" Germany. It's conceivable that the French and the English - consistently and often nastily at each other's throats - share what one might simply regard as an enormous superiority complex, which is harder and harder to justify as the glorious memories of Louis XIV and the Empire fade away.

These pretensions - which are in fact not all that overweening in day-to-day life - have the unfortunate consequence for the French (and similarly for the British) of earning them more than their share of sarcasm and criticism, all of which tends to belittle their importance (one does not reproach the Italians or the Spanish, or even individual Germans for having an exalted view of their country's historical stature).

France, by being much in the public eye, lays itself open to its critics. And the small francophone countries, whose only privilege (virtually) is to be able to criticize larger ones with impunity, are quick to unburden themselves of their little frustrations at the expense of the French - on the assumption that such a great nation would hardly take offence at low blows from little worms that decide to turn.

A mistake. The French, even as they strut their stuff on the international scene, are extremely thin-skinned and don't like to be criticized. Very often, diplomats posted to North America, or even ordinary journalists or travellers, will react bitterly to what is being said "over there" about their country, as if suddenly all the powers on earth were in league against a small and unhappy France, alone in the midst of barbarians. "I was very shocked by what the Swiss and Belgian journalists had to say about France on Polac's show," a veteran Parisian journalist confessed to me one day. A Frenchman on his high horse only proclaims his vulnerability all the louder. And I've always been rather taken aback by the cries of anguish emanating from the French when they've been publicly attacked for being haughty. Can you imagine someone treating the Americans, the Russians, or even the British with kid gloves?

One must bear all that in mind while reading or browsing this book. It's a gallery of portraits and snapshots, some never before published, others taken from articles written for *La Presse* and *L'Actualité*.[1] I've probably not made it clear enough that France is perhaps the most cultivated country in the west, where for many mysterious reasons the quality of life is at its most delightful, or all things considered, at its least disastrous; one can never say too much for the trains that arrive on time. There should be more here about women, and about the refined and diabolical bargain struck between the sulfurous south and the democratic and Protestant north: France is a mix of Mediterranean tortuousness and northern liberalism. On the other hand there's a lot about money, for one of the idiosyncracies of France is to deny its obvious dominion in an age of post-industrialization and unbridled capitalism. In this it is unlike Britain or Germany.

Ultra-conservative and therefore at times so revolutionary, defending - like England, China, and now the United States - its inalterable right to be universal in all things, France is a work of art, a precious gem, an anthropological curiosity, and a land long buffeted by the tumultuous and contrary winds of history. As she sometimes goes too far without really noticing, she is amazed at the nasty things people say about her. But these brickbats are by definition flattering, and they are aimed at a country that, even though in decline and impenitently unbearable, is still, at the end of the twentieth century, one of the three or four great cultural touchstones among nations.

---

1   Which are a major newspaper and the most important monthly magazine in Montreal, itself the largest city in Quebec.

I.
The Uncertainty Principle

The Uncertainty Principle

In *Pulp Fiction*, John Travolta, a hired killer who has just returned to the United States following a "posting" in Amsterdam, chats with a colleague about his European experience:

"You know what the funniest thing about Europe is?"

"What?"

"It's the little differences. I mean, they got the same shit over there that we got here, but it's just, just, there it's a little different."

"Example?"

McDonald's, it turns out, is one example.

"You know what they call a Quarter-Pounder with Cheese in Paris?"

"They don't call it a Quarter-Pounder with Cheese?"

"They call it a *Royale* with Cheese."

"What'd they call a Big Mac?"

"Well, Big Mac's a Big Mac, but they call it *Le* Big Mac."

A modest but invaluable lesson for anyone venturing into France. France with its traditions has undergone such upheaval over the last thirty years that on every corner, MacDonalds are displacing century-old eateries. Last spring, Place de la Bastille's remaining traditional *brasserie* was replaced by a huge and chaotic *Tex-Mex*. Has France, like Germany and Holland, become just another clone of North America? At certain hours of the day, you would almost think so. And then you realize that even a Big Mac, in Paris, is not *exactly* the same as an American Big Mac. It's like the trendy English vocabulary you find in France: *le pin's*, *le footing*, and other linguistic concoctions, that in fact represent a language found nowhere else, certainly not in any known dictionary.

Many similarities, then, and here and there tiny little differences that change everything, and at the same time almost nothing. That blur the image. Uncertain whether France is really and truly a different planet, the North American is constantly assailed by doubt and hesitation. When he lands in Paris for the first time in his life, he may very well see nothing out of the ordinary. After all, the French drive cars (they're small), use the telephone like everyone else (at long last), and even have freezers, though not air conditioners as yet. You can get fast food on every street corner. As for the historical monuments, they hold no surprises either; they look just like the postcards and the countless scenes from films you can see even deep in the Midwest. If he's there for three years, the same *homo americanus* risks falling into an even more dangerous trap: he *thinks he's understood* the true nature of Paris and of France, that he's isolated all the little features that distinguish them, subtly, from America.He makes the fatal error of thinking he'se got the hang of it! It will take him at least twelve or fifteen years of careful observation to return to his initial, very modest, and more legitimate position, something akin to Jean Gabin's "I know, I know..." which leads to a triumphant "I know that you can never know..." When you get right down to it, all you can say for sure about Paris (and France) is that whether or not it's on the same planet, it is a Land of Supreme Complexity, and you're kidding yourself if you think you can understand the French (even if, from time to time, it's possible to have the odd insight into one or two of them). Here the uncertainty principle must be invoked every hour of the day. Besides, after fifteen years you'll see that even the French don't really try to figure each other out; people from Brittany won't dare try to explain the natives of Nice, and vice-versa. They're also reluctant to probe the mysteries of their own deep selfhood. Are they primarily peasants from the interior, people of the plain, or Mediterraneans? Latins or Gauls? These basic questions provide fodder for endless speculation, itself often impenetrable, all year long in trendy papers and in the Paris publishing world. On a day to day basis, the Frenchman is happy to wear all hats at once: faced with the frivolous and disorganized Italian, he'll play the role of an efficient and sober northerner. Next to the industrious and awkward German, he'll present himself as the perfect *Latin lover*, sparkling in the salons and a virtuoso in bed.

You could almost say that no one understands anyone, and stop there. And the French are just as hopeless when they think they understand North Americans, except it's not the same kind of misunderstanding.

If North Americans, seen from France, seem unpredictable, it's because lacking deep roots (they cut all theirs when they crossed the ocean) they can from one day to the next change their sex, their religion, leave New York for Nebraska, give away their fortunes, become serial killers. Beneath an apparent conformism, anything and everything remains possible, as there are no great models from the past that command allegiance. Of course, a married accountant will likely continue to be a married accountant, and the director of a lesbian art gallery will wear her hair short. That's a simple matter of statistics. But to spin out of control is always a possibility, and nothing - to a Franco-European eye - will provide any hint that a mutation is in the works, or where it will occur or what its consequences will be. The French are made very uncomfortable by this lack of predictability.

What frustrates the curiosity of a North American where the French are concerned is not their unpredictability, but rather the complexity of what has gone before and made them what they are. What's complicated in France has nothing to do with confusion, or anything random. If the country is virtually impossible for a foreigner to understand, that is not because it is incoherent, but on the contrary because everything has been determined by a profusion of influences that overlap, interconnect, and blend into each other.

The differences among the French do not arise from any transgression of society's overall rules, any abrupt departures or mutations, but rather from the fact that the French scrupulously conform to their own personal code, history, and roots, which subdivide ad infinitum. The controlling influences are both geographical and historical; they spring from countless regions or French towns and villages (some 36,000 communes), each with its own history going back ten or twenty centuries, where one finds, piled one on top of the other, Gallo-Roman, Merovingian, Cathar, Protestant, Chouan, Jewish, Anarchist, Republican and Jansenist strata, and more. The problem in dealing with a given Frenchman is not any difficulty in determining his future (that was largely taken care of at the time of his birth), but the impossibility of ever assimilating all the data - there's no end to it - regarding his origins and his roots. The French are not hard to fathom downstream; they are complex and mysterious upstream. If only one could gather together all the relevant information and plug it into a powerful, appropriately programmed computer, one would be able to accurately determine each individual's motivations, and plot out his personal and professional path within a scientifically acceptable margin of error.

*   *   *

With a few exceptions, the most obvious being Manhattan, North-American cities are not really complicated; they're young, simply designed, functional and easy to decode. One level of urbanization sweeps away the last, the opposite of what happens in Paris, where they are superimposed. The only sensible approach to Paris is to assume that it is, ultimately, inscrutable.

Seen from above Paris is like a giant automaton, where every morning at the same hour tens of thousands of moving parts come to life and assume once more the roles that have been permanently assigned to them: the ballet of garbagemen and postmen at the crack of dawn; dreary traffic jams as upper and middle managers advance from the west; gendarmes and policemen taking up their posts at predetermined intersections; cafés opening at 6 o'clock, cafés opening at 7:30, cafés not opening until 9; train stations disgorging their floods of commuters.

At least twice a week, early in the afternoon, the police make routine preparations for a demonstration that will take place between Place de la République and the Bastille. In some cases, shopkeepers will have taken the precaution of lowering their iron shutters for the duration of the event. But not always. On Boulevard Beaumarchais, where it joins the square, the ladies in uniform at the venerable pastry-shop B*** talk of this latest parade with resigned irony: "So who's marching today? We don't even try to keep track any more." The procession of protesters and the traffic jam that goes with it start right on time, with a green armada of Paris street cleaners bringing up the rear. After which the routine anarchy of the boulevard reasserts its rights. Paris is a long-running spectacle of teeming humanity that ought to degenerate into total chaos, but is in fact perfectly planned and runs like clockwork. Two, three, five million people know just where they belong in this well-proportioned toy - nine kilometres by fifteen. But there are so many different parts to the mechanism that it's folly to think one can take in or grasp the whole picture. The only viable approach is one of confirmed doubt and uncertainty; we can identify and observe the toy's gears and wheels, but we can never assimilate it as a whole.

Even if we restrict ourselves to a specific neighborhood and its day-to-day activities, we must be prudent and learn to live with our perplexities. Take for example the Bastille, and some of its most ordinary and down-to-earth institutions: its cafés, its newsstands, its bakeries. It doesn't matter if you have lived there 15 years, what you in fact come to realize after all that time is that the closer you get, the more byzantine its micro-reality turns out to be.

The newsstands, for instance - the real ones - are particularly numerous on this square: there are five or six, depending on how you count. Having patronized most of them over the years, I've been vaguely conscious of a rather curious ballet, conducted to all appearances according to rules that are strict but impenetrable to the uninitiated. It's a bit like the mating ceremonies of wild animals that you see late at night on television: you know something rigorously choreographed is going on, but you can't make out the moves or the code unless they are explained to you in patient detail. I don't know if running a newsstand is a marginal, comfortable, or very lucrative operation, or if it all depends on where you're located; I've seen some manned all day long by one person, others that seem to be run (more or less) in tandem, and others that appear to support a whole family quite happily (in some cases it would take a Lévi-Strauss, at the very least, to unearth the *elementary structures* of this kind of kinship). The kiosks have changed hands over the years, but with no particular pattern: some managers have stayed put for a long time, others have made a brief appearance and then vanished. I have seen them move from one location to another, on the next sidewalk, without knowing if this meant a promotion or a decline in status. Another newsdealer whom I had come to know turned up mysteriously on Avenue Victor-Hugo, where I encountered her entirely by accident. "I can't tell you what a pain it is here," she declared. "Such snobs! Unbearable! Ah, I really miss the Bastille." How had she ended up on Avenue Victor-Hugo? A few years later I ran into her on the Place du Colonel-Fabien; she still didn't seem very happy. "But I'm a candidate for the Bastille," she added, with a touch of nostalgia, but also with the common man's deference and modesty vis à vis real power.

Did she say *a candidate*? The word threw me into a quandary. I have to admit that, despite a bit of casual research into the question, I have absolutely no idea what mysterious system controls the 360 newsstands in the city. Or what subtle ballet the dealers dance, who are the lords of their profession. I know that a terrifying "parity commission" assigns the kiosks, but I haven't the slightest notion of what lies behind this very French title, whose intent is to be reassuring. I suppose the distributors must be involved, because they are wherever there is printed matter; the publishing union, to a degree, because there's no getting around it; perhaps also the Paris City Hall, because nothing human is foreign to the Paris City Hall when it's a matter of doling out jobs to clients and friends. In practice, it must be as dangerous for an outsider - someone not already a member of the clan - to force his way into this profession, as for a panhandler to set up shop at the entrance to a fancy Parisian restaurant or for a Hong Kong businessman to thumb his nose at the various local Triads. To get a foothold in the trade, I'm sure it's not enough to satisfy the official criteria of excellence - if such exist - that the afore-mentioned commission lays down; you have to be allowed into the family, perhaps recruited. The Paris newsdealers certainly do seem to be a family; along with the motorbike couriers and taxi-drivers, they are the last incarnation of popular Paris. Almost always true Parisians, ironic, grouchy, shrewd, they are often outspoken on world affairs, as well informed on what's happening in their neighborhood as in the hinterlands of Chechnia, and while hostile to the bourgeois they are cynical about politics.

The newsdealer is one of the many constituents of Paris, which is like a Rubik's Cube for which no one has the solution. Not even native Parisians. But in their case it doesn't matter, because they belong to the Cube and are a natural part of its functioning.

Take the bistros. For you, a foreigner, they are certainly not all interchangeable. Between the grand *brasserie* that sits majestically on the square with its trained waiters in regulation dress, and the *bar-tabac* on the street-corner with its tiny sidewalk terrace, formica tables and odors of Gauloise and Clorox, there can be no confusion. But at first sight they are all just Parisian bistros, with their mandatory hard-boiled eggs in a little carousel on the counter, and their cigarette butts ground into the floor. In fact, if you take a closer look, and take your time about it, you realize that they're almost all different from one another, subtly or radically different. Each has, not just its own habitués, but its own *population*. It's not only that the indigenous Parisian is set in his ways and has his favorite bistro, but that, for reasons that are beyond your grasp, he will *never* go into other cafés. What you dimly sense to be a certain kind of bistro, the Parisian-born will immediately identify as a place with a bad reputation - *unpleasant*, or *snobbish*, or *tacky*, or *old*. The population of café B***, middle-class with vaguely smart pretentions, will never cross paths with the population of F***, much more simple. At B*** a lunch table is set aside for the dentist on the corner; at F*** the carpet-layers and couriers empty glasses of beer at the counter, and leave messages for the owner to pass on to "Jean-Yves." Diagonally across the boulevard, you're more likely to run into marketing people, and sales reps driving Audis equipped with car-phones. Farther on there is a rather marginal café that has always had a *bad name*, despite its many renovations and the turnover in its clientele. Even when it changes its furnishings and its decor, an old Parisian bistro never manages to rid itself of the ineffable spirit of place that haunts it or escape its class destiny. The bistro where, during the 1930s, the Henry Miller of the *Tropics* hung out occasionally to sample its hookers, will always bear that invisible stamp. At least until the day it's bought up by some truly modern establishment, a fast-food outlet or a chain of steak houses, or even wine bars; these new entities have no identifiable clientele, you meet there whoever turns up or anyone at all, and find yourself bathed at last in a serene and absolute anonymity, with nothing French about it. There are no codes to be broken or problems to be solved when you make a hurried pit-stop at a Macdonald's or a Hippopotamus. It's all perfectly slick, neutral, functional, occasionally restful, always utterly bland.

Something else I don't know is how much a baker earns who, if he makes his own bread, must work a schedule that would seem more appropriate to ancient Rome. There's one in my neighborhood whom you would take to be an agricultural worker from the south of France, and his wife to be someone on welfare. The other day I saw them come out of their bakery and climb into a sparkling new Audi. I didn't assume from that that they were rich, but my perplexity blossomed anew.

*   *   *

In France there are an infinite number of rituals, customs and codes of behavior that you must grasp, assimilate, and respect to the letter if you want to live in society. North America, by comparison, is almost virgin territory, where you can - with rare exceptions - greet people, meet people, dress, and behave however you want. The social system there, even in a very structured milieu, is so loose that it resembles the current European monetary system, which allows for fluctuations of fifteen percent one way or the other. You have to go pretty far to make a mistake or commit a faux-pas that will compromise your future.

All French society is codified to the last detail, as much as in

Italy, and much more than in northern Europe. This is true in the countryside, where it's very easy to make a gaffe. It's even more true in the large provincial cities, Brest, Bordeaux, Lyon or Marseille, and the closer you get to the Meditteranean, the more complicated it becomes. But in Paris this codification attains new heights of intensity and complexity, as it includes all the local refinements. Greater Paris has a population of about ten million, ten or twenty times that of the largest provincial cities; it's on a totally different scale. This population, historically, has always lived in close proximity to absolute power (for something like a thousand years) and has acquired, as a result, certain distinctive traits: sycophancy, a muddled anarchism or a taste for regicide, corrupt practices. Today Paris is home to all who wield absolute power, in every possible domain. In the provinces, your quest for the powerful does not take you very far; once you've met the deputy mayor, the archbishop, the prefect, perhaps the director of the opera (if there is one), you've done the "corridors of power" and you can go home for a nap or think about your retirement. In Paris there are ten or fifteen important ministries, with their ministers and their private secretaries. There are all the great names in television, cinema, show business, banking, industry, not to mention the greatest concentration anywhere in the world of the international jet-set, lodged at the Ritz, the Plaza-Athénée, and the like. One could spend three lifetimes exploring each of these micro-societies, especially since they all naturally have their own codes, customs, behavior and vocabularies. Not only that. The nuclei of all these different powers-that-be consist of people from all parts of the country representing all the French tribes - and some from abroad - and while they are recast in the Parisian mould, they bring with them a residue of their native ways. The result: Paris is a jungle of codes and signifiers, a landscape teeming with impenetrable enigmas. How to behave properly in such circles and under such conditions? How to know, first of all, where exactly you are and to whom you are talking? If the riddles and options are already legion in Bordeaux, they are mind-boggling in the capital, where every step can be a faux-pas, and where, amid the apparent confusion, newcomers must try to pick out certain coded expressions, little signals shared among initiates.

What is unique to Paris (it doesn't exist in the provinces) is that everyone here is constantly alert for transgressions to the code. It allows you to put to the test someone you are chatting up, detect the non-Parisian, take the high ground. The practice is not primarily directed at foreigners who can barely mumble a bit of French; these are the tourists that you can spot a mile off, and you just rough them up and shake them down a bit as they pass, without wasting much time making fun of them. The real prey are the francophones: Belgians, Quebeckers, foreigners who have put down roots and speak fluent French, and most of all the provincials with little experience of the capital.

All visitors, even the slowest on the uptake, have noted the Parisian inclination, either to pretend not to understand an expression that is perfectly comprehensible but that departs slightly from the norm, or to take the speaker to task for the fault committed, even if no misunderstanding ensued. For example, a tobacconist, after a painfully obvious moment of feigned perplexity, will respond to a client who has asked for Marlboro *légères*: "Ah! You want Marlboro *light*!" And just try to ask for an *"avance de fonds"* on your credit card at the local bank, where the employees are hardly multilingual: "Ah, no, I'm afraid we don't do that." Then, after some reflection and consultation: "Ah! You mean a *cash advance*!" Apart from the garden-variety snobbery involved in lacing one's conversation with a few words of Paris's inimitable *franco-anglais*, there is the exquisite pleasure to be found in manipulating the code perfectly oneself, while exposing the abysmal ignorance of the person one is talking to. Language in Paris is not first and foremost a tool of communication; it's an arena of self-affirmation, social differentiation, and perennial combat. The Parisian takes great pleasure in relegating his interlocutor to the status of non-Parisian, hick, know-nothing, who asks for an *expresso* (and not an *express*) or a Perrier with lemon (rather than a *rondelle*). Not to mention the countless errors in vocabulary committed by foreigners with some experience of Paris who, thinking they've got the hang of it, try their hand at the latest slang or the lingo. It's a very dangerous exercise, as the lexicon is always in flux, the changes unpredictable: an expression that was fashionable in 1993 can have fallen into total disrepute a year later, and you find yourself once and for all branded as a hopeless fuddy-duddy. If all this takes place around the dinner table - or at a cocktail party - there is sure to be someone ravishingly worldly to say, with a suave smile: "Ah! They say that *chez vous*?" Or even better: "They *still* say that *chez vous*?" (The *chez vous* in question can be the provinces, Quebec, or Belgium. Whatever, it still means "your neck of the sticks.") Of course, the codes are so varied and complex that no one is immune to errors, not even the most hardened and knowledgeable Parisian. His technique - tried and true - is first to be prudent at all times, not to stray too far from the beaten path, and to watch for someone else to make a mistake on which he can pounce. But if, despite everything, in a moment of inadvertence a fault is committed, the true Parisian will choose to brave it out with style, to bluff, to persist in his error, either to pretend that it was all done deliberately as a joke, as a provocation, or to convince his adversary that it's *no longer* a mistake (hasn't been for a week, a day, a month). The rule of thumb in true Parisian society, whatever your origin or class - even in the direst of circumstances, or perhaps then above all - can be summed up in the words of the murderer Landru, as he was being led off to the guillotine: "Never confess!"

* * *

If you take up residence in Paris you will soon notice that people are highly attentive to the social gaps that mark them off from each other, and spend considerable time trying to place each other and be placed.

A caricature of the North American would be someone who, when he wants to introduce himself, pulls out his visiting card and recites his curriculum vitae, his professional status, and the state of his finances. In Paris, everything is and must be implied by the way one behaves, one's terms of politeness, one's vocabulary, and one's cultural and worldly references. Someone really important - but who has not been introduced as such - will never stoop to giving you a rundown of his achievements; instead he will take pains - no, he will take pleasure - in sprinkling his conversation with little gems that, put end to end, get the message across quite clearly. The game is played that way because only rubes, parvenus or crooks flaunt their power or their fortune (or have showy cars and clothes). Also because with the indirect approach, you can discern whether your opposite number is a rustic or a true initiate.

And so in Parisian society there are countless little signals that enable people from the same milieu to pick each other out in a crowd, and to exclude those who would like to penetrate the inner sanctum. The signs are as varied as they are subtle: dress, vacation spots, books read, plays, films, and exhibitions seen, people met (whose names are slipped into the conversation at opportune moments). In a salon Mr. S*** can be perfectly polite for as long as it takes to put Mr. W** to the test, and set him a few traps. If he falls into them, Mr. S*** will remain very correct, but a subtle shift in the tone of his voice will tip off an initiate that he wants nothing more to do with this Mr. W**, who may henceforth be considered of negligible interest. If you attend dinner or cocktail parties, and have made a long enough study of all these subtleties, you will eventually be able to recognize or sense the almost limitless palette of intonations and polite expressions: all the forms of obsequiousness that inferiors employ with their superiors; the tone of serene, or blunt, or feudal superiority on the part of the truly powerful; the false familiarity that often implies utter contempt, and has nothing at all to do with genuine simplicity; the impromptu introduction of vulgarity that can be a means to forging a certain complicity, or of banishing you once and for all from the charmed circle; the light irony, which can equally be a mark of sympathy or frank dislike.

In North America, not only is it hard to make a gaffe, but most of the time it really doesn't matter. Someone who doesn't know how to behave himself in society, or who dresses very badly - and in both instances you have to go pretty far - will not be judged on that basis. In France you'd better not walk the city in a sloppy raincoat, or in clothes that are too new, or shiny, or showy, like the North-American yuppies on American television. Not only will you expose yourself to a poisoned barb from some beauteous sophisticate, who will exclaim, "Oh, a brand new suit, how nifty!", but you'll be slotted indelibly, if invisibly, into a low-grade category. You should also avoid appearing in trendy establishments with a young lady on your arm who is boringly plain, or you'll hear it commented on, cruelly, at regular intervals for months on end, and the headwaiter the next time round will give you a table near the washrooms at the back. You'd be better off, in fact, turning up with an old lady or a woman who's spectacularly ugly, in which case people will think you're stepping out with a relative (always a commendable gesture in this country with its sense of family), or possibly a literary editor.

In America, people long ago dispensed with the social nightmare of formal address. It doesn't exist. In theory, *you* is equivalent to the formal French *vous*, and it's the *tu* (*thou*) that has vanished from the scene. So everyone says *vous*, from Liverpool to Miami. But if you ask me, in England it's still all formal except in very special cases, while in America it's anything but. In the States, questions of protocol don't come up except with the Chief Justice of the Supreme Court and the President himself. And even then. One *Mister President* and you've done your duty, and then you can go on to *Yes, Bill*, and *You're darn right, Ronny*.

Not only does formal address exist in France, but it's still employed with much more rigor than in Spain and Italy, for example (and doubtless Germany). Crude and blatant errors in this domain are very much frowned upon. And the ongoing game of *vous* and *tu* provides new opportunities to underline social differences. You can say *vous* out of politeness and respect, but also with contempt, to mark your distance. There are people who, after having said "Let's say *tu*, now we're friends," will keep backsliding, excusing themselves with an ingratiating smile: "It's funny, but I don't seem able to call you *tu*." There is the inappropriate *tu* on the part of the rich businessman who thinks he will make inroads into fashionable circles by being casual with everyone: he risks being sorely disappointed. Take the example of the late president François Mitterand, who, in all his years of public life never allowed himself to be addressed as *tu* except by a handful of intimates. One day he was approached by an official in the

Socialist Federation: "So, Comrade Mitterand, shall we say *tu* or *vous*?" The famous reply: "Comme **vous** *voudrez...!*" ("As **you** *wish*.") There are also the persistent tactics of café waiters or owners - if you're a regular customer - designed to lure you into the murky waters of familiarity. The deluxe treatment, reserved for brasseries and their terraces, gives you the benefit of both *vous* and *Monsieur*. Then, a little later - or in a neighborhood café - you'll only get *vous* or *monsieur*. At the counter, which is reserved for regulars - almost always male - informality is the order of the day. You'll still hear *vous*, but prefaced by some ironic salutation (Young man! The Canadian! or simply Eh! Canada! Or: The American! Or again: Chief! Boss!). Next comes the famous *he*, a kind of linguistic no man's land where the *vous* that you were no longer exists, and the *tu* has not yet come into force, but that is an unmistakable move in the direction of greater intimacy: "And what is HE having today?" That's the point at which you can still back off without really offending your opposite number; you just pretend not to have heard the come-on. Afterwards, it's too late: you don't go back on a *tu* that's been offered and agreed upon, and a return to *vous* is considered, often rightly, as a declaration of cold war.

The handshake is another nightmare. Even in Italy, a country where everything is complicated, you don't find this precise ritual; the Italians greet each other by shaking hands, but also by patting cheeks, pinching cheeks, resting a friendly hand on a shoulder. In France, a population of 58 million people (minus small children and paralytics) spends entire days shaking hands. At least that's what it looks like to North Americans passing through, mesmerized by the spectacle of someone coming into an office or a bistro and shaking the hand (or kissing both cheeks twice, as has been the practice in Paris now for some years) of each of the eleven people present. So that the North American who settles in Paris and wants to do the right thing - or, woe is he, thinks to pass for a Frenchman - tries all day long to apply what he believes is a simple, universal law. Anywhere at all and no matter what, he shakes the hand of every Frenchman in his path, including café waiters, shopkeepers, and little old ladies. This earns him either a little surprised reaction of shock or amusement, or a diplomatic smile, like that accorded by the Chinese when you hit the wrong pitch.

Because there's the rub: the French spend a lot of time shaking hands, but even more managing not to do so. In his brasserie of choice, a Parisian will sooner or later shake the hand either of the headwaiter or of his usual server - but under no circumstances all the staff. With young ladies, the code is not absolutely strict but is even more unforgiving: you generally shake hands in a professional setting, but not necessarily; at a cocktail party or on an evening out it depends on the circumstances, the atmosphere, mutual rapport. In every case, to abstain is completely unthinkable and unacceptable. But to shake hands indiscriminately will make you a laughing stock; it's a mistake that will be forgiven a foreigner the first time round (or for the first five minutes), but beyond that will be held against him. People will say, "He's so refreshing! So natural! So rustic!" Don't take it for a compliment.

It certainly can be discouraging: what with this plethora of rules, both shifting and extremely strict, it's impossible to live one's life without stumbling, or at the very least making a lot of missteps. Even some hardened Parisians trip up now and then (others, never: since I've known them, they've always been impeccably dressed, have adopted just the right tone with everyone, have played in every key with equal virtuosity, have known everything that had to be known, and have never once been caught mouthing tiresome platitudes.) Remember Landru, and keep in mind that the worst violations of the code can be gotten away with if you just have the nerve.

When in doubt, keep a low profile (but stay alert), and play a defensive game. Watch how foreigners behave who are familiar with Paris. Some are much better at blending into the landscape than others, or at any rate are more naturally at ease. They pick up one local trait, ignore another, never try to pass for a native, and above all show the poise that will sometimes win respect all on its own. They are often Argentinians, Brazilians, or if (rarely) Americans, they are invariably New York Jews. Foreigners with a real gift for adapting to Paris have their own legacy of complex codes (from Mediterranean or Asiatic countries, but not Scandinavia or Holland, and North America even less), or codes impossible to crack (Russia, at the top of the list). In Paris nothing surprises these people, and so from the start their behavior is pragmatic. They don't try to understand the works of the giant machine, or to mimic its behavior in every detail. Do as they do: don't try to understand the Rubik's Cube, or to pretend you understand it; just behave like someone who has his own code, just as complicated, at home. In short, behave like someone who's seen it all before, and you'll be ready to start your day in Paris.

II:

Getting One's Bearings

1: Literary Overtures

My literary adventures in Paris began on a July evening in 1965, and definitely got off on the wrong foot. Dressed in a velvet suit and turtleneck, I sat myself down on the terrace of the Café de Flore, my left elbow lodged in one neighbor's ribs, my right hand with about six inches' leeway before it would capsize my other neighbor's glass. I thought I spotted, on the edge of the terrace, the delicate profile of Françoise Sagan - which seemed perfectly normal, and a happy omen for events to come. Having ordered a coffee, I flipped open the notebook I had placed in front of me, and took out a pen. No sooner had I done so when a terrifying waiter, strapping and mustachioed, boomed out in a voice that could not be ignored: "No writing on the terrace!" Now, Simone de Beauvoir had made the neighbouring Deux Magots famous by spending entire days huddled up to the coal stove during the Occupation, putting words to paper. A few photos, along with the cut lines, had gone around the world. And this notoriety had rubbed off on the Flore, as well.

One would think that the owners of such establishments (owned, like most Paris cafés, by *Auvergnats* from the south-west of France) would have been flattered by this worldwide cultural consecration. On the contrary. They were appalled by the ensuing invasion of penniless scribblers from hither and yon, who threatened to monopolize indefinitely - in exchange for the modest price of a small espresso - a precious table that could bring in at the very least the price of a large beer every half-hour. And so the order went out: not only to oblige customers to have a refill every 60 minutes, but to identify the wordsmiths as soon as they appeared on the scene, and stop them from pulling so much as a notepad out of their pockets - otherwise it would be harder to get rid of them without causing a fuss.

It's not hard to sympathize with the waiters at the Flore. That intrepid breed, the apprentice writer, is as much a threat to Paris as is the New York fine arts student to Tuscany. All the good terraces of Saint-Germain and Montparnasse together could not accommodate them at the same time.

More than any other city in the world, Paris attracts the writer - the writer of fiction in particular. And so I spent the year 1965-66 composing a first novel, whose only copy I lost in the gents at Heathrow airport the day I returned to Montreal.

I spent those eight months in a hotel; a standard room cost ten francs a night, and you paid at the end of the month. To use the shower on the floor cost extra. In those days most of the hotels in the Latin Quarter, Saint-Germain and Montparnasse, which now cost at least 400 francs a night, were overrun year-long by a large population of intellectual or "artistic" young people: they were foreigners, "provincials," or just Parisians waiting for an apartment.

Among the foreigners, who were Americans for the most part, the number of self-styled "writers" was considerable. They were primarily New Yorkers, habitués of the Sélect in Montparnasse or the Café de la Seine on the street of the same name. They had written, were writing, were going to write. Some had been working on the same novel for five years; others had barely covered three pages. A few, having taken root in Paris without ever producing anything, became freelance translators at Associated Press, proofreaders, or anonymous authors of porno novels. Already they had drunk as much as Hemingway and were as broke as Henry Miller. Well, it was a start.

Paris is unquestionably a city of writers, the world's prime literary capital by demographic weight, the quality of the writers, and above all the diversity of their origins: Britons fleeing smog, lukewarm beer and boiled beef with mint jelly, real American authors, many varieties of Latin-Americans, plus Romanians,

Croats, Hungarians and other refugees from Eastern Europe. At the time you could find Samuel Beckett at the Petit Suisse across from the Odéon, Arthur Adamov at the Old Navy, Sartre at the Coupole: they were walking myths. Today the myths aren't what they used to be. All you're liable to find - and that not very often - is Philippe Sollers at the Closerie des Lilas, or Bernard-Henri Lévy at the Balzar, or perhaps Jean-Edern Hallier at the Place des Vosges. And most of the time not even that. Thanks to television, celebrated writers who value their privacy - Duras or Sagan for example - rarely set foot in the Flore, unlike thirty years earlier. Paris is still the world capital of literature, but you don't see it so much in the streets.

*　　*　　*

Paris continues to attract foreign writers, who pass through with varying degrees of regularity. But very few "full-time" writers, with no other professional pretext for living there, have taken up residence, other than the Canadians Anne Hébert and Mavis Gallant, or the American Jerome Charyn. Even the Englishman Robin Cook, my amiable neighbor near the Bastille, only makes flying visits, quickly heading back to his Provençal property to write. Some come and browse around for a week now and then; others rent an apartment and stay six months, enough to finish a book; still others, more rarely, settle in for two to four years. But even those who think they will stay forever end up leaving after a few years, often for economic reasons, because for North Americans at any rate, life is twice as expensive and three times as complicated as it is at home. But also, I'm convinced, because Paris, in the long run, is lethal to inspiration.

Let us be clear: some writers can write absolutely anywhere, in the city or countryside, in a plane or in a café, in a room that looks out on a wall, or on a park bench. For them, Paris is a place like any other. They write there as they would in a museum.

Others, quite a few I suppose, write better when they are elsewhere - away from their natural habitats and their daily routines. For someone who lives all year long in Montreal, Paris is as disorienting as Rome or the west of Ireland, as long as one does not visit too often or stay too long. It's a matter of keeping intact a certain mystery, not knowing exactly where you're going when you step into the street.

Now if Paris is extremely complex, with its customs, its codes and its secrets, it is in no way mysterious. Culture and society there have always been shaped by the same influences. The laws of the clan, of the family, of commerce, of the Mediterranean, Catholicism, Bonapartism and history rule the lives of all. So much so that Paris is, as Mavis Gallant has said, "a toy in motion": more precisely, an enormous automaton with millions of working parts, that gears up without fail every morning, in every season. The French are only complicated, like a giant puzzle for which you don't have all the pieces; they are never surprising, as they might be were they ever to transcend those forces that make them what they are.

After the first shock, everything you see seems already familiar: can one be surprised by the Venus de Milo or the Mona Lisa? Even if the overall picture remains elusive, there comes a moment in Paris when one realizes, to one's chagrin, that one KNOWS once and for all that THIS scene has already been played out a thousand times, that THIS individual is already there in Balzac or Dumas or Eugène Sue - or, of course, Proust. And that the scene will be replayed, with the same characters, next year and ten years down the road. Everything has already been made and done in Paris - murders, masterpieces, exploits and dastardly crimes - all has been said and described, and the plum roles were handed out a long time ago. Where the novel is concerned, there is nothing more to invent; the best writers, with their genius and brio, spend all their time paraphrasing, explicating, dissecting the Great Texts: one reheats Dumas in a sauce of Robbe-Grillet, flavors Zola with Borges, serves up endless varieties of Proust, Benjamin Constant, Madame de Sévigné, Flaubert, Stendhal. But it's been an eternity since someone has produced the Great Novel that you find today in Latin-American and Anglo-Saxon literature. There is no national equivalent, even, to Günter Grass, someone to write the novel of his time or at least of this fin-de-siècle.

Where formal excellence is concerned on the other hand, Paris is a stimulating - or daunting - city. Everyone speaks with ease his own French (popular, conservative, chic, snob, regional), and the art of conversation has here reached a pitch of perfection unequaled anywhere in the world, including Italy. What is more, many people - even very ordinary people - write well, or very well, quite naturally. The major newspapers boast journalists and columnists who are also remarkable stylists. Where esthetics are concerned, Paris continues to dominate French language literature. And it is always a good and bracing idea to see this first hand.

But to come here to dream, no. Certainly one is taken aback, bewitched, overwhelmed at first by the beauty of Notre Dame or the quays of the Seine. But wait six months or a year, and the astonishment will have fled. Well, almost. Now and then when you least expect it you'll be dazzled anew, on an autumn evening, say, as you cross over the Seine. What endures is the respect and admiration you feel for the Beauty and Perfection you behold as you try to recall, just as it was, that first sense of wonder, the colors and the smells. To dream of Paris or to have it as inspiration, it's perhaps better just to stay home, or to have left it behind long ago. To write there while you live there, to escape the museum without fleeing it, you have to follow in the footsteps of Bernard-Henri Lévy, and rent a suite at the Hôtel Raphaël. You can always lose yourself right around the corner, provided you can pay the price.

2: *Some Crucial Data*

The other day, between cheese and dessert, a Quai d'Orsay diplomat attached to what is commonly referred to as the "North American desk" was kind enough to show some interest in the supposedly impertinent articles I had written about France, or the French, or the two together.

"For example," he chuckled, "I very much liked your piece on how dirty the French are. Besides, you're not off the mark; one toothbrush per year for six people is not a lot..."

"Of course," added another diplomat, "it speaks well for French thriftiness: we share toothbrushes..."

There are two possibilities here. Either I'm being credited with a malicious streak out of all proportion, even for me, or this nasty accusation of insalubrity, doubtless initiated and nurtured by perfidious Albion and then passed on from capital to capital, has so often echoed in the ears of the French that now they've been convinced: yes, they are dirty; yes, the whole world considers them filthy.

In fact, I have never written any such thing, because, of course, I rely entirely on established scientific truths. It's not because a few French lady friends with a flair for hyperbole claim, after a meal well anointed with wine, to have declined to bed down with their compatriots purely out of a concern for hygiene, that I'm going to jump to conclusions and take all that at face value: I see it rather as a figure of speech, poetic licence.

Before I pronounce myself on the question, I need irrefutable data, rock solid! Well, here it is: a book of over 400 pages has just

AND GOD CREATED THE FRENCH

been published by Albin Michel, written by Jérôme Duhamel. It's called *Vous les Français* ("You the French"). In this compilation of 2,200 polls of all sorts, you'll find everything you ever wanted to know about the average Frenchman, but never dared ask.

Very well, then: unclean or not unclean? You be the judge.

French women adore luxury, that we know. Eight percent of them dream of taking a bath in champagne. On the other hand, only 26 percent of the population takes a bath or shower every day. That doesn't seem like a lot. However, 47 percent of women use a bidet, which has its usefulness and often its charm, and this is a rare occurrence in North America, where the number of bathrooms equipped with such an accessory is so insignificant that their owners - assuredly decadent, if not degenerate - don't even figure in a representative sample.

Let's be honest. French women hold their own better than the men. Some 82 percent of the women change their underpants every day (only 56 percent for the males), one in a hundred reserving this operation for Sundays. Only three percent brush their teeth as seldom as once a week (eight percent for the lads), so you'd have to be rather unlucky to happen on one of those.

The situation, then, is not so appalling as the British, for instance, never very well disposed toward the "froggies," would like you to believe.

Of course, another poll reveals that 30 percent of the French "find it agreeable not to wash for several days." Perhaps they're honoring the spirit of Napoleon's injunction to Josephine: "Don't wash, I'll be there in a week!" An august and lofty example.

But, since we're on the subject of toothbrushes, let it be known that many more are sold than one might think: no fewer than 41 million units per year (for 55 million inhabitants). That seems respectable. Less so, however, are the numbers for men's undershorts: only 3.5 sold per person per year, compared with 9 in Germany and 12 in the United States. The French will claim, obviously, that their shorts are of superior quality, and resist multiple washings as well as wear and tear.

There are 4,000 polls in this country every year, most sponsored by industry, but lending themselves all the same to refined analysis and the most intricate cross-checking.

One of these surveys - they can cost up to 50,000 francs - made possible a crucial correlation between political allegiance and the use of deodorants. Not so silly: it is not just a choice between cleanliness and inferior hygiene. It also denotes a commitment either to nature or to synthetic modernity. The humorist Claire Bretecher has, with good reason, characterized brown sugar as "sugar of the left." Similarly, France is an arena where a century-long conflict has been played out between the proponents of natural odors (the majority, my nose tells me) and those who swear by soap. As for deodorants, I would have thought their most loyal adherents would be urban dwellers, and so, logically, socialists or followers of Giscard d'Estaing. A huge error! It's the Chiraquians who win by a nose: 59 percent are users. Next come the Communists with 58 percent, then the socialists (57), and finally the Giscardians (56), who, for all their refinements, still place last. I admit the results are inconclusive, and perhaps even meaningless.

As there's more to life than dirt, you can also learn that the ultimate in obscenity for 32 percent of the population of either sex is "to make love in public with an animal." That's understandable. And, too bad for the Woody Allens of this world, 51 percent of French women prefer men to be "tall." 60 percent of men who read Lui Magazine (the French Playboy) favor big breasts - although current wisdom on the subject constantly assures us that this "infantile" fixation is exclusively American. Of course, it still has to be determined at what point, exactly, breasts qualify as big. No doubt we have another survey to look forward to.

What else? 27 percent of women admit to having peed in a swimming pool. To the question: "Have you ever caressed your 'zezette'," 17 percent of girls under 12 replied yes, they had masturbated, although the French way of putting it seems so much less utilitarian. But only 2 percent of French women like making love on Tuesday (Tuesday seems to have a dismal reputation in this country; it's a day that's inordinately empty and inconsequential, when to the rote question, "How are you doing?", many are moved to reply: "Bof! Like a Monday.")

On a higher plane? One percent of households boast a tortoise. Of 5,000 dog bites recorded over the year, 31 percent of the victims were not unfortunate postmen, employees of the State, but the animals' own masters (which seems to me only just deserts). 15 percent of Communists are left-handed, which is enormous, and must be a clue to something. The female personality whom the largest number of men would like to see nude in a magazine is TV journalist Anne Sinclair. The man most sought after by women seems to be the owlish "culture vulture" television host Bernard Pivot (but sought after for what, one might ask, and for how long?). The most attractive Frenchwoman, pollsters found, is by far Catherine Deneuve, neither an imaginative, nor particularly original choice.

Finally, note that the country most dear to the hearts of the French is none other than Canada! (It scores 75 percent, one more point than Italy!). However, let's not get carried away: in a crunch, your average French woman will prefer to have sexual congress with a French man, which would indicate that endogamy still has a future, while that of the European Union is not so certain. Italians come second, but follow far behind (35 percent). As for other nationalities, they hardly count. Which raises the painful question: is France's love affair with all things North American strictly platonic? We will need further polls to elucidate this complex issue: stay tuned.

3. Good Manners

On the 4th of April 1975, in a lost and lugubrious corner of Normandy, a squadron of police laid siege to a farm where dangerous bandits had taken the residents hostage.

French television had not yet reached the point of instant video or knee-jerk real-time reporting, so we had to wait for the evening news to get the visuals. As my set was still black and white, the sense of a 1950s gangster film was all the more pronounced.

Hunched studiously behind a car, a mean-looking man in his fifties with a bull-horn, wearing hat and glasses, was conversing with the gang leader from afar. "Awright, toss out your rods, don't be jerks, you ain't gotta chance, don't play games. Don't try anything smart, come on outa there." Just like in a Humphrey Bogart movie.

The man couldn't even claim to be from police headquarters in Paris, where you have no choice but to use bad guys' language; he was the prefect himself, that is, the State's highest authority in the department. His "odious" choice of words made for a huge scandal across the land and within the administration. The very next day the prefect in question, Jacques Gandouin, was transferred, as a disciplinary measure.

The same Gandouin is the author of a celebrated reference work on good manners, the *Guide du Protocole et des Usages*, or "Guide to Protocol and Etiquette," regularly revised since the 1970s, and whose 1991 edition runs to 598 large-format pages. The prefect ousted for his bad manners is one of the acknowledged arbiters of elegance and good taste. Some might find this strange, but the French see nothing untoward here, no contradiction in these terms.

The essence of French savoir-vivre consists not only in making the right choice of riding-boot tops for the hunt, or devising a proper seating plan for a dinner-party that includes a duchess, two prefects, a descendant of the throne of France and a coadjutor bishop, but also in knowing how to talk "man-to-man." If a vulgar individual starts assailing you with insults in a public place, you must avoid replying with an "Excuse me, sir," or "How dare you, you filthy cad?". Like a great lord, you must be able to speak, when need be, the language of drunken sailors in a low dive. The issue of style is, in fact, addressed for all to see in Monsieur Gandouin's manual, and one of the seven great principles governing protocol and behavior is what he terms "the reciprocal similitude of forms." The unfortunate episode of the gangster film did not, in any case, compromise the esteem in which the Duc de Brissac, who prefaced the work, holds Monsieur Gandouin. The two men have often gone to the hunt together, and, according to the duke, our prefect is a man with an excellent mastery of "the language of hunting," which is reassuring. How could such an accomplished hunter and rider be anything but a man above suspicion?

The terrain of good manners is, as the wise Duc de Brissac makes clear, perilous, if only for the countless official decorations one must commit to memory in hierarchical order: 18 crosses, 22 commemorative medals, 15 Orders of Civil Merit, 3 Orders of France Overseas, and 32 medals of honor. (And that's not counting all the minor or "local" decorations.) In this matter, as in rinsing your fingers at the table, you are in deep trouble without your "Gandouin."

Everything is covered, from the relatively simple to the exceedingly complex. The art of the pocket handkerchief, closely associated with that of the tie, and which is only worn after five o'clock. The double-breasted suit, which must never be unbuttoned, unlike the single-breasted jacket, which is unbuttoned as soon as one walks in the door. The table setting, with the tines of the fork turned toward the tablecloth (to draw attention to the family initials, for example LT for La Trémouille). Kissing the hand: one bends toward the lady's hand, one does not pull the hand toward oneself, one brushes it with one's lips, without pressing down and slobbering. You do not engage a lady in conversation without removing your hat, although a lady who knows what "social security fund deficit" means will immediately invite you to put it on again.

There are 63 different ways to end a letter, of which some are reserved for correspondence between women. You never present your "humble respects" to a very young woman, but only your respects. You never write "Monsieur le comte," unless you're an inferior (a notion that seems harder to imagine with each passing day) or a merchant, but in any situation you can say "Monsieur le duc" without demeaning yourself or appearing ridiculous. To an Orthodox priest you write "Monsieur l'archimandrite," and to a rabbi, "Monsieur le rabbin." British peers, as is too often forgotten, are simply called "milords," as in Edith Piaf's song. And if you want to write to a cardinal, "I have the honor to beg, with the deepest respect, the most humble servant of your eminence." There are little tricks that can help you save time, while maintaining correct behavior: the use of visiting cards for instance, which allows for a number of shortcuts, such as the abbreviation "P.F.C.," which means "pour faire connaissance," or "to make your acquaintance." The mastery of proper practices is not only the sign of a true gentleman, but is what saves him from spending a good part of the day puzzling over questions of etiquette.

France is, compared not only to North America but also to the other European nations (with the exception of England), the country where good manners are most important. For several centuries it was a monarchy and a great power, where a centralized aristocracy set the tone and established the rules of the game. Then the bourgeoisie decided to give itself aristocratic airs, while the aristocrats who were not too dim-witted tried to make money. All that has left its mark, despite the devastation wreaked by television and the urbanization of the last 30 or 40 years. The day-to-day protocol surrounding political power remains among the most onerous and elaborate in Europe, especially where the presidency is concerned: ceremonial dinners, republican guards, and so on. The result: the French (a bit like the British) make fun of customs and etiquette, but continue to be preoccupied by them.

On French radio you can still, in the middle of the afternoon, hear a lady discussing with the utmost seriousness whether it's proper to mop up one's plate with a piece of bread (on the end of one's fork, naturally). No, if it's a real dinner party. Yes, if it's among friends, and a simple meal, on the express condition that one ask prior permission of the lady of the house: "That will even introduce a note of humor and fantasy into the dinner," concludes the expert. One can imagine the irrepressible flurry of amusement rippling through the little group in the wake of such audacity.

If the "Gandouin" remains the uncontested authority, it's perhaps a bit too detailed for the common of mortals, who do not spend their lives entertaining the diplomatic corps, apostolic nuncios, or what remains of the local aristocracy. Here, then, is another, more modest reference book: *Le Savoir-Vivre Aujourd'hui* ("Today's Savoir-Vivre"), by Christine Géricot (only 230 pages!).

Madame Géricot is tall and thin, and dresses in the best possible taste and the noblest of material: wool, silk, linen, all in muted tones, as is only fitting. Far from being a specialist in good manners, she is content to be an enlightened practitioner. An artist and painter, she was to have illustrated the book in question, and ended up writing it. Not entirely by accident. Madame Géricot's pedigree seems to have been most respectable, and she was, to boot, "married for 25 years in Bordeaux, France's most bourgeois and conservative city." That is, before being "demarried," and returning to Paris.

She's not an extremist and doesn't try to complicate matters. With a touch of disdain, she talks of "the etiquette invented by the parvenus of the First Empire; prior to that, the true nobility had no need of a code of conduct, for it was born to good manners." Her more or less utopian ideal would be that we wear our good manners naturally, without ostentation.

Alas, I wouldn't hold my breath! Where the male animal is concerned at any rate, the bare minimum is far from assured, at least according to Géricot's standards, and she is uncompromising. If one's licence could be suspended for poor conduct in society, how many (French) men would still have theirs?

There are those who refuse to give up their seats on public transport to ladies of any age, or who guffaw noisily while taking up an inordinate amount of room. There are those who poison dinner parties and closed spaces with fat cigars, and those who make a variety of mouth noises while chewing food or tasting wine. There are those who tap their cigarettes on the package before inserting them in the corners of their mouths, who talk with the butt hanging down or even — horror of horrors — stick it behind their ears "for later." There are those who never open doors, don't hold the chair for a lady, don't light her cigarettes. There are those who wear more jewelry than a simple wedding band: a chain over the chest, a heavy signet ring, even a link bracelet! Heaven preserve us! Finally, there are those who do not understand that when the waiter brings the cheque, it's up to them to fork over the cash, and no one else. Madame Géricot is intransigent on that point. The men in the party go discreetly over the tab and split it. Even if the male is on his own in the company of three or four women it's up to him to shell out, and without any comments like "Geez, it costs an arm and a leg here!"

But there are more complex matters: organizing a dinner party, an engagement, a marriage. How long should one wait before sending out the announcements? Two months. What if it's a remarriage after a divorce, or a widowhood? Is it appropriate to organize an engagement party for a son who has been living for two years with his paramour? (Reply: NO! But one could envisage a lunch for the two families, with the lovebirds seated side by side at the end of the table. Besides, at dinners one NEVER separates engaged couples, or those who have been married for less than a year.)

We live in troubled times, and often the marrying children are burdened with unworthy parents: the mother is divorced and not remarried, and one wonders if she has a gigolo; the father is remarried, but with a Barbie Doll 25 years younger than himself - how on earth is one to word the invitation? And if the parents are separated but not divorced? And if the mother has been so gauche as to remarry? Reach for your Géricot, it takes care of everything in 250 questions and answers. Including the hypothetical nightmare of a marriage cancelled a week before the ceremony, with the presents already starting to arrive. Ghastly!

As for the table, one thing is sure: after having read this book you'll never again serve your spaghetti and meatballs in the same old way. First, to ensure an acceptable seating plan where male and female alternate on either side of the master and mistress of the house, themselves face-to-face at the centre of the feast, it is recommended to have 6, 10, 14 or 18 guests, and never 8, 12 or 16. (Should you be feeding an heir to the throne, a head of state or a cardinal, he supplants the master of the house.)

When the moment arrives to summon the guests to the table, don't shout: "Dinner! It's going to get cold!" After 30 or 45 minutes you should be heartless, and remove the place-setting for a late arrival. Avoid bringing the conversation round to such subjects as the washing of dirty laundry, toilets, illnesses and cemeteries (but also, today: homosexuality, Aids, cancer, car accidents). NEVER offer a second helping of soup, salad, cheese or fruit. Unless it accompanies the entire meal, never serve champagne with dessert ("a heresy") and, of course, offer coffee in the living room (if you have one).

Besides advice on how to serve wine, proper modes of address, proper form for letter writing, how to summon a waiter in a café (not too much "Psst!" or "Hey!"), and how to behave at the cemetery, Christine Géricot devotes the last part of her book to professional relationships in the office, and how to present oneself for a job or put together a C.V. At this point we are dealing more with a survival course or a first-aid kit. And it's true that in the current climate, being blessed with employment, remunerative if possible, stands as a prerequisite for being able to hang on to one's good manners. Unless, of course, one is oneself heir to the throne.

4. The "de" is Not For Burning

Everyone agrees on this: in our day a noble title - even an authentic one - means nothing. It's more likely to provoke sniggers than marks of respect.

Never mind. More than 200 years after the night of August 4 and the abolition of noble privilege in France, an impressive number of people try each year to join the ranks, officially and administratively, of the vague dead letter which is all that remains of French aristocracy. Others are content to raise doubts by appending to their banal plebeian cognomens the well-known nobiliary particle plus the name of some family property or nebulous ancestor.

Why should Raoul Benet, born in Hyères on October 10, 1912, and whose surname in French could be rendered as "ninny," have to endure mocking smiles and bad plays on words throughout his life. "What if I called myself Benet de Lamothe?" he thought. In May 1949, his request for a change of name appeared in the *Journal Officiel*. It was, alas, rejected, which probably didn't stop him from adding "de Lamothe" to his visiting cards. Likewise for Alain Froc, doubtless of the venerable bourgeoisie, who tried in vain to append "de Géninville" to his family name.

The second demise - legal and definitive - of the nobility may date back 125 years (to the end of the Second Empire), but many continue to move heaven and earth to give at least the appearance of having blue blood. And even if it's been a tired old trick for generations, these visible signs still impress the onlooker. During the 60s, at the Coupole (the famous Montparnasse eatery), the head waiter would point out an elderly, portly gentleman, dressed in a worn tuxedo, sitting every evening by himself. "He's a descendant of Louis XV," he would whisper, with both mock amusement and authentic respect, and that hint of irony native to the Parisian-born who are heirs to the French Revolution, but still, when all is said and done, impressed.

Similarly, a hostess will not be able to resist telling you that one of her old friends is a real Romanian princess (for reasons that are not too clear, the Romanian princess in exile is a classic of the genre). Finally, it cannot be denied that, even in highly educated circles, which are rational by definition, those who possess a family name with a noble ring to it attach a certain amount of importance to their particle: the Poivre d'Arvors, the de Closets, and the Carrère d'Encausses are visibly happy not to be called Dupont or Martin.

There was a time when the peerage had real social and legal status. In France in 1789, the true nobility consisted of about ten thousand families at the most, and represented less than one percent of the population. It had the right to reserved seats in the church and low bows from the peasants, but also exclusive access to official posts and exemption from certain taxes. A bogus title, foreign if possible because more difficult to check, might gain one access (without breaking and entering) to the very best salons, where one could play cards and perhaps win the hand of a richly dowered young lady with an illustrious name. This, by royal decree, one would append to one's own, and along with it all the privileges thereunto attendant. In the days when it meant membership in a real caste - in France up to 1789 - nobility, over and above the prestige that it accorded, was serious business, for it brought with it riches and power. That is why the King's justice considered impostors to be thieves and criminals.

A dozen years after the abolition decreed by the Revolution, Napoleon I established a "noblesse d'Empire" (nobility of the Empire), which the Restoration of 1814 was quick to recognize, at the same time as it reestablished the old titles (but without daring to restore their former status). Titles continued to be bestowed up to 1870 and the coming of the Third Republic, but only on an honorary basis. The former privileges - other than the church pew - were never revived. Nobility now caters only to the vanity of those who seek it. But the usurper doesn't risk much either, just a snigger here and there. There is no dearth of candidates, therefore, for an expanded name.

The historian Pierre Dioudonnat has found fertile ground here; he has devoted a good part of the last 25 years to establishing a list of truly noble families, and above all tracking down the bogus aristocracy. In the 1994 edition of his *Encyclopédie de la fausse noblesse et de la noblesse d'apparence* ("The Encyclopedia of False or Ostensible Nobility") we are treated, over 669 pages, to some 4,000 names that fall into this dubious category. Let's be frank: the book shatters most of our remaining illusions and casts down our idols from their pedestals.

There are, however, different degrees of falsity. Thus De Gaulle and De Beauvoir - who had no need of it to shore up their haughtiness - never for an instant pretended to blue blood. The General, for example, was simply the issue of a very old bourgeois family, and we find as of 1720 a Jean-Baptiste de Gaulle who was prosecutor in the Parliament of Paris.

"Once again," Dioudonnat reminds us, "the *de* is not in itself an attribute of nobility. Many ancient noble families did not initially sport the particle, whereas it was found among some of the common folk. But it is true that, since for most people the two little letters were synonymous with aristocracy, nobles tended to affix them to the name of one of their fiefdoms. And families of the grand bourgeoisie followed suit to give themselves a semblance of nobility."

It is likely that the famous *de* did exist from the beginning in the Beauvoir or Closet families, but if it was added it was a very long time ago, and not by those now concerned, or even by their parents.

What makes it more dubious - or ridiculous - is knowing just when, more or less, the bearer of a banal commoner's name made the decision to cloak himself in aristocratic garb.

Thanks to M. Dioudonnat, we learn, for example, that the star broadcaster on French television, Patrick Poivre d'Arvor, flat-out

tacked on a "literary" d'Arvor to his family name. Where civil law
and his passport are concerned, he remains the simple Monsieur
Poivre of his childhood. That doesn't stop him from pursuing his
career under this pseudonym (although his colleagues in the know
just call him Poivre). Nor does it stop him from believing in it a
little. In 1972, he tried to inscribe his daughter under the name
Poivre d'Arvor at the registry office. It didn't work. But that didn't
prevent his own brother from rechristening himself d'Arvor, as
well. As for Hélène Carrère d'Encausse, she was content just to
include on her visiting cards the little spelling mistake that transformed plain old Dencausse into d'Encausse.

There are of course truly noble families, some flourishing and,
more common, some destined for extinction. According to Dioudonnat, there are between 2,000 and 4,000 today in France.
What is a true aristocrat? He is the descendant in a direct line
(exclusively masculine) of someone who was genuinely noble at
the time when nobility had legal status. That applies to those so
honored before 1789, but also to the Empire nobles or those from
after the Restoration. No succession through the female line or
through adoption (even less thinkable), is accepted. Two special
cases give grounds for appeal, Pierre Dioudonnat admits: first, the
descendants of a family that was in the process of being ennobled
when the proceedings were so regrettably interrupted in August
1789 by the French Revolution; second, those bearing titles
accorded in the nineteenth century by the Vatican, which is
apparently more supple in this area than on questions of sex.

The moral of the story: it is utterly impossible today to become
noble, because that would suppose that you could transform
yourself into a true descendant of someone who was noble back
when nobility had legal status. You can, however, take on the
appearance. The ideal is to get your new name on the register,
either by official parliamentary decree or, more shrewdly, by
making an arrangement with the mayor of your village or (small)
town. The forgery, once inscribed and correctly executed, will be
there for you till your dying day. Or, finally, you can have yourself
officially adopted, even at the age of 50, by an elderly impoverished
aristocrat whose gambling debts you will pay.

But this touching attempt to hoist yourself above your station doesn't always pay off. Take the case of former president Giscard d'Estaing. True, his ancestor Giscard did, in 1818, marry into the *real* nobility, in the person of Élise-Marguerite Cousin de la Tour-Fondue (the name alone must have been a daunting challenge to the gallant knight when the time came for pillow-talk). But there is no succession through the female line, and the Giscards remained commoners. The name d'Estaing to which they subsequently laid claim is itself upstream in the genealogy of the Cousins de la Tour-Fondue. None of that stopped Valéry's father from obtaining by decree, in 1922 and 1923, the right to reassume the name d'Estaing, after having tried in vain to revive the name of Tour-Fondue, which has, nevertheless, lived on, but in Montreal, which boasts one of its illustrious descendants.

Mildly obsessed by his (bogus) aristocratic ancestry, Giscard d'Estaing has been dealt, on this subject, a number of disagreeable rebuffs. In 1974, he was refused entry into the Cincinnati Society, whose members, in the United States, are descendants of the heroes of the War of Independence. "My ancestor Admiral d'Estaing took part," pleaded the French president. "He certainly took part, but he wasn't really your ancestor, old boy," replied the uncooperative Americans.

Many years earlier, when as Minister of Finance he was setting up a large public bond issue under the De Gaulle presidency, Giscard had posed the question, in cabinet: "How shall the loan be called?" The General's well-known retort: "Why, the Giscard d'Estaing, of course! Is that not a good 'borrowing' name?"

5. Louis XVI, The Discomfiting Ghost

We saw it when the time came to celebrate the momentous anniversary of January 21, 1793: two centuries after Louis XVI's execution on the Place de la Révolution - today Place de la Concorde, although it could just as well be called the Place de la Traffic Jam - the ghost of the late Capet continues to weigh heavily on the memories of the French and to divide them. The worthy man, dull, obtuse and relatively uncultured, was no political genius, nor was he an impressive orator or an innovator, but he was certainly not, either, a true tyrant. His main interest was locksmithing. He gave Dr. Guillotin, inventor of the guillotine, some good advice, and he parroted the ideas of his time, though without doing much to stand in the way of modernism.

In other climes, those nostalgic for the monarchy and the hard-line proponents of the Revolution would probably find common ground; the figure of Louis Capet is not a major point of contention, even in debates on the Great Revolution. His disappearance was not a huge loss for political and intellectual history, although his execution probably served no purpose. It was arbitrary, its legality was questionable, and its consequences were disastrous. It meant that the Republic was founded with blood on its hands, and it legitimized political murder in spectacular fashion, paving the way for the Great Terror of 1793-94. It's not even certain that to banish such a colorless individual would have posed more of a danger to the new Republic than his public execution, which risked making him a martyr.

With three million unemployed (and more to come) across the

country, with legislative elections due two months later which were to prove an unmitigated disaster for the socialists, the 200th anniversary of Louis XVI's execution on Thursday, January 21 at rush hour was certainly not the event uppermost in the minds of 58 million French citizens. But the imminence of this date was enough to cause quite a political flap in the media and to resurrect a 200-year-old debate, with everyone taking the same old sides. Granted, it was a muted debate, with weary antagonists. Whether or not to erect a posthumous mausoleum for poor Capet or to strike him once and for all from History's rolls, was not going to bring millions of Frenchmen into the streets.

In many countries some sort of gentleman's agreement would have been concluded, and the fight called off; whether it was a constructive act, error, or crime, the execution of Louis XVI belongs to the past. The British, who have had a number of more down-to-earth problems with their House of Windsor, including the telephonic effusions of Prince Charles and Sarah Ferguson's predilection for topless toe-sucking in Provence, have nevertheless settled once and for all the philosophical problem of the monarchy. Charles I was decapitated in the seventeenth century, his son Charles II was set back on the throne with full honors, and that in large part erased the sin of regicide. However, one way or another royal absolutism had been given a mortal blow, and England drifted smoothly toward the most liberal kind of parliamentary government without ever doing away with the monarchy and without it being clear at what precise moment the old order had given way. At the same time, the aristocracy with its divine right succeeded in transforming itself, quite serenely, into the bourgeoisie, and shed the visible signs of power so as better to conserve it in reality. The British Crown, then, is neither a divisive topic, nor really a genuine preoccupation. It's part of the sentimental, historical backdrop for the British, but nobody really asks what purpose it serves, and even less whether its existence compromises the purity of their democracy.

In France, where the luckless Louis XVI has been dead for two centuries, all it takes is a good pretext or an anniversary such as this to resuscitate in dramatic terms a debate which is in fact that of the French Revolution itself. Yes, we had to guillotine him, it was a salutary act, claim some. It was a sanguinary crime which we must publicly expiate if we are ever to achieve a national reconciliation, claim others. Never mind the "centrist" group which, following in the path of the philosopher Jean-François Revel, is of the opinion that it was a good thing to do away with absolutism, but that it was regrettable, given what followed, to have thought one could found a state grounded in law while setting up an extraordinary tribunal and proceeding with an arbitrary execution. This not unreasonable historical point of view, however, falls far short of rallying majority support.

On the right, the "partisans" of Louis XVI are not satisfied just to deplore the violence and pointlessness of the gesture; they assert that January 21, 1793 was the day of the Great Crime, which opened a wound that has never been healed. They remain loyal to their odd yearnings, not for absolutism of course, but for some old gingerbread aristocratic society, paternalistic, and - in their dreams - consensual. In fact, even if they know it to be unthinkable, there are some 25 or 30 percent who would be in favor of some sort of Restoration. It seems a difficult matter in this country to deplore the execution of January 21, 1793, without at the same time shedding tears over the old order.

At the other extreme, and this is just as remarkable, a solid minority of again about 30 percent still asserts that the execution of Louis XVI, far from representing a blot on the escutcheon of the Revolution, was the crucial founding act of the nascent Republic. Needless to say, if the first third is rightist (and sometimes extreme right), the second is loyal to the orthodox left, and generally includes those who want to rehabilitate the amiable Robespierre, architect of the Great Terror. Him they view as the innocent victim of the spanking new reactionary bourgeoisie, which thwarted his desire to give all the power to the people (an ambition that Lenin, of course, was to realize brilliantly in October 1917). From time to time one is buttonholed in the capital and asked to sign a petition in favor of naming a street after Robespierre in Paris.

In those days of January 1993, other petitioners were roaming the Paris streets and haunting the antechambers of the media: the "partisans" of Louis XVI, who were demanding that at last, come what may, he be given his due. They even held a press conference to express their desire for an official commemorative ceremony. Then they formed a procession, on notorious Black Thursday, and laid flowers at Place de la Concorde on the very spot where the guillotine had stood.

Heading the committee was a novelist of some talent, but with an unfortunate tendency to uphold in no uncertain terms the positions of the extremist right, Jean Raspail. A few figures representing the more officially conservative parties were by his side. But they were joined by others who are eminently moderate and respectable, such as the former minister (and novelist) Jean-François Deniau, and the writer Michel Déon. Even more astonishing: Thierry Ardisson, a vulgar-chic night-time television host on France-2, who said he "had always been a monarchist." And the art expert Maurice Rheims, academician and descendant of an old Jewish family from Alsace. Curiously, the Chief Rabbi of France almost became a member of the committee, not only because Louis XVI had taken the initiative of signing decrees favorable to French Jews (unprecedented at the time), but also to express his commitment to consensus.

Obviously, the time for a detached assessment of the dossier has not yet arrived. The French state made it through the bicentenary of the Revolution in 1989 by studiously avoiding any serious historical debate, and by organizing a magnificent spectacle on the Champs-Élysées for July 14 that was as extravagant as it was hollow. It also commemorated the bicentenary of the Republic's proclamation in 1992. This year, there was not a peep out of the official authorities on the anniversary of the last Capetian's execution, after 800 years of dynastic rule. What is more, the Prefect of Paris tried to prohibit the Concorde commemoration on the grounds that it would block traffic! The committee asked the Archbishop of Paris, Monseigneur Lustiger, for permission to celebrate a solemn commemorative mass at Notre Dame. A silent refusal, with no appeal. In 1993 poor Louis XVI, crowned at the age of 20, lover of locks and keys, who on July 14, 1789, wrote in his hunting diary, "Nothing," still constituted a threat to civil order in France.

6. The Specter of the Count of Falloux

Twice in less than ten years, it appears, some zealots or madmen have amused themselves by tampering with the cadaver of the Count of Falloux, a less than progressive minister under Louis-Napoléon Bonaparte. Although the count in question is less renowned than Louis XVI, Napoleon, Danton or Robespierre, his corpse has conserved its magical powers: dare to touch it, and the country comes close to civil war. Parisian ladies in Chanel dresses who have almost never set foot outside their peaceful neighborhoods surge into the streets crying bloody murder. The mass rally empties the religious institutions - what's left of them - of their good sisters and cassocked priests. Choir boys join in, and the imposing cohort of French bishops assembled on the dais calls to mind nothing so much as the Bolshevik politburo in wartime. A delicious whiff of History wafts through Versailles once again.

It's much the same when the other side gets a chance to play. Any attempt to call into question the famous Falloux Law - adopted March 10, 1850 on an ultra-conservative platform, then revised in a *republican* direction in 1882, 1886, 1901, 1902, 1904 - works miracles in the ranks of the left unlike any seen within living memory. The countless union organizations, sworn enemies under normal circumstances, bury the hatchet and fall into each others' arms; the Socialists fraternize with the Communists; the Catholics of the left and the Freemasons (dressed in their most splendid finery) march arm in arm.

We know how in May 1984 the Socialists first touched off the crisis. Their common platform - and even that of then candidate François Mitterrand - had made a formal commitment to do away with that shameful blemish, private schooling, which continued to sully the republican ideal and no one, on the right or the left, paid much attention. This promise was regarded as just another of the left's utopian prophecies. But there was to be a surprise. By the end of 1983, the left and Mitterrand had absolutely nothing more to say or to offer in economic terms, having executed a 180 degree turnabout and set their course, irrevocably, for austerity and the sacrosanct market economy. Had the economic situation not been so disastrous, with no hope at all for a return to socialist orthodoxy, a way would no doubt have been found to put off the minister Alain Savary's reform long enough to for it to languish and expire. But the political and economic impasse provoked an ideological offensive, and one thing led to another. The socialist deputies seemed to be chanting in unison: "If they have no more bread, let them eat ecclesiastical cake." A vote in the Assembly, which slightly toughened Savary's law, was enough to scuttle the compromise that had been painstakingly negotiated and only grudgingly accepted by the supporters of private schools. In quick succession there followed two of the largest demonstrations of the last forty years in Paris: half a million people at the Bastille and then, as I noted earlier, a million kilts, cassocks and lodens at Versailles. For having dared to shift by only a few millimeters the Count of Falloux's sacred cadaver, the Mitterrand regime found itself on the verge of toppling. One could almost catch a whiff of Restoration in the air. As it turned out, only the heads of Savary and Prime Minister Pierre Mauroy rolled. An impeccable Jacobin, Jean-Pierre Chevènement, was put in charge, and he lost no time putting the cadaver back where it ought to have been left in the first place: unseen, unheard, under wraps.

Nine years and a few months later, having forgotten the still fresh lessons of History, it was the sedate right that succumbed to a spell of madness, when, euphoric after a very successful 1993, it gave in to the old temptation. Was it in response to specific instructions from that ordinarily reasonable man, the Prime Minister Édouard Balladur? Whatever the case, in the dark of a

December night a young man, so reasonable, equally worthy, François Bayrou, launched a lightning attack on the front lines of secularization, breaking 1984's cease-fire. The "territorial adjustments" targeted by this winter offensive were doubtless less drastic than those demanded by the enemy camp in 1984, but no matter. The civil war was on again.

Despite that other sacrosanct tradition, the Christmas truce, the result was not long in coming. Crushed by their defeat in March 1993, the left had virtually ceased to exist; the Socialist Party was marginalized, the unions had for some time been weakened and more divided than ever. Then Monsieur Bayrou took his awkward initiative and instantly everyone was united and out in the streets. And on January 16, despite their advanced state of demoralization, no fewer than 500,000 of the left's faithful marched between the Place de la République and the Place de la Nation. There they were, shoulder to shoulder, socialists in their caps, all factions of the FEN (the teachers' union), the Masonic lodges in full regalia. It had been fifteen years, if not twenty-five, since so many left-wing demonstrators had been seen in Paris. And in the meantime the Balladur government had already reversed itself unceremoniously; like a lapsed alcoholic who has awakened with a hangover, the unhappy François Bayrou had the sobering experience of seeing the Constitutional Council reject certain measures in the new legislation, which gave him his cue to scurry in front of the television cameras and declare that *of course* the latest sorry revision of the Falloux law had been withdrawn in its entirety, and that would be the end of it forever. Ten days later, the mere memory of this dastardly ecclesiastical offensive was enough to draw half a million republicans into the street yet again. There was no more threat on the horizon, only this fleeting but unconscionable affront: THEY had dared to "lay hands on the non-denominational public education system"! Who knows what might have happened had the right persevered for only another two months? Could the taking of the Winter Palace not have been entirely ruled out?

Édouard Balladur, in the ten months after he became Prime Minister, had been able with no problem at all to increase taxes, cut social benefits and allocations, privatize institutions, and let unemployment soar, without provoking any popular unrest. He had banned smoking cigars in public, had appeared on television to announce more bad news and new sacrifices, then gone back home, reassuring everybody: "You can count on me, it's all for the best!" And it worked like a charm; even the poor rushed up to offer him money as he left! But no sooner did he nudge the mummy of President Louis-Napoléon Bonaparte's Minister of Education, than Balladur felt his extraordinary magic. The reform was dead in the water.

The war of the schools, some 150 or 200 years old (the first shots were fired, according to historians, even before the Revolution in 1789), is a truly French affair, in a country that is both deeply Catholic by culture and tradition and 90 percent non-practicing. Every time the question comes up, each camp behaves just as it has for the last century, as though nothing has changed. On one side, the notorious Catholic lobby (where the bishops are far from the most zealous) claims that the state wants to stifle freedom of thought. On the other, the lay faction sees in private schools (the Catholics call them *free* schools) a Trojan horse of the old order, Pétain, the Restoration and obscurantism.

The reality, both simple and very complex, is something like this: private schools in France account for 16 percent of the students (more at the secondary than the primary level), while the Ministry of National Education grants them 13 percent of their budget - paying, essentially, operating expenses and the teachers' salaries, in keeping with criteria adapted from the public sector. In exchange, these establishments, "private and affiliated under contract" (and not to be confused with truly private institutions receiving no government support), agree to apply rigorously the programs and schedules of the Ministry of Education, but they have freedom of movement where admissions, fees, and the size of their schools are concerned. It's a hybrid sort of arrangement that can be found in one form or another in most European countries.

What's different in France is that initially and historically, private or free schools were truly Catholic; that is why, despite a certain decline, more than a third of students in Brittany, a stronghold of Catholicism, still go to private schools. And across France, most private schools are run, if from a distance, by the Catholic establishment, which always negotiates with the government in this area.

The reality on the ground is quite different. Except in regions like Brittany where they are both popular and truly *catho*, private schools in France have for many years been devoid of religious content. Only 10 or 15 percent of parents claim that they send their children there for confessional reasons. The private school has become, as in most countries, a kind of backup school, which most people want to maintain as an alternative to the rigidities of the public system.

For a few, it's a matter of tradition (and in these regions the schooling is not expensive). For others, in the cities, the private institutions represent a safety net for children who have problems in their public schools. For still others, those from an affluent milieu, the private school is a sign of social distinction. (But this only goes so far, and is a bit of a mirage. The great French schools - Louis-le-Grand, Saint-Louis or Henri-IV in Paris - are all public).

Over the years and through the decades, with a little adjustment here and there under the Gaullist right, then under the becalmed left, France developed and maintained a modus vivendi between a very good public system (with wide discrepancies in quality, however) and a private sector which was variable but standardized, surviving fairly comfortably on government grants and parental fees. No one can really say, because the figures in any case are often fudged, whether the current balance is perfectly equitable. Besides, who can really determine what would be equitable in this affair, between the 100 percent subsidies that the Catholics think would be proper and the zero percent envisaged by the heirs of Robespierre? One thing is certain: in 1984, it was for strictly ideological and political reasons that the left had tried for a public victory in this area, before coming a cropper. In December 1993 - perhaps in a state of euphoria following the conclusion of the GATT agreement, and doubtless to please the "hard" right and the lobbies - Balladur insisted on tampering with the delicate power balance then in place, opening the way for municipal subsidies to private schools, when he could just as easily have freed up some funds at the national level without making a to-do. But the school question in France has nothing to do with rationality or even clear-cut special interests. Rather, it harks back to the venerable culture of the civil war. Everyone knows it, the leaders above all. But from time to time they forget what they ought to know, and thoughtlessly give way to the old urges. It's like the scorpion crossing the river on the frog's back, who mortally stings his mount even though he knows he'll also drown when the frog sinks. He just can't help himself. It's his nature.

7. The War of Words

Surely there was no connection between the one thing and the other; it was the day after the outbreak of the war with Iraq, January 17, 1991, when the Académie Française officially ratified its new spelling reforms, under the guidance and sponsorship of that noble institution's permanent secretary, Maurice Druon himself. In any case, this great victory for the Modernist cause went largely unnoticed.

The Gulf War, in fact, couldn't have been more timely, and the quiet media reception afforded the reforms was not unwelcome. While clarity has always been considered a defining quality of the French language, the vote of approval from the academicians clearly meant the opposite of what it was just as clearly proclaiming. In truth, the reform was being laid to rest once and for all, with a few wreaths of flowers on its grave, plus some unspoken thank-yous to Saddam Hussein for having launched his spectacular foray against Kuwait. The resulting media smoke screen conveniently masked the turnaround of the academicians who had to reverse Monsieur Druon's decisions, and their own into the bargain. All the while pretending that all was well.

At the Académie Française, two weeks later, the permanent secretary's personal assistant, Monsieur Daniel Oster, shouted into the telephone: "But not at all! The Academy has never gone back on it's acceptance of the reform! To the contrary! On January 17, by 25 votes to 6, it ratified the proposals, which, as is customary, will be subject to the test of time and of usage."

The vice-president of the *Conseil Supérieur de la Langue*

Française, the linguist Bernard Quemada, chief architect of the reform and director of the monumental *Grand Dictionnaire de la Langue Française*, said approximately the same thing. Yes, the Academy did give ground in response to the hue and cry, "but the reform project has been accepted, and it will prevail as usage dictates."

His enthusiasm did appear a trifle forced, and called to mind the famous words: "From defeat to defeat until the final victory!" And to play it safe he called on other francophones, especially Belgians and Quebeckers - "who are less conservative than the French" - to urg the innovations on the "mother country." Monsieur Quemada made it clear that the improvements will be *appended* to his own dictionary (we are never so well served as by ourselves). In fact, TV host and culture maven Bernard Pivot, who had sat on the reform committee before distancing himself from it, settled the question bluntly: "The Academy found a way to save face for Maurice Druon, while burying the project - or was it the other way round?"

For those linguists and grammarians who had dared to challenge a few hyphens and double consonants, it meant a rude awakening. At the beginning of February I talked with Claude Kanas, one of those responsible for the *Petit Larousse* dictionary, the most popular printed matter in France after the Bible and Doctor Spock.

Madame Kanas's verdict: "Everything was in place to annex the text of the reforms to our 1992 edition. For each of the words concerned, a symbol would have referred the reader to the text, which we would have published in its entirety. After the January 17 vote, we eliminated both the symbols and the annexed text."

It couldn't be any clearer. When the new school year began in September, 1991, there would be no sign of the reforms in either the *Petit Larousse* or the *Petit Robert*. And the Ministry of Education, which the reform's enemies suspected of wanting to produce a circular on the subject, took no action either. Where then would this elusive "reform" appear? In the Academy's own dictionary. But wait: in the annex. That is, simply for the record. And the assumption is that if the reform is not soon backed up by usage, the annex will eventually be dropped.

Now, contrary to what one would like to lead us to believe, there is no evolution in spelling "as a result of usage," as there is for the spoken language. You only change the way things are written by decree. The self-appointed authorities in this matter are, in no particular order, the Academy, the two or three most widely consulted dictionaries, and the educational system.

The Academy already spends a good part of its time proposing spelling changes. For example: *impresario* becomes *imprésario* and takes an "s" in the plural (even if one may still amuse oneself with the plural, *impresarii*, as in the popular ditty: *Sorry papa, you say/ impresarii/ with two "I"s*). After a few years, the *Larousse* will bit by bit include some alterations, but as variants, and with the qualification "Acad. Franc.". Thus a (true) *credo* in the *Larousse* still has no acute accent. And although there are two or three thousand variants and discrepancies among the major dictionaries, teachers consult them as if they were bibles. No infringement of their law is conceivable and *chariot* written with two "r"s remains an inexcusable error in French.

Why then did this modest reform, supported by educators, accepted by linguists, and negotiable to boot, run up against a blank wall?

It was a quintessentially French psychodrama. The initiative came from Prime Minister Rocard - which meant that President Mitterrand, great man of letters under God, was opposed, by definition. He nursed a quiet but profound hatred for his prime minister; over every project dear to Rocard there hovered Mitterrand's curse. Maurice Druon, a man of the right if ever there was one, became the great helmsman of the reform; the right saw him as a traitor to tradition, and the left assumed that any reform he backed could only be reactionary. All the conditions for a stalemate were in place, even if they had not yet manifested themselves. As the reform was rather prudent, and as public opinion and the media were otherwise engaged, Monsieur Druon, who was the only one dealing with the question full-time, had no trouble convincing the academicians that the committee was unanimous, while assuring the committee of the Academy's wholehearted support. The Academy members ratified the text to a man in November 1990 (with 21 of their number voting), and it seemed to be in the bag.

It just took one spark to explode the powder-keg: a petition signed by ten "prominent intellectuals," and Pivot's change of heart when he decided he had been misled about the Academy's unanimity.

With the exception of three or four valiant journalists and three heroic academicians, all the Paris media giants and luminaries went to town on the poor reforms.

For some, it was a perfect example of political power imposing arbitrary reforms by dictatorial means, without consulting anyone. A matter of republican principle. Mitterrand's circle spread the rumor that this was a fresh instance of Michel Rocard's incompetence and irresponsibility. Many others raised the specter of a new Tower of Babel for, they said, "the new literate generation won't be able to communicate with the old." The Mitterrandian singer Renaud even vowed that while he lived he wouldn't allow the circumflex accent to be removed from the word âme (soul) - not realizing, it appears, that no one had ever suggested doing so.

Alerted by this rumor of civil war, the academicians, who had initially accepted the reforms without paying much attention to the details, instantly went into reverse and noisily denounced this "butchery," still without having examined the proposals.

*   *   *

"We'll no longer be able to read Corneille as it was written!", bemoaned - among others - the (ultra-gallic) academician Jean Dutourd, thereby committing two serious errors in one sentence. On the one hand, the reform would have changed no one's current reading habits. On the other, if we still read Corneille today, it's because indeed we do not read him in the original.

According to the Belgian linguist André Goosse, a member of the reform committee and director of the celebrated *Grévisse*, a reference book on correct French usage, the proposed revisions affected only six out of a thousand of the most common French words (such as boîte (box), maître (master), and août (August),

whose unpronounced circumflex accents were to be eliminated).
For Bernard Quemada, it would have amounted to changing on
average one word per page in Proust.

What is undeniable on the other hand, is that Corneille's
spelling (not to mention that of François Villon) for us today
verges on the unreadable.

- *"Sçais-tu que c'est son sang?*
- *A quatre pas d'icy je te le fait sçauoir...*
- *Que nostre heur si tost se perdist..."*

In the eighteenth century, Voltaire fought to have "je savais"
(I knew) written the way it was pronounced, and not "je savois."
It was not until 1835 that a solemn decision by the Academy
transformed the "o" into an "a." Similarly, formal decrees were
required to distinguish "f" from "s" and "u" from "v."

For a long time spelling was left to each individual's imagination, and Montaigne wrote the verb "cognoître," today "con-
naître," (to know), in eight different ways. Lamartine wrote "âme"
without the circumflex. And Baudelaire put a hyphen after "très"
(very). The renowned "genius of the French language," invoked
by so many writers and other figures in the course of the January
"war," was in times past permissive and easygoing, until the
adoption by decree of a number of partially successful reforms
which led both to simplifications and anomalies. But there was
never an overall reform, as in Spanish or Portuguese, that sys-
tematized or rationalized the written language.

According to the linguist Henriette Walter, the French language, unlike Italian or Spanish, can never be truly phonetic,
because it has lost all its Latin endings and very often the same
sounds correspond to several different words, for example *vert,
verre, vers, ver* (green, glass, toward, worm). There is a point
beyond which no spelling reform can ever go, and therein, truly,
lies the (evil?) genius of the French language.

To assert that even so, French literary and scholarly spelling has
remained constant for three centuries would be to proclaim one's
ignorance. On the contrary: after having fixed its rules, the
Académie Française spent two centuries adapting writing to the
language - as far as it was possible - in order to simplify usage, and

LOUIS-BERNARD ROBITAILLE

eliminate occasional glaring absurdities. If at the end of the nineteenth century it had eliminated the "Greek" letters (th, ph, y), as other Latin countries have done, everyone today would see it as perfectly normal. Spaniards don't find their "crisantemo" any less poetic than the French "chrysanthème" (chrysanthemum). The Italians don't find their "fisico" any less learned than the French "physique" (physics). "To claim that a rigid and exact written language is synonymous with the genius of French is totally absurd," says Henriette Walter, who considers that spelling can only be "adjusted" by repeated decrees. And preferably, by embodying plain good sense.

In *Que vive l'orthographe!* ("Long Live Spelling!"), Messieurs Leconte and Cibois, close associates of the teachers' union, make the case for radical reform, which for them implies a rationalization of writing guided by simple and universal rules, and allowing for no confusion in meaning. They would do away with mute consonants, circumflex accents, the horrible, pointless doubling of consonants, and so on. Their proposals also include the elimination by main force of the notorious "Greek letters."

The official reform proposal is, by comparison, a model of restraint. Disappointingly so to some, who used that as a hypocritical pretext for joining the crusade of the old guard.

In fact, it amounted to no more than a reduction in the number of anomalies so flagrant as to have become the frequent butt of jokes and the staple of spelling competitions.

A few examples. Hyphens were to be replaced by a general rule for agglutination, so that "porte-monnaie" (change purse) would be consistent with "portefeuille" (wallet), men would from now on play "pingpong" (not ping-pong) and ladies would don their "froufrous" (frills). The plurals of compound words were to be simplified, so that they would behave like normal nouns, on the model of "gendarme", which was originally "gens d'armes" (men-at-arms). Inconsistencies in words from a single series were to be eliminated, such as "combattre," "combatif" (to combat, combative), "trappe," "chausse-trape" (trapdoor, trap), and so on. Verbs ending in ETER and ELER were all to be declined according to the same rules. The circumflex accent on *i* and *u* was to be done

66

away with, except where it made for a different sound or meaning. "Voute" (vault) would be consistent with "route" (road), and "abime" (abyss) with "cime" (summit). As for the notorious "nénuphar" (water lily) - as Proust and Mallarmé wrote it - by changing the "ph" to "f", one would simply be restoring the original spelling, as it is a Persian word.

These modifications were perfectly in line with those that dictionaries had gradually accepted over the years, but that had never provoked any great controversy. Even if the reform of January 1991 was reasonable, it contained a flaw that in France is fatal. It was not its daring but just its scope that gave rise to a debate over fundamental principles and dragged the French genius into the fray, along with the spirit of the language, the survival of the culture, and the ghost of Molière. To disturb a few commas was tantamount to calling the established order into question, along with a thousand years of History and the soul of the nation. That was going too far in a country where the tiniest reform smacks of the barricades and anarchy, and where anarchy and the barricades ultimately force the powers-that-be to bring in much more momentous reforms, in a state of panic and under the worst possible conditions. After all, years after the monetary reform of 1958, almost everyone still talks in terms of old francs. Old francs, no doubt, are part of the French soul.

8. *French Women, Try a Little Harder!*

I don't think France is a country that is particularly unfair to
women. On the contrary, overall their status in society and
their relations with the opposite sex place them less at a
disadvantage than most anywhere else. Françoise Giroud, former
Secretary of State for the Rights of Women, wrote not long ago
that these relations were "among the most delightful in the
world," which may seem overly enthusiastic but not far from the
truth.

The same Françoise Giroud is the first to confess, her sorrow
leavened with humor, that if there is one area where the female
condition seems to belong to a different tradition, this one ancient
and immutable, it is certainly politics. Within the EEC, France
remains the country which, by far, reserves its harshest treatment
and its lowest placings for women who have the gall (or gaul) to
meddle in governmental affairs. With only five or six percent of
woman deputies, France trails far behind even Italy or Spain. Only
in Greece is the situation worse. It's as though political conven-
tions had remained frozen while the personal and professional
standing of women was changing in all other sectors of society.

It's easy to blame built-in machismo of the political class, which
is never that welcoming to competition. Still it is an astonishing
phenomenon in the age of television and the massive influence
of image and the polls; even when women achieve huge popularity
with the public, their own parties prefer to discredit them rather
than to capitalize on that fact, for fear of turning them into real
aspirants for power. For the last twenty years, since women first

took centre-stage in political life with Giscard d'Estaing's blessing, the story has been repeated over and over again.

So it was during the campaign for legislative election in March 1993.

As always on such occasions new stars and new heroes appeared on the scene, and this time attention was focused on two young women.

The first was Dominique Voynet, 44 years old, a doctor and a longtime militant for the Green Party, the most mainstream faction of the Ecologist coalition. Unknown before the campaign began, she rapidly eclipsed the other leaders of the group, beginning with the sinister Antoine Waechter. Much in demand for the major political television shows, she came across as natural, spontaneous, and politically astute. Compared to the president of *Génération Écologie* (Ecology Generation), Brice Lalonde, whose effortless fluency led him to make slips and commit gaffes, Madame Voynet consistently showed remarkable political aplomb. On the night of the first round of voting (which saw a disastrous 7 percent for the *écolos* instead of the hoped for 15) she was one of only two candidates for the coalition in the whole country to qualify for the second round. In the midst of the electoral gale that had swept away both Lalonde and Waechter, she had survived. Not only that, she had garnered what under the circumstances was a most honorable score, with 44 percent of the votes, running against the mayor of Dole.

The other heroine was Ségolène Royal, 41 years old, mother of four, Minister of the Environment during the last two years of socialist rule. The night of the socialist rout, while the leaders, devastated or otherwise occupied in their distant constituencies, were mostly invisible, the lovely Ségolène was everywhere on television, holding her own against the young carnivores of the right or daunting crocodiles such as Charles Pasqua. Three hours later she had become in-dis-pen-sa-ble to the Socialist Party. Three days later, militant socialists who had been shattered by the results were asking themselves out loud whether the renewal of their party didn't require a new leader, from a totally new generation. That would be Ségolène.

The catapulting of these two *young* women into the limelight had something about it that was refreshing. This does not mean that Miss Ségolène, with all her charm, is not ambitious and calculating, or that *Doctor* Voynet is the greatest political strategist and philosopher of recent years. But overall they compared most favorably to many of the big names on the right or left, none of whom is presumed to have superhuman gifts. However, it must be said that their moment of glory was rather brief. Ségolène worked the media quite well for a while without ever getting any real control over the Socialist Party; then she was cast aside when she made her first mistake by objecting to the method used to choose a presidential candidate. As for Dominique Voynet, she ended up doing badly in the presidential elections, even though the terrible duo of Waechter and Lalonde declined to run. Both women were victims of political professionals. Ségolène never really managed to infiltrate the Socialist Party apparatus. Nor, frankly, did Dominique Voynet ever manage to impose herself on the Ecologists, despite her popularity. It was as though when push came to shove the militants, even the Greens, preferred almost any man as their leader, even Waechter. To make it in French politics, you need at the very least to have a clan, troops behind you. These two women were solo performers, and so it was easy to brush them aside at the first false note.

Since then a new star has appeared in the firmament: Martine Aubry, serious, solid, ambitious, daughter of an illustrious father, a prudent strategist with long-term goals who has built herself both a personal network and a political base in Lille. Her prestige today is great. What remains to be seen is whether it will stand the test once she really tries to capitalize on it in the political world.

Because for twenty years, it's been the same story. Some women - a small number only - suddenly acquire considerable prestige, which remains secure as long as they don't try to cash in on it. Simone Veil is the most prominent example. She was for a very long time the most popular political figure in France; her past, her fight for the liberalization of abortion, made her almost immune to attack. Her influence in the media and in the political arena was enormous and long-standing. But, apart from running as a centrist in the 1989 European parliamentary elections, she always abstained from the real power struggles, even within her own party, and never even tried for a seat in the French national assembly. Her disappointing performance in 1989, which fell short of even the most pessimistic predictions, confirmed the rule that she herself knew well: the popularity of an individual means little when the political chips are down unless it is backed up by the party apparatus. Who wields the knife, and wins, is at the head of a pack. Not alone.

A few other women have succeeded for a time, both in getting a foothold inside their party apparatus and in topping the polls. Édith Cresson, France's first prime minister, had herself won her fief at Châtellerault, then had played an important role in the government. Georgina Dufoix had started off well at Nîmes. Michèle Barzach had a perch in the Assembly and the conservative RPR, and was very popular. With Mmes Cresson and Barzach, however, what ensued was a political lynching that began the day they were perceived to be getting too big for their boots. And the punishment inflicted on them, having the political rug pulled out from under them, first by their "comrades," then by the media - served as an object lesson for anyone who wanted to follow in their footsteps.

From Veil to Cresson, and including Edwige Avice, Yvette Roudy and Françoise Giroud, the common denominator was that their power, when it was real, always emanated from the protection of a Prince. They were given good and sometimes important ministries, and all had reason to be proud of the popularity they brought to their government. But none of them was able to build a real political base, either in electoral terms or within the party. Plain good sense and electoral self-interest, properly understood, ought to have led the major parties like the Socialists or the RPR to run prestigious woman candidates in crucial legislative (or even municipal) elections. Yet what invariably happened, what with the infighting of clans, personalities or political factions, and the respect due to party notables and loyal militants, was that in the 580-odd ridings in the country there were never more than 50 female candidates of any significance. What is more, when a woman politician succeeded on her own in winning a riding that she had been allowed to contest only because it was deemed unwinnable, in the following election she was asked to give up *her* seat to a real party man and try her luck at the other end of the country. The most frequent reason given for this extraordinary policy of exclusion is that the local nominations are decided by majority vote, which gives rise to violent struggles that are difficult to control at the national level. The height of absurdity was achieved in the legislative elections of 1986, which were conducted differently, on the basis of proportional representation with party lists. When, department by department, the lists were drawn up, and after all the country-wide haggling about who would appear where on the lists, it turned out that there were even fewer women in a position to be elected than under the old system! In fact the March 1986 Assembly was even more dominated by males than those that had preceded it.

What is incredible is that despite all the worthy and reasonable declarations on the part of every important political leader you can think of, the situation was no rosier in 1995 than in 1993 or 1981. In forming the Juppé government, newly-elected President Chirac was inspired to include twelve women in the inner circle: a historic record. The problem was that they were all either young and lacking in experience, or complete unknowns, or second-fiddles, or all three. Simone Veil was thrown out of office, Michèle Barzach was not forgiven her sins, and even the ever-popular Alliot-Marie was dropped because she converted to Chiraquism too late. One might have thought that the prime minister would have called on a prominent female figure from the private sector (it wasn't as if it had not been done before). It didn't happen. The result: we're almost back to the days before Giscard, 21 years ago.

"To go into politics in 1975," Françoise Giroud once declared, "was for a woman like invading the locker-room of a football club after a game." Twenty years later, the old guard and the young Turks of French politics are a little more accustomed to seeing the occasional woman in the locker-room doorway, but only in the role of majorette or president of the fan club. French women, you'll have to try a little harder if you want to make it in politics!

9. *The De Gaulle Monument*

What's left of Gaullism, fifty years after De Gaulle's famous radio appeal of June 18, 1940 to the French to continue fighting the Germans under his leadership? At first glance, everything and nothing. Everything: the entire political class - other than a few extremists - sees itself in his image, or at the very least pays him homage. Everyone has become a Gaullist of sorts. Nothing, if one takes literally the dreams of glory the General brandished on the world stage, and which vanished when he did.

The flamboyant assertion of independence, the leadership of Europe, the membership in an exclusive club of four Great Powers, the prophetic vision of a great Europe (with France as a driving force), all these now seem like bygone mirages utterly divorced from reality. Were the British, who could never stand him, right when they said De Gaulle was a Don Quixote who heard voices, like Joan of Arc?

Jean Lacouture, the biographer who for the moment is the recognized authority on Charles De Gaulle,[1] has also coined a somewhat denigrating, if revealing, equestrian metaphor: "De Gaulle was unfortunate," he tells us, "in bestriding a mount whose stature was, in the last analysis, modest in the extreme." The France of Louis XIV would certainly have suited him better. His

---

1   De Gaulle, by Jean Lacouture, 2 vols., London: Collins Harvill, 1990.

old friend and rival Churchill had more luck in 1940 when he took over the helm of a Great Britain that could still with some credibility call itself a superpower, and that was to play a crucial and glorious role in World War II, before experiencing its own decline.

Did De Gaulle fail in just about everything? Was he only a dreamer, a role-player, a slightly ridiculous actor? Even within France the hard-line Gaullists, guardians of revealed truth, resemble nothing more than a modest circle of old gentlemen living off their memories. Almost the entire political community honors De Gaulle's legacy. And yet his first successor to the presidency was Valéry Giscard d'Estaing, who was instrumental in the *Grand Charles'* departure in 1969. And the presidency then fell into the hands of François Mitterrand, who was his main political adversary from 1958 onwards. Mitterrand was followed by the "Gaullist" Jacques Chirac, who had played an important role in the election of the "traitor" Giscard in 1974. What his successors have essentially retained of Gaullism is the independent nuclear deterrent force which they had all initially condemned and had criticized as costly and laughable. Giscard and especially Mitterrand effortlessly assumed the monarchical style they had so self-righteously deplored in the General - but perhaps that is more a national trait than a legacy of De Gaulle.

If one is to believe their most reliable biographers, both Giscard and Mitterrand were intent on keeping up appearances, especially at international gatherings of heads of state, but they had no illusions about playing a major role on the world stage. Now, when France speaks *urbi et orbi*, it is, more modestly, to present itself as an embodiment of the rights of man. It no longer sees itself as anything but a middling world power. And what with German reunification, it can no longer even delude itself as to its eventual role in Europe. If you add 80 million Germans (compared with 58 million French) to a huge balance of trade surplus and an all-powerful mark, the dream of an autonomous Europe with France at the helm resembles an adolescent joke. Still, given its central position in Europe and the historical restraints that prevent Germany from using all its political muscle, Paris can reasonably hope to play an important role in a sort of unofficial Franco-German condominium.

However, if we're taking stock of Gaullism, we have to know what its creator himself had in mind. De Gaulle was certainly not the visionary the British and Americans took him to be, nor even a dreamer or a naïf. According to Lacouture we're dealing here with a superb performer, an actor who, while striving after an outsize goal, had no great illusions as to its attainability. In London during the war he played at being the incarnation of France, but he knew perfectly well that it was a bluff and he had no cards in his hand. The same was true when he demanded to be treated as an equal by Roosevelt. It's not that he took himself for Joan of Arc, but that he knew he had to play the prophet to garner a little respect. It was true again after the war, when thanks to him, France, a conquered and officially collaborationist country, moved into the camp of the conquerors (he was neither at Yalta nor at Potsdam, but he got a seat at Berlin, as well as on the UN Security Council). De Gaulle was a great political artist who gave grandiose performances in the public arena in order to attain relatively modest goals. And he did not entirely believe everything he said.

He knew perfectly well that he didn't have the power to dictate American monetary - not to mention military - policy, and that his clout where the Soviet Union was concerned was extremely limited. But did he not succeed for years in pretending otherwise, and in keeping France - a country of "calves," as he sometimes called it - in the media limelight? And was he not taken most seriously by Adenauer, Kennedy and Nixon?

"De Gaulle," says Lacouture, "forced France to surpass itself, to live for a time beyond its own capacities." De Gaulle, who behind the rhetoric was a profound pragmatist, had only one aim: to ask the impossible in words in order to gain a small advantage in reality.

To assess the De Gaulle legacy, let us try to imagine what would have occurred in this country if the man from Colombey-les-deux-Églises had not been part of its history.

- *During the war*. France, a great military and colonial power, had been defeated and was the only major nation to have collaborated with the Germans. Without De Gaulle, liberation by the Americans would have led to a long-term eclipse on the world scene. The status of France could have been similar to that of Italy today.

- *The Algerian crisis*. All De Gaulle achieved was to manage a major political defeat, cynically misleading the political forces that had returned him to power while allowing the terrible violence to drag on for another four years, and failing in the end to maintain the French population of Algeria in place. A depressing record. But one has to bear in mind the situation in France in 1958. The Algerian war could not be won politically, the political class was totally powerless to find a way out, things had reached a point where the army was threatening to take control of the state. "Of course," says Lacouture, "it's hard to believe that in a country with a tradition like that of France, with its close ties to the United States and its links to the Atlantic Alliance, a military dictatorship would have been tolerated." Nevertheless, with a Fourth Republic in tatters and the Algerian war even more virulent, what condition would the country have been in five years down the road?

- *The institutions*. This is the least spectacular of De Gaulle's achievements, but it is perhaps the most important. In any case it's what has most deeply affected the position of France in today's world. Without the Algerian crisis, De Gaulle would never have been returned to power. But without him, the political class and the electorate would never have accepted the imposition of the Fifth Republic, which, while fairly authoritarian for a Western country, is an outright constitutional corset for the tribes of Gaul. Anthropological tendencies have always inclined France toward a regime similar to that of the Fourth Republic, with its ineffectual parliamentarism and its taste for back-room deals, favoritism and scheming. From 1946 to 1958, the France of the Fourth Republic boasted only one strong figure, Pierre Mendès-France, elected in the course of another crisis, that of Indochina. Eleven months later all sides in parliament ganged up on him and swept him out of office.

France at the end of the millennium is perhaps not the great preeminent nation wished for out loud by De Gaulle. But without him, its bad old habits would certainly have endured: a parliament that makes and unmakes governments that have no authority, governments incapable of governing except in terms of short-term survival, an industrial and banking private sector tied to the bureaucracy and infected with cronyism, and a non-existent foreign policy (as under the Fourth Republic).

A France that had never known De Gaulle? It would doubtless be a great European country, relatively prosperous, inflationist, politically unstable, and with no clout compared to Germany and Great Britain. That description more or less matches another European country, one that is economically dynamic and prosperous, but that unfortunately no one takes seriously on the international scene: Italy, with its 55 million inhabitants. It finished the war on the side of the losers, it never transcended its sterile political system, and, given its potential, it's not doing that well.

*   *   *

De Gaulle is one of those mountain ranges that you can never explore completely.

It was thought that Jean Lacouture had sewn things up, for several years at any rate, with his excellent three-volume biography of some 2,000 pages (two volumes, abridged, in English).

But now, reading what is only the first third of the recently-published notes taken at the time by Alain Peyrefitte, one soon realizes that where De Gaulle is concerned, there are still secrets to be unearthed. Lacouture goes into detail, but Peyrefitte, who saw the General in person daily almost without interruption between 1959 and 1969, as his adviser and then as a minister, took down verbatim what De Gaulle said, and above all how he said it. There are the dates, the circumstances, comments on his facial expressions and his intonations. Nothing conflicts with what we already knew, but it's as though we had been given for the first time detailed close-ups of the man.

Seen at close range, De Gaulle is, if anything, even larger-than-life than we knew: wittier, more mordant, more cynical in his assessment of political situations, more visionary.

A true cynic, De Gaulle was returned to power in May 1958 by partisans of French Algeria, to whom he had made clear and unambiguous promises.

The first time the young deputy Peyrefitte met him in private was in March 1959, that is, at a time when the very idea of Algerian independence was still unthinkable in official discourse. It is clear that for De Gaulle even then, to keep Algeria in France and to integrate the Algerian Arabs was out of the question. "For that would mean," he said to Peyrefitte, "that my village would no longer be called Colombey-les-deux-Églises (Colombey of the Two Churches), but Colombey-les-deux- Mosquées! (Colombey of the Two Mosques)"

The tone is set at once. The General, in private, does not shy away from using blunt and aggressive language, bordering on the coarse.

"He had three levels of language," says Alain Peyrefitte, "one of the statesman, in public, carefully weighing his words, and learning by heart his speeches and declarations to the press; one for his Cabinet where he spoke freely and played with ideas; and one for his private circle, where he was deliberately provocative, brazen, and sometimes brutally frank."

Algeria, then, in 1959. On the one hand, we are struck by the clarity of his political vision. Independence is inevitable, with *if possible* the maintenance in place of the French Algerians, or *pieds-noirs*, and all the rest is nonsense, a product of those with "the brains of a hummingbird."

De Gaulle didn't try to masquerade as a liberal: "The Muslims, have you been to see them?" he said to Peyrefitte. "Have you had a good look at them, with their turbans and their djellabas?" he asked. "You know perfectly well they're not French! Arabs are Arabs, the French are French." And a little later, concerning the tactical formula of "self-determination" he was proposing, both to the Algerian liberation front and the *pieds-noirs*: "It will be a snare for idiots." Still later: "Can you imagine France, ten years from now, with an Arab president in the Elysée Palace?" In short, De Gaulle, from the moment he arrived in power, followed a cold and intelligent course of reasoning that only Raymond Aron, and perhaps a few others, dared to espouse at the time: France could not hope to hold onto Algeria except by integrating it totally, a project that not only would make no sense culturally, but would be disastrous for France itself. "We can't be responsible for these people who multiply like rabbits."

As the pages turn - sometimes we skip, depending on the subject at hand - Charles De Gaulle emerges as a veritable encyclopedia of geopolitics and a consummate master of strategy. He seemed to know everything about the African countries, about the standing of the United States and Great Britain, and was much more forthright in private than in public regarding the real power of France. And so, in the course of a conversation regarding the fate of the Algerian *pieds-noirs*, he made this comparison in 1962: "The French-Canadians are a majority in Quebec. There they were able to survive, to defend themselves. In the other provinces, where they are in the minority, they were overwhelmed, wiped out." In 1965: "The French-Canadians are fighting for their freedom. We have to help them." (In a later volume, we learn that "the French-Canadians must no longer be the flunkies of the Anglo-Saxons.")

In private, De Gaulle is willfully provocative - but it's hard to tell when he's ironic and when he's serious. After Peyrefitte had been named government spokesman, the General said to him: "You've studied Latin. The word minister, means servant." On another occasion he laid down the law: "When I reach a conclusion after due deliberation, then the government is speaking through me. Without me the government has no substance. Only I endow it with life."

An unbearable autocrat, De Gaulle spent his time complaining about journalists. Where television, part of Peyrefitte's "responsibility," was concerned, he always said "your journalists." "On TV they're all leftists, they've created soviets, get rid of them!" For him, the entire press corps was hostile: "To the point," he said, not quite joking, "where if Le Figaro and L'Immonde[2] were one day to support me, I'd see it as a national catastrophe!"

To my knowledge, even the political superstars that were his contemporaries did not in private exude this constant energy, this enthusiastic appetite for irony. Being somewhat fixated on the British, for a while he banned whisky from intimate dinners at the Élysée, explaining that Napoleon, by blockading England, had encouraged the development of that drink, about which he had nothing good to say. And when one of his advisors asked him to send a courtesy message to the British on the occasion of Shakespeare's birthday, he replied haughtily: "Now your Shakespeare, we don't even know if he existed. How are we supposed to know when he was born?"

---

2   This is a play on words. The newspaper *Le Monde* –The World– becomes *L'Immonde* –the vile. (Translator's note)

III.

Unease in
"La Bonne Société"

1. *The Serene Comfort of the "Bonne Société"*[1]

The seventh arrondissement, especially that noble part of it still referred to as the Faubourg Saint-Germain, always reminds me of the *Fronde* salons in Alexandre Dumas's *Twenty Years After*, and is in certain respects the most mysterious part of Paris. At first sight, to the tourist passing through it on the way to the Rodin Museum, it seems austere and unwelcoming. Later one views it differently, having discovered how many august personages, descendants of old families, possessors of solid and discreet fortunes, its high walls house. Its streets are no less arid and sterile for all that, but they do at times inspire the sort of awe one feels before the grand and historic symbols of absolute power. It's in the seventh that the heart of real Parisian society beats, and nowhere else; so much power linked to so much discretion commands respect.

Like the aristocracy in the past, *la bonne société* hates the display of money in all its forms - showy cars or villas, a sumptuous and extravagant lifestyle - and it does not appreciate the vulgar flaunting of huge incomes. Being of it means old family property, and if one holds a job it is preferably a public office, within a university,

---

1   A relatively unique French category, which groups, loosely speaking, the "right crowd," the "people who count" in the media and the state, the defenders of culture, intelligence, refinement and reassuring good taste. This cultural bourgeoisie will be hereinafter referred to by its French name, i.e., *la bonne société*.

in the upper ranks of the civil service, in the museums and colleges of France, in the major media, publishing, the Council of State, the academies, possibly even in the banks. Salaries are relatively modest, even if, especially if, they represent only a quarter of one's actual revenue. Thus a professor at the *École Pratique* will concurrently hold down a job or write a column in a prestigious newspaper, while keeping his hand in at one of the great publishing houses where at regular intervals he brings out a book highly regarded by the *happy few*. At the same time he enjoys the occupancy of a beautiful apartment he's inherited at the top of Rue d'Assas or Avenue Denfert-Rochereau, plus a house he's acquired in the Lot or the Pyrenees. And from these stately heights, where one rubs shoulders at will with authors, scholars, researchers, who are often of very modest means, one rails against the new barbarians with their Bentleys, their best-sellers, their money or their mass appeal, who pander to the cheap media. And with a clear conscience one espouses what is worthy, cultivated, intelligent, enlightened, refined, and reassuringly tasteful.

This propensity for discreet comfort is reflected in the habitat and preferred neighborhoods of the Parisian elite. The truly chic parts of the capital are not necessarily the most opulent or the most expensive, or even the most striking.

Long ago when I still frequented real estate agencies, I often heard, in response to the routine question: "Where would you like to live in Paris?", the equally routine response: "In the west." This could also mean the suburban west, improbable districts with names such as Boulogne, Puteaux and Levallois-Peret. I came to the conclusion that to keep up appearances, middle managers from outside Paris had to have an address somewhere in the bourgeois west, even if it was dreary, if they were not to be suspected of poverty. It's true that for the longest time, the well-off Paris neighborhoods were to be found in the west and the "prole" neighborhoods in the east, just as in London, or other great metropolises elsewhere in the world. In one direction you have Saint-Cloud, Neuilly and the sixteenth arrondissement, where you're not likely to stumble across any slums, and in the other, Montreuil, Belleville or Barbès, where villas and *palazzi* are not too thick on the ground. It's easy to see where the money is. Even today, bourgeois in quest of refinement and upper managers climbing the social ladder would immolate themselves in the town square rather than live beyond the confines of these visibly opulent enclaves.

What makes things complicated is that true chic must not be confused with the bourgeois west, nor even with those neighborhoods where you pay the most per square metre. The Parisian *bonne societé* may not lack for money, but neither does it consort with the Moneyed.

When it can afford it, it sets itself up in a lovely apartment dating, from, say, the eighteenth or nineteenth century, and in the noble part of the seventh arrondissement, the venerable Faubourg Saint-Germain. In utter simplicity. A hundred and fifty square metres, sometimes much less. You find Parisian celebrities and intelligentsia installed in relatively restricted quarters, where at times one must push aside piles of books and pull out the table in order to serve dinner for eight.

Although all of the seventh arrondissement is desirable, and very expensive per square metre, there does exist a kind of Golden Quadrilateral, a Forbidden City, where practically everyone "belongs" and where, with few exceptions, everyone living there, even in a maid's room for two, is not ennobled exactly, but let us say invested with an invisible *right-of-way*. On the west, this Forbidden City is bordered by Les Invalides, on the south by the thoroughfare that will become Boulevard Montparnasse, on the north by the Seine, and on the east by a less precise frontier that overlaps the sixth arrondissement, extends as far as the Rue de Seine, and beyond that includes, conceivably, the territory south of Boulevard Saint-Germain that leads to the Luxembourg Gardens.

Its main arteries - Rue de Varenne, Rue de Grenelle, Rue de Babylone and a few principal cross-streets - all run in a straight line and at first seem quite barren, shut off as they are almost end to end by walls that protect the villas, gardens and ministries, by the uniform and well-preserved façades, and by the monumental doorways, always closed. A telling feature: there are in these streets few or no cafés or businesses, except for the occasional old-fashioned shop selling notions or stationery, or, a modest concession to human weakness, an Arab grocery store discreetly open in the evenings. In the Forbidden City one finds many of the important ministries, doubtless because at a certain point the ministries laid their hands on the most beautiful private mansions in Paris and they happened to be located in the Faubourg Saint-Germain. There are venerable religious institutions and old hospitals with gardens. There's the Rodin Museum, a solitary and unusual cinema, the exotic *Pagode*, a few cultural centres, an old Italian bookstore, and finally the *bonne société*'s general store, appropriately named the *Bon Marché* (The Good Deal). But the Quadrilateral is not a neighborhood for businesses, and even less for bistros. There are hardly any restaurants, large or small, as though, in this global capital of gastronomy, the vulgar practice of eating heartily and expensively ought not to be indulged inside the walls of the Forbidden City. Unless of course the meal is taking place in a private apartment. In short, we are not far from Bunuel's *The Discreet Charm of the Bourgeoisie*, where the guests relieve themselves in public but retire to the toilet to gnaw on a chicken leg, unobserved by prying eyes.

These long avenues may appear sad, their passersby not especially captivating, their street life non-existent, but it must be said that there are people who would burn in hell rather than be exiled from them. Every day one can meet someone who would prefer, for 6,000 francs a month, to rent a two-room walk-up flat rather than a beautiful apartment with a view and an elevator in, say, the fourteenth - which is itself nothing to be scoffed at.

In the seventh, the choice and the less choice real estate costs a lot per square metre, whether one is buying or renting. But, and here is the charm, these astronomical sums are in large part theoretical; most people there don't pay anything, or have never had to dip into their pockets for real money, or in any case have never paid the real, the market price. Many apartments, including some of the most impressive, have been in the same family for generations. They have no known value, other than sentimental ("My mother was born there, we heated with coal, that's where my nurse died, we all adored her!"). I'm not at all sure that, even with piles of dollars or petrodollars, just anyone, if you follow my reasoning, can acquire property in the Quadrilateral. There is no sign, certainly, of any significant turnover. If you were not born yourself in the Faubourg Saint-Germain, it's far better to hold a lease on a 180-metre apartment belonging to the Bank of France, old insurance companies, the Académie Française, or Paris City Hall, than to buy. It's common practice, it costs two or three times less than the market price, and it's a sign to one's neighbors that one is on good terms with individuals well placed in venerable and reliable national institutions. Finally, it just isn't fair. The most bourgeois neighborhood in Paris is also one of those where you can still find rents unchanged since 1948, or little apartments that are well kept but antique (postwar plumbing and no elevator), set aside by their easy-going owners, in exchange for a small sum, for friends or relatives or country cousins visiting Paris. The Quadrilateral is not a moneyed domain, but belongs to this elite, and many university and publishing employees live there modestly enough, with salaries of from 11,000 to 14,000 francs per month.

As the Quadrilateral can't accommodate all of *la bonne société*, its members are scattered here and there around Paris. But not just anywhere, and not where you'd expect. What's unique about Paris is that if you can't make it into the Quadrilateral, or even into the less prestigious part of the seventh, you don't automatically fall back on a typically bourgeois neighborhood or the residential west. When you carefully examine a list, compiled at random, of *people who count in Paris*, it's clear that very few of them, despite their affluence, have chosen to live on Rue de la Pompe or in Neuilly or Saint-Cloud. Those who have settled there sometimes even offer the (acceptable) excuse that it's due to their affection for an old family property. But it's much less chic, unquestionably, than certain old working class neighborhoods, Maubert, the Marais, the Bastille, etc. I am always struck by the fact that the Parisian high-flyers hardly ever live on Avenue Foch for example, in those gleaming buildings so well protected from interlopers, with their frontage roads and high fences separating the gardens from the sidewalk. Every time I've found a celebrity there, he or she was either foreign, most often American, or "nouveau-riche." It was the perfect spot for Jackie Onassis.

In two recent books, one dealing with well-known Parisian journalists, and the other the elite intelligentsia, this geographical phenomenon is quickly confirmed. There is the Quadrilateral and its noble outskirts: all of the sixth, the fringes of the thirteenth and fourteenth arrondissements. Add to that certain small enclaves whose status is at least as high: Place des Vosges, the gardens of the Palais-Royal, the best part of Montmartre.

There follow a few areas in the process of becoming noble, and whose territory is expanding. The Marais, whose rigid western boundary is the Rue du Renard and its extensions, is, despite its unevenness, a perfectly acceptable place to put down stakes. By osmosis, the edges of the eleventh have become legitimate (especially since the construction of the Bastille Opera). The twelfth, neat and petit-bourgeois beyond words, is one of the least acceptable arrondissements in Paris (along with the nineteenth, much of the twentieth, and the depths of the fifteenth or thirteenth), although Place d'Aligre is an exception to the rule.

The criteria determining these choices (as they have evolved slowly over the years) have little to do with comfort or bourgeois opulence, but rather with a certain idea of History and Culture. Outside the sixth and seventh, one might as well live in neighborhoods that do boast a History. Which enables an intellectual of some stature, reasonably well off, to declare brusquely, "I live in a real working-class neighborhood, it's fantastic. It's so authentic." What's important is not that it be necessarily true, but that everyone agree to believe it and to repeat it. A neighborhood that yesterday was beneath contempt, today is declared chic by the arbiters of taste for the elite, and becomes acceptable. So goes the sociology of living space in Paris, and the price per square metre follows not far behind, at a moderate but constant speed.

A code almost as strict governs moves into the countryside and the establishment of secondary residences. *Bonne société*, overall, locates its vacation homes in very specific regions that have inevitably become expensive over the years, but which were not in the beginning moneyed districts. Doubtless, in earlier times, it frequented the Côte d'Azur with Fitzgerald, and the port of

AND GOD CREATED THE FRENCH

Saint-Tropez just after the war, but today these are vacation spots for parvenus, rich bumpkins, supermarket moguls and rowdy racketeers who specialize in real-estate. One cannot decently have a second home there unless, as we saw earlier in the case of a principal residence in the sixteenth or Neuilly, it's a family dwelling, ennobled by two generations of occupancy, preferably in a place like Ramatuelle, or even better in Grimaud.

The two locations of choice, outside Paris, have this in common: they were for a long time discreet, even secret places. They are the Luberon, the hills behind Avignon, and Belle-Ile-en-Mer, near Nantes. I remember an article fifteen or twenty years ago in the *Nouvel Observateur*, by Jean-Francis Held, that caused a small uproar in Saint-Germain: "Where do *THEY* go secretly at Christmas, Easter, and in summer?" Swimming pools invisible except from a helicopter, ancient farms surrounded by low walls at the end of a country road, the discreet (then) charm of Rousillon, Saignon or Lourmarin. An acquaintance with an illustrious name, who frequents only celebrated figures of the *bonne société*, told me quite seriously, "Now Held is one of the traitors. No one will speak to him."

As for Belle-Ile, its clandestine character has endured much longer than that of the Luberon, and its being an island protects it from all sorts of undesirable invasions. There one encounters left-wing intellectuals who have called it their "home away from home" for thirty years, and Parisian architects for whom it forms part of their childhood memories. There are few hotels - the most sought after, l'Hôtel du Phare à Sauzon, is the cheapest on the island - hardly more rental properties, and a preponderance of family homes. Belle-Ile, with its bicycles, its old cars left there year round, its tourism that is exceedingly ordinary to the untutored eye, gives all the appearance of modesty and frugality and is even so perverse as to hide the fact that life there (restaurants, hotels, rentals) is far more expensive than anywhere else in Brittany, as expensive as in the Luberon itself. But you will never have to endure busloads of tourists there and, finally, is it not worthwhile paying an arm and a leg in order to *appear* of modest means, when that is a quality *la bonne société* holds so dear?

2. *The Abolition Of Money*

ARISTOCRATIC NOSTALGIA

It took me a long time to get a handle on the widely accredited truism that the French do not like money, or as they say, *have a problem with money*. After all, I've seen them lining up to buy electrical appliances at Darty's discount warehouse, or counting pennies after their vacations or at month's end. In fact, the French, even in the best circles, do not detest money at all, or at least what it brings them in the way of luxury, power, black limousines, mansions, fine restaurants, and above all beautiful and good real-estate; what they do detest is *counting* it. They hate - even in working class circles - seeming to care about money or to scurry after it. Nothing for them is more gauche than displaying it in full view as though no one had ever seen it before, or on the other hand appearing to count every sou, as though they were afraid there might not be enough. Money exists, like bathtubs and toilets, but should not be shown off, nor publicly discussed. You may think about it all you want, just don't talk about it.

From the French point of view, America is like a huge public WC where people from all social circles talk about money at the dinner table, show off their pay cheques, compare the buying prices of their houses and cars. At the end of the meal, they receive - just like that, without having to ask - separate checks, wherein every penny is accounted for, including the mineral water, the coffee, and their share of the red wine. Around the table, each diner can tell you within a few thousand dollars what is the salary of the next, how much tax he pays, and how much net income he has. In North America, people know how much a university professor earns, or a bank manager, or (garden-variety) print and television journalists, and even the members of the liberal professions. Only captains of industry and a few top television stars are immune from the general rule, but sooner or later their income too crops up in the newspapers.

In France separate checks don't exist (except grudgingly for American tourists): the very idea seems incongruous and vaguely suspect. Other than for a modest office lunch or a meal shared by a few penniless young friends, you rarely see anyone at the end of a dinner putting the bill under a microscope and pulling out a calculator to figure out how much each person should pay. In exceptional cases, the bill will be divided by the number of people present, including women, but it will frequently happen that the men discreetly split the tab among themselves while the women pretend not to have noticed. Often enough, and not only in affluent circles, someone will take the bill and settle for everybody before anyone has had the time to react, making the grand gesture on the pretext that someone else treated last time, or just because he's in a good mood. Everyone will know that given his probable monthly income it's a lot of money, but that's the whole point. In working class bistros you never drink "*en Suisse*," or Dutch treat - you have to pay your turn without really counting. When it comes right down to it, pleasure for the French prole (and of course the Italian) is a matter of playing at being a great lord, and putting the constraints of cash out of one's mind long enough to indulge in a few libations and say: money's no problem, or even better, *no money between us*.

The flip side of this generosity is that, generally speaking, the French don't like you to know the exact state of their finances. For a humble employee to pay an extravagant round is also a way to distract people from the modesty of his circumstances or to sow some doubt in their minds: might he be hiding something? Has a rich uncle passed on? Even in fairly modest and well documented milieus - those of workers, employees, civil servants - most people manage, often with some success, to generate a smoke screen around their true income, making it seem either higher or lower; they can't stand anyone knowing what's in their bank account. You hear everything from: *I'm as poor as Job, if you only knew!* to: *No problem, I make out all right!* And most often they achieve their goal. One never knows if M***, a simple government employee, is also profiting from the rent on three apartments, or if W*** has received a generous bonus, or perhaps holds down a second job.

Even in the middle ranks of *la bonne société* it's often impossible to tell what this person or that one really earns in a year. On many Parisian newspapers, to take an example with which I ought to be familiar, pay scales often vary considerably and there are, for no apparent reason, differences in salary as great as four to one (the disparity is even greater in television journalism). Moreover, at a certain point you realize that F***, while receiving his full salary on a certain weekly, also teaches at a university and is on the payroll of a publishing house. Not only does F*** not divulge his annual income - assuming anyone would be so gauche as to pop the question - but if he does spill the beans he provides what is almost certainly an inaccurate figure, because it reflects only one of his sources of revenue.[2]

About two years ago, the newspaper *Libération* caused a small scandal by publishing the salaries of hosts and star journalists for public television (France 2 and 3 for the most part). It turned out that, in the secret high echelons of French television, a talented journalist, a star in his field but who did not necessarily attract a large viewing public, earned six times as much as an ordinary

---

2   In the 1970s, the famous bandit on the run Jacques Mesrine kidnapped, somewhere deep in France, a certain Monsieur Lelièvre, and obtained a ransom from his family of six million francs in small notes, even though the gentleman's bank accounts were frozen by the police. M. Lelièvre was a total unknown who dressed like Paul Léautaud, that is half-way to being a bum.

well-known television journalist, who himself already earned four times the guaranteed minimum wage. Certain producer-hosts for major political or cultural programs, prestige items with modest audiences, earned even more. That meant that the highest salaries were about thirty of forty times the minimum wage. This sort of gap was a legacy of the 1980s, and was especially absurd in public broadcasting, where the programs concerned were not particularly profitable. These "revelations" were instantly condemned by the interested parties as infringements of their privacy, and a large part of the French population agreed. Even some of those who are eager to believe that the bourgeois, the media stars, and the highly placed are capable of the worst sort of baseness and affluent debauchery, thought it was not right to divulge people's salaries, never mind if they were paid from the taxpayers' pockets (the publication of the annual income - seven million francs - of Peugeot's chief executive officer, Jacques Calvet, had provoked the same sort of controversy, but this was in the private sector). To reveal someone's true income - even if he is the worst sort of class enemy - is like printing a picture of him in a brothel. It's considered morally repugnant in France. You can debate important political issues here, polemicize on philosophy, chew over insurrections or Restorations, but nobody wants to hear about money, not even those whose business it is to attack the ruling class. Both the left and the right in this country will tell you this: money is a *false problem*.

Seen in that light, François Mitterrand was an exemplary president. A bit less so than Charles de Gaulle, who charged private dinners at the Élysée Palace to his personal account, but much more so than Georges Pompidou, who bore the ineradicable stigma of having been a banker (in the private sector!), and Giscard, who was notorious for his stinginess. Catholic and Jansenist, President Mitterrand, who ostentatiously disliked money, never (at least officially) had a personal fortune, only one of those discreet but comfortable lifestyles that are the envy of good society and public opinion. In Château-Chinon he stayed at the Hôtel du Morvan, and in a room without bath. In Latché he had an old country house, doubtless bought in the old days for a song. In Paris, a private mansion, but in a student quarter, and he shared the property with his brother-in-law Roger Hanin. A perfect picture, both for those who held to old family traditions, and for the republican enemies of the *bastions of money*. Monsieur Mitterrand enhanced the picture by taking care - according to a very old legend - never to weigh himself down with banknotes when he went out, whether to Chez Lipp, the restaurant, or to a bookstore in Saint-Germain. When the bill came, he turned to someone else around the table, a wealthy lawyer or the owner of a fashion house: "Good! You take care of it, and we'll settle afterwards." And there was never any afterwards. Even for those who considered him the worst sort of ambitious schemer and an opportunistic adventurer, Mitterrand had this one sterling quality of not being a man of money. And he was able to sustain this reputation almost to the end, even if it was generally agreed that for someone with such contempt for coin it was odd that he allowed influence trafficking and the misappropriation of funds to reach such unprecedented heights during his two terms, including among his close associates, and without his ever bothering to separate his private and public accounts.

La bonne société doesn't operate so differently; the (aristocratic) ideal is that money never see the light of day even if we know that it exists, just like realpolitik, wars, and the sort of delinquencies alluded to above. If you want to be accepted, you are well-advised to exercise the greatest possible discretion in this area. The big businessmen and other nouveaux riches who flaunt their gleaming BMWs and Hollywoodish villas in Saint-Tropez are not well regarded by the "real" French high society, and in any case, they'll never be part of it.[3]

* * *

Such discretion, so important to the French where their per-

---

3   The French don't like moneyed professions - unless they're within a large bank, co-opted by the State. Merchants are not highly regarded. On the other hand, practitioners of traditional trades such as agriculture and crafts are respected. Engineers as well, darlings of the Republic.

sonal fortunes are concerned, applies also to affairs of state. Compared to Anglo-Saxon countries, Germany or Scandinavia, there is very little control over public administration in France, whether it is a question of major industrial or technological initiatives, government, municipalities, public sector banks and enterprises, the allocation of procurement contracts, or, of course, political parties. To the extent that it is itself an active player in the handling of public affairs, *la bonne société* with its aristocratic principles would find it most unfitting that any Tom, Dick or Harry stick his nose into the account books of Paris City Hall or the Académie Française. And so one settles for a few rough appraisals and seasonal reprimands from the government ac-counting office that are simply laughed off by initiates. In fact, where the political class is concerned, it's clear that no one really wants the public sector books to be systematically audited in the Anglo-Saxon manner. On the one hand there is this aristocratic ideal that places leaders somewhere above the law. On the other (left) hand, there is the legacy of the French Revolution and the anarcho-syndicalist tradition that is in favor not of improving or modernizing public finances (which would be tantamount to endorsing the power of money), but of doing away with what is left of the old order, of the bourgeoisie and of money altogether. Why bother reforming bourgeois democracy, which is corrupt anyway? All this allows the traditional left, for the best of reasons and while awaiting the new dawn, to bankroll itself with public money just like the right, through the mayoralties and Depart-ments it controls. To complete the picture, the left (beginning with the French Communist Party) has always been of the opin-ion that any interference in the financial affairs of political parties by the justice system was an affront to political freedom.

As a result, the list of activities not subject to any serious control, and involving public moneys, is almost endless.

Here are some taken at random.

In the wake of the business boom in the 1980s, a few leaders - Chirac, then Michel Rocard in particular - suddenly got the bright idea that one could, at least in part, set guidelines for legal political financing. And after the March 1993 elections of three deputies were invalidated, the idea of a reasonable ceiling for electoral expenses may indeed be taking hold. But it's not at all certain that such standards would apply to presidential campaigns, or that any significant irregularities would much inconvenience the two main candidates, or the elected president. The French president remains untouchable. As for the financing of the parties themselves, all indications are that surreptitious practices continue, but at a slower pace and more discreetly. Finally, where the country's leaders are concerned - in every camp - no one, particularly in the media, has ever thought to look into the financing of their Paris offices, their rents, the salaries for press officers, secretarial expenses, etc. The reason is simple. These notables generally have at their disposal a non-profit organization - dedicated to some appropriately noble civic cause - which can legally accept millions, even billions of francs in contributions each year, as long as no kickback or influence peddling can be established after the fact. So who takes care of the monthly Paris budget, totalling 100,000 francs or more, of, say, an ex-Prime Minister of the Republic? No one, apparently. Unless perhaps said minister gets a little help from the Association of Sunday Cyclists for Democracy, which gives him unlimited use of its secretarial staff and its offices in St-Germain des Prés. Why pry any deeper?

As for the Paris mayoralty, there had to be leaks before a major real estate scandal was brought to light, even though the *Tout-Paris* always knew how the system worked. What is astonishing is that for a good twenty years it never occurred to the left opposition to poke its nose into the management of so-called "private sector apartments" that belonged in reality to the municipality of Paris and whose ownership may have been seized from deported French Jews during the Vichy regime. The newspapers were just as indifferent. The truth is that, on the one hand, even certain individuals on the left benefited from the favoritism, and on the other hand everyone else saw such arbitrary management as pretty well normal. As for whether it was normal for the mayor to have a personal staff of ninety (with as many chauffeured automobiles), there was a routine article on the subject in the satirical weekly *Le Canard Enchaîné*, mostly ignored by the other Paris press.

The French state, in the best Colbertist tradition, still controls a large part of the economy, even where private groups are concerned, and gets directly involved in industrial strategies. As a result we find the same budgetary opacity in the economic field. The Concorde supersonic jet that De Gaulle wanted had "no price," no budgetary ceiling, no obligation to make a profit. We don't know how much it would really have cost the taxpayer if, by some miracle, it had been a commercial success. As it turns out, that was not important. Now the official line is that it's thanks to the Concorde that the Europeans were able to develop the Airbus - an authentic technical and commercial success, as was the Ariane rocket - and so it's absurd to try and determine the real cost of the supersonic airliner; the decision was political and so had no price tag.

The *Train à Grande Vitesse* (High Speed Train) is also an impressive technical and commercial achievement. The only problem is that no one can really say how much it has cost since the project was launched, nor even how much the new lines cost; certain research expenses are the responsibility of ministry X, certain infrastructure falls under budget Y, certain loans are quietly absorbed into the overall national debt. "I really couldn't tell you if the TGV is profitable," I was told by an executive with Bombardier, the Quebec-based transportation conglomerate and manufacturer of rolling stock in Europe: "To know that, you'd have to know how much it cost."[4]

And finally: in what other Western country (with the possible exception of Italy) could one witness the mad escapade of the Protestant Giscardo-socialist banker Jean-Yves Haberer who, during five years at the head of the Crédit-Lyonnais bank, loaned 12 billion francs to suspected Italian ex-cafe waiter and fraud artiste Gian Carlo Paretti and 1.4 billion more to Bernard Tapie (former

---

4 Among the more spectacular budgetary sinkholes, we can mention the Hermes space-shuttle (ruinous, and since abandoned), the Cable TV plan which swallowed up 25 billion francs and barely got a million subscribers, and the TDF1 satellite, that is orbiting largely unused over our heads.

owner of the Adidas sports shoe empire and the Marseilles soccer
team, deputy in the French national assembly, only recently freed
from an extended stay in a Paris prison as punishment for various
economic crimes), bought at astronomical prices all the Paris
property that caught his fancy, finally leaving in the wake of his
grand design a debt of 50 billion francs and 150 billion in dubious
loans (which will be paid off sooner or later by the taxpayer)? But
in France, among senior civil servants in high society, asking for a
detailed accounting from a highly-placed public-sector banker is
just not done.

* * *

And so the right had to return to power, in the person of Jacques
Chirac, before anyone thought, even for a moment, even theo-
retically, of imposing a bit of restraint on the French state's
grandiose life-style. Starting with the presidency. The least one
can say is that the *socialist* François Mitterrand never seriously
considered cost-accounting. At no time prior to his two seven-year
mandates was there ever a court so teeming with presidential
advisers, or so much globetrotting on the Concorde or government planes, or so many personal friends or cultural guests invited
on so many presidential junkets. At the Élysée budgets were free,
by definition, of all commonplace, human constraints. Money was
never a problem for Mitterrand.

In any case, why should it have been otherwise? The right of
any French leader or employer, even of the middle rank, is to
behave like an august aristocrat. While a lunch with the American
Embassy press officer is liable to be in an unsavory cafeteria with
a fixed-price menu, an invitation from the Quai d'Orsay - the
French State Department, which isn't afraid to lament over it's
tight finances in public - will find you in a restaurant (with
Michelin stars) in the seventh arrondissement, or at the Bristol
Hotel, with a bill of 1,000 francs per guest. Even the press services
of French industrial concerns do not stint on their expense
accounts. As for the New Year's cocktail parties organized by
practically all the ministries - at least twenty of them - they're the
talk of the town in Paris, a city where one's greatest fear is to be

seen as mean and miserly. And what is there to say about the fourteenth of July garden party at the Élysée, where, at least until Chirac's arrival, champagne and expensive wines flowed freely for more than 5,000 guests? "One garden-party like this," a Canadian diplomat told me darkly, "would be enough to bring down the government in Ottawa."

The journalist Michel Schifres, who wrote *L'Élysée de Mitterrand* (Mitterrand's Élysée) in 1985, told me that he understood perfectly why Mitterrand had chosen to continue the tradition of "republican splendor." "If he, a socialist, had not done so, the French wouldn't have respected him." The republican faithful, when it comes right down to it, still want to be led by a monarch. And extravagant, he must be extravagant. As that's a popular demand that's relatively pleasant to satisfy, we'll see if Chirac I will long honor his election promises of (relative) modesty and frugality.

As everyone knows, the Republic has become well entrenched in France, especially since the Commune was crushed more than a century ago - but on the express condition that it behave like a monarchy.

PHARAONIC

Here is a phrase the French utter under their breath, and with a certain pious reverence: the *great presidential works*. It's as though one were entering another world, a magic circle under the exclusive sway of the Prince, and so immune to ordinary laws.

"How do you distinguish a *great-presidential-work* from an ordinary project?" I naively asked one a manager of the work site for the *Cité des Sciences et de la Musique* (City of Science and Music) at la Villette at the beginning of the 1980s.

"Ah!" he replied, with feigned dismay, as though I had asked him to cite, off-the-cuff, the various proofs for the existence of God. "Ah! You know, in such instances, there are no budgetary constraints." He gestured vaguely, and sighed, as though he were contemplating the Infinite or the Great Void. "There is, as it were, no budget at all."

My source was exaggerating, of course. There are at least two fairly precise and accessible budgets for a GPW: a sort of starting budget, which seems often to have been quickly scrawled on a napkin in a fine restaurant, and which serves to satisfy the initial curiosity of the press. Then there is the final budget, two to eight times higher than the first, which corresponds, if not to all the money spent, at least to all of it that has not been palmed off on other budgets or ministries. The more malicious newspapers dutifully call attention to how far the project has gone over budget, and cite the names of various chums and cousins of the powers-that-be who were insinuated into the organization chart of the GPW in question. Then the dossier is closed for the rest of eternity. At the most the GPW will provide ample raw material for the next government auditor's report, always a reliable source of amusement for those in the know at elegant soirées.

Let's look at the positive side first. It is reasonable and proper for a great and ancient country such as France, which boasts one of the major world capitals, to be mindful of its prestige. The system of presidential "works" is an effective means to that end. To quote a Canadian diplomat responsible for culture and for relations with the French-speaking world, "What I find admirable is just this capacity of the French State to free enormous sums at the drop of a hat for a prestigious cultural project. At home there will always be a gang of members of parliament to protest that it's all money we're not spending on hospitals or the unemployed, and then the bureaucrats put in their oar, and it takes forever. In France the decision is made, no one protests, and it's done."

And in fact, among the Great Works - most of which were commissioned and completed under Giscard and Mitterrand - many are absolute jewels and great achievements: the Musée d'Orsay, the Arab Institute, the Grand Louvre, the City of Science and Music. And as for the French National Library, currently under construction, one can at least say that the reading rooms, with space for 1,900 researchers, are alluring, seductive, luxurious.

So much for niceties.

For the rest, one wonders why in the upper echelons of the State, no one ever thought - even if we're dealing with the express wishes of the Prince - of instituting a few budgetary controls for these projects. For at the end of the line, they all cost an enormous amount. Some have been frankly ruinous, while others are financial sinkholes, conceived and executed in defiance of good sense, and administered with a total absence of rigor.

Those initiatives that experts view as simply very expensive include the Grand Louvre and the Musée d'Orsay. In both instances we know that the budgets were enormous, and nothing was too beautiful or too luxurious for these renovations. But no study, no persistent rumors point to any sort of scandal. The costs were considerable, they're expensive to run, but reasonable French limits were not exceeded.

In an intermediate category, both the City of Science and Music and the Arab Institute have been targets of criticism, although it's generally agreed that they are pleasing to the eye and successful. In the latter case, it's the administration, the choice of those in charge, and budget management that have been questioned as high up as the government accounting office. To be blunt, the Institute is both a bottomless pit financially and a gravy train for various friends of the Mitterrand regime. In the former case, there was much talk of cronyism, wasteful management, and extravagant salaries for the directors. And even if overall it's a great success, certain North-American museum professionals think it cost twice to four times as much, proportionately, as it would have on their side of the Atlantic.

Even making allowances, why could the work not have been done almost as well, but for less money? For in the end, even if it's the Prince who gives the order, it's the people who pay.

Then there is the last category: the GPW that is far too costly, unnecessary or poorly conceived from the start, and which is destined to be a budgetary drain forever.

Where the library is concerned - it was called, initially, the *Très Grand Bibliothèque*, or the Very Big Library - we are in the realm of the burlesque. It goes without saying that this was an important project. It's not every day that you shell out 7 billion francs, and it was known that the construction of this TGB would take several decades.

Did Paris need a big new library? Certainly we shall miss the sumptuousness of the old National Library, but today almost everyone would say the answer is yes. With its 11 million volumes, it had reached its saturation point. The 600 cramped places reserved for researchers were inadequate. Even if adjoining buildings were annexed, a true modernization of the Richelieu site was problematic. It seems reasonable today that Paris should have a major modern library, computerized, linked to other large cities in the country, and on a par with Washington, which holds first place, Frankfort, which could be compared to the new French library, and London, which has experienced its own fiasco with the Saint Pancras library, still not finished after 23 years!

Given this relatively clear objective, one wonders how it is that some of those responsible didn't sit down for an hour or two around a table, long enough to consult a few experts and to decide what the new institution would be expected to accomplish. Would the TGB be intended primarily for researchers, or would it be a center for the public at large, like Beaubourg, the modern art museum? If the former, would it simply replace the old National Library, or would it be a large annex to it?

Had they been consulted, French and foreign experts would in all likelihood have come to the same conclusion: it wouldn't do to divide up the library's collection and give one part to the new building, everything would have to be transferred to its site at Tolbiac; the TGB could not be both a large public gathering-place like Beaubourg and a temple of research; finally, a mega-library of this sort had to respect certain simple ground-rules in its design.

But why bother consulting? The project sprang fully armed from the brain of François Mitterrand, perhaps with the help of some enlightened counselling from advisor Jacques Attali. The verdict was the following: the National Library's budget would be divided; it would keep all publications dating from before 1945 and the rest would go to Tolbiac. The TGB would be a total library, both public and popular, ultramodern, and of high quality. Finally, this opportunity would be used to initiate a renewal of the desolate thirteenth arrondissement.

With all this in mind the young architect Dominique Perreault prepared the project: four million books would be stored in the basement, four glass towers would house the offices and reading rooms. Priority would be given to public spaces and the creation of a vast esplanade extending behind the building all the way to the Seine. Having set in motion such an ambitious undertaking, President Mitterrand entrusted it to someone who was neither a city planner nor an architect nor a librarian, but instead an ordinary right-wing journalist whose chief merit was having rallied behind the president before his reelection in 1988: Dominique Jamet.

By the time the intellectual and academic communities woke up and saw how incongruous the project was, work was already under way. After several months of scandal and debates in the newspapers, the plans were all turned upside down: the entire collection would be moved, and the new library would be first and foremost dedicated to research.

No problem. The Perreault design, which was not at all conceived with this in mind, would be stretched to accommodate the library of the twenty-first century, which would hold 12 million volumes when it opened, plus 150,000 new works per year for the next hundred years.

"A Very Big Library is a perfectly simple architectural concept," says Emmanuel Le Roy Ladurie: "an enormous rectangular cube buried underground - because that makes it easy to maintain a constant temperature - where the reading rooms are as close as possible to the reserves of books..." (Apparently that is the model for the Frankfort library.)

But at Tolbiac, it was already too late to start from scratch. The Boeing had been in the air for some time before the flight plan was suddenly changed. And so they improvised. The glass towers would be protected from the sun, air-conditioned, and converted into storage for the books. The reading rooms would go underground (below the level of the Seine), but would give onto a garden of giant pines three stories deep. The concrete basement would be considerably enlarged to accommodate the several million books most in demand. Complex, tortuous and undoubtedly costly solutions. Certainly, at its (sham) opening last March, the perspective offered by Perreault's esplanade was full of promise, and the underground reading rooms with their lofty ceilings, set in a natural sanctuary of pine trees, were positively sumptuous.

All the same, being below the level of the Seine represents a pointless risk, as does the storage of books in the towers, where they will be vulnerable to any failure in the air conditioning or even in the conveyance system that has to ferry the books to the reading rooms. All that at a cost difficult to pin down, and we'll see in practice whether the system works. Dominique Jamet was replaced by a respected professional, Jean Favier, in a thoughtful move. But the muddle in 1994 concerning the computerization of the catalogue and the choice of terminals - these are not minor details - left yet another bad impression. Would the giant liner be ready for launching on the date foreseen? And finally: how much would it cost per year? Disturbing figures were being circulated; there was talk of 10 percent of the French cultural budget being set aside. No one really knows, but one of the defining features of all the GPWs is their ruinous operating costs. Where the library is concerned, it's certainly an open question. What can be said is that if a rational and competent individual had decided to build one of the four or five giant libraries in the world, such as the one at Tolbiac, he would have gone about it differently and arrived at a more simple and effective solution, and much more cheaply. But why should the Pharaoh make things simple when all the charm lies in making them complicated and expensive?

*　*　*

With the Bastille Opera we reach heights never before equalled, and unlikely to be attained ever again. Whereas the great industrial and technological disasters (Hermès, Rafale, the plan to cable every French household, TDF 1), at least had a definable goal at the outset, the Opera was a meaningless gesture, a three-billion-franc fantasy that had no reason to be. Maryvonne de Saint-Pulgent, who has written an entire book about the *Syndrome de l'opéra* (The Opera Syndrome), boils it down to this: "The Bastille Opera is a bad solution to an inexistant problem."

François Mitterrand and his Minister of Culture Jack Lang, using the bicentenary of the Revolution as a pretext, decided one day to erect a Popular-Opera-at-the-Bastille-for-1989, even though Paris had no need of another lyric theatre. This opera, as I said, was to be popular. No one knows what that really means, but the seats are as expensive as they were at the old opera, the Palais-Garnier, and they are just as hard to get hold of for the major productions. It cost at least twice as much as what had been estimated; the much-touted convertible hall demanded by conductor Pierre Boulez, and which served to justify the entire project, was never built; and the ruinous, futuristic system for changing the sets never worked. The Palais-Garnier was one of the most beautiful opera houses in the world, with good acoustics, and it only needed a bit of modernization: it had 2,200 seats (20 percent of which had an obstructed view) compared to 2,700 today at the Bastille, not an enormous difference. You could also see lyric theatre at the Théâtre des Champs-Élysées, at the Chatelet, and the Favart. And, if you really wanted to do something *popular*, you could always put on *Aïda* or *Carmen* at Bercy, and everyone would be happy.

Rarely has there been a concept as muddle-headed as "popular opera." In the first place, opera is certainly not such a popular business that it's going to pose a threat anytime soon to Michael Jackson; it's an extremely onerous and costly art that is of interest to an enlightened and enthusiastic minority, but a tiny one. Its public is limited and always the same, barring the odd casual devotee. Of course, when there is a production of exceptional quality, with stars and a high-profile conductor, all the aficionados line up to see it at the same time; not only is it impossible to obtain a moderately priced seat, you can't find a seat at all. That's what happened at the Garnier when Rolf Liebermann took over the direction. His *festival* policy, favoring original productions with great directors and conductors and world-renowned singers, made for riots at the box-office and gobbled up enormous government grants. But - again according to Mme. de Saint-Pulgent - when the Garnier was content, before the Liebermann era, to be a repertory company, doing good work but without big names or stars, its followers, rich or not, found seats without too much difficulty and it all cost much less in grants. Only the public did not swarm to see productions that were not particularly spectacular. In order to appear popular, the opera had to stage a permanent festival, with ruinous creations and great world-famous stars. It all cost so much that the number of performances had to be limited. At the opera there is a crowd every day for Pavarotti, but you cannot afford Pavarotti every day. And when there is no Pavarotti, there is no crowd.

If during the 1980s it was thought that there really existed an opera public frustrated by the cost of tickets and the shortage of seats, the logical solution would have been to alternate repertoire and festival at the Garnier, or to open the Favart and Chatelet sites to less demanding productions, already paid for. It's a flexible, manageable formula that has already been adopted in England and Germany.

The Bastille project had all the flexibility of the *Titanic* bearing down on an iceberg. To justify itself, it had to be popular, and of course, *totally new*. There would be 250 performances a year. For that there would be a system unique in the world, with a main stage flanked by five lateral stages of the same size, plus a rehearsal stage, all shunted around by computer command on the principle of a Rubik's Cube (that Cube again!). Add to that six underground floors to store the sets. In other words, one would be able to rehearse *La Traviata* with its set in the afternoon on the main stage and in the evening present *Der Rosenkavalier* in the same place. All you'd have to do would be to press a button.

Needless to say, the futurist system never worked, and they still pull and push the sets by hand the way it was done in the nineteenth century. Following continual delays, with personality conflicts and other major crises, the Bastille finally opened two years behind schedule. Six years after its official launching, it was able to stage about 120 performances in a year, just like the Garnier in the good old days. How, in any case, could it do much more? Since it had become the foremost lyric theater in the capital, the Bastille Opera had to present new productions or productions of very high quality, and so very expensive. The result:

to stay within its budget, it had to curtail the number of performances. With annual grants of 450 million francs, the Paris Opera monopolizes 90 percent of the money given to French opera, but does not do as well at the Bastille as at the old Palais-Garnier, which was much more prestigious and much less of a money-guzzler to boot. What is more, the eruption on the scene of the Bastille Monster threw the opera world in Paris all out of kilter: inflated fees, outlandish contracts for conductors (quickly denounced in public, then cancelled), boycotts of the new opera house by great European stars (orchestra conductors or stage directors) who preferred to work at the Châtelet. The disaster was and remains very costly. In exchange for a huge increase in public subsidies, all that was accomplished was to erase the memory of Liebermann's years of glory, when the opera world's attention was focused on the city of Paris. And to transform the Garnier into a half-empty hall consecrated to dance, an ironic fate for a house with 400 obstructed seats!

AFFAIRS TO REMEMBER

I n France, "affairs," or scandals, are a bit like Stalin's terror in the Soviet Union during the 1930s: once the train is rolling down the tracks, there's no real reason it should ever grind to a halt.

At the beginning of the 1980s, judges began to bring charges against mayors, deputies, even former ministers for bribery, political interference or influence peddling; it was something new in French political life, then it became routine. And under the Balladur government, in 1994, there was a sudden flurry of activity. Like ducks in a row, three ministers were charged: first the young and promising Communications minister, Alain Carignon, then two other prominent figures, Gérard Longuet and Michel Roussin. All three were forced to resign, their careers destroyed. In October, another thunderbolt: the same Alain Carignon, former minister, mayor of Grenoble and president of the regional council, was placed in preventive detention for having obstructed the investigation and destroyed evidence, and he stayed there for

seven months! An enormous taboo had just been violated, for, to
say the least, Carignon's character and the misdeeds with which
he was charged pale next to those, for example, of Senator Maurice
Arreckx, or of Jacques Médecin, former mayor of Nice, who fled
to South America to avoid prosecution. Alain Carignon was far
from being the black sheep of French politics, and no one has
accused him of lining his own pockets.

After that, one could ask why France did not experience the
sort of national upheaval that occurred in Italy, with the indict-
ment (and often the imprisonment) of a large segment of the
political class, along with bank directors and captains of industry?
Even if - putting all the cases together, and they include a number
of very local ones - the number of charges laid totalled close to
forty, that's a very far cry from the Great Terror set in motion in
Italy during the Clean Hands campaign. And it must be confessed
that the French state enjoys a stability and a credibility the Italian
state has never dreamed of.

But if you come right down to it, is there any part, even a minute
percentage of the French political class that could never be
accused of at least minor acts of illegal financing, influence
peddling, kickbacks or bribes received in exchange for construction permits or government contracts? Is it credible that the four
giant firms that receive most of the building and public works
contracts have never issued false invoices or paid out secret
commissions? Could tainted knowledge of the public housing
scandals in Paris and the Hauts-de-Seine, for example, not have
reached the higher-ups in the government party? And finally - not
to go on forever - what large municipality in the country has not,
one way or the other, skimmed off its share of commercial development money in its jurisdiction?

During a monthly luncheon in the fall of 1994 that brought
together the elite of the French economic community and the
highest levels of public administration, an industrialist indulged
himself in some black humor: "If French judges were to initiate a
Clean Hands operation like the one in Italy, half the people here
would be in prison."

At about the same time, in a small village in the south of France, an artisan stonemason gave me, in microcosm, his version of the system: "Strangely, when 200,000 francs have been approved for a piece of work, only 150,000 end up in your pocket. The rest disappears into thin air. But you're asked, of course, to provide invoices for the entire 200,000 francs. And then, if there is trouble, the boys can't even cover you. You're on the hook for fraud, when in fact you're the one who has been robbed. I've had it. Never again."

Of course, that was in one of the five *départements* on the Mediterranean coast, where it's generally agreed that the most dubious practices are well-entrenched: widespread bribery, and a "tip" at every level. "Provence-Côte d'Azur is a world unto itself," say the experts in government corruption and "affairs."

"In this region, the morality of the political class is, let us say, elastic, and the strong presence of the Mafia doesn't help," explains the investigative journalist Jean-Marie Pontaut, whose books include *Les Ripoux de la Côte* ("The Swindlers on the Coast"), his account of a number of notorious scandals in Nice, Marseille and Toulon. On the coast, it's true, the number and seriousness of these affairs assume Pagnolesque proportions, proper to Marseille; that is to say, enormous. All this against a background of rumored rampant racketeering, settlings of scores, and the assassination of the Hyères deputy, Yann Piat.

Let's concede that the Mediterranean departments, traditionally, do represent a world apart, where business and banditry have much in common. But what is unprecedented is that across the country, whether in the north or the east or the south, emerging scandals now implicate *honest* political figures. No one suspects them of links with the Mafia, or of having secret bank accounts in Switzerland. They are simply accused of having pocketed money one way or another, often on behalf of their party; they usually took an undeclared commission and handed it over, scrupulously, to the bag-men. It was for a good cause, and it was THE technique for political financing in general. Some went a bit further; they allowed businesses and wealthy friends to finance their political activities and their professional lifestyle: the rental of a Paris apartment, a car with chauffeur perhaps, salaries for a secretary or a publicist, etc. So what if in the process some rich protector landed a lucrative contract in the municipality or the region? The deputy mayor's conscience was clear. The contract in question was perfectly *normal*, and in no way represented a payoff for contributions received. He, of course, never "benefited personally." Others went still further. For example, a local industrialist, who receives contracts from the municipality, offers (purely out of friendship) to do a bit of work on a country house. That might range from redoing a kitchen to the 20 million franc restoration of a property owned by a certain Roger-Patrice Pelat, a close friend of President Mitterrand who had lent his talents as go-between to a construction company to facilitate an enormous contract in Korea.

Cases as striking as that of Pelat are, it would appear, the exception, as are those of Médecin or Boucheron (a former mayor of Angoulême). What is more common, in varying degrees, is a *normal* commission received on behalf of the party, or a welcome boost to a political figure's lifestyle: private planes, limousines, the paying-off of electoral debts. There surely must exist, somewhere in the country, deputies or mayors who have scrupulously lived only on their salaries (the most generous in Europe, outside of Italy). But if one were to go so far as is now done in the United States or Canada, as to make a poor politician tremble in his boots for accepting a color TV or a week of paid vacation in the sun, how many would survive the test?

The reality is that in France until very recently, everyone considered it normal that the political class - the elite in general - attend to the financing of its activities and sometimes its lifestyle, without the police and the justice system poking their noses in. It was taken for granted that this same elite had enough moral fibre and good sense not to go too far; to elicit a 2 percent commission from a developer for the building of a shopping center represented a normal and honest practice if the percentage was within the limits accepted across the country, and if the money was earmarked for political activities rather than personal enrichment. At the low end of the scale, everyone found it normal as well that officials at the Paris City Hall, for instance, provided publicly-owned apartments to close relations, friends, or those to whom they owed a favor, at derisory rents. As for the little gifts to those in office - a car, a trip, etc. - well, they were considered signs of a civilized life and worldliness. "After all, you're not going to jump down a deputy's throat just because he had his kitchen fixed up by some local businessman!" protested a newscaster on the *France-Inter* radio network. When the Botton business bribery affair hit the headlines and it was learned that this particular golden boy had showered a good part of the media with coin - at the top of the list a one million franc gift to star newscaster Patrick Poivre d'Arvor - the loudest protests came from those who thought the accusations were tantamount to an inquisition. In the words of a well-known journalist, "Do you expect us to ask who's paying every time an airplane ticket arrives on our desk?" Well, yes indeed, that would be uncouth.

Let's be blunt. Good Parisian society, infused with Pascalian pessimism, considers it normal and inevitable that political figures take advantage of their situation, as long as certain norms are respected. It's up to the political class to maintain order in its own house, and to discreetly rid itself, from time to time, of a sheep that's really too black. But no one would think of reproaching Raymond Barre for having bought, at an especially reasonable price, a mediterranean property on which to build at Cap Ferrat at the time he was prime minister. Not a word to Mme. Giscard d'Estaing for having played the market during her husband's term as president. Nor even to Chirac - as long as it was kept under wraps - for having accepted a paid week's vacation in a Persian Gulf palace, with a private jet thrown in for the transportation.

"If you talk to political journalists in Paris," says journalist Stéphane Denis, "they can all point to such and such an individual, penniless when he became a deputy, who within a few years was the owner of a luxurious apartment on the Champ-de-Mars, where he gave lavish dinner parties. No one was ever very surprised, or even thought to find out where the money came from."

Those in the know had a similar reaction to the interest-free loan of a million francs offered by Mitterrand's wheeler-dealer crony Pelat to minister Pierre Bérégovoy. It was a thinly-veiled gift from someone who had profited handsomely from the regime, but it was judged, in the light of Bérégovoy's long career, that such a modest sum, (whose only purpose, poignantly, was to pay for a modest 100 square-meter apartment in the ritzy sixteenth arondissement), reflected the inveterate honesty of Beregevoy, a former worker for the French Electricity Board. Bérégovoy was certainly not a profiteer - even if during the 1980s he took to rubbing shoulders with dubious operators, such as Traboulsi and Tapie. Nevertheless, in many more "Nordic" democracies, this business of an interest-free loan would have been enough to spell the end of a politician's career, "honest" or not, and might have led to serious difficulties with the justice system.

Many scandals that erupt today were for a long time nothing to write home about. And the law of silence prevailed all across the board; those elected on the right - when the right was in power - had no reason, obviously, to spill the beans. The left, it was said, took it for granted that anything to do with money was tainted, whether it be legal or illegal. It chose not to denounce the right, and followed its example by profiting from the system. It brought along on its coattails the largest unions (already closely linked to the state, which subsidized them). And finally, the most important political journalists in the country, whether from Paris or the provinces, maintained such an incestuous relationship with the political class that they would never dream of betraying those who had become intimate friends, and sometimes benign benefactors. In short, the political and media class lived - and considered itself - above the common law, which is only for car thieves, petty crooks, and people who cheat on their income tax.

Today the system is in a shambles, and this well-ordered world has been shaken to its foundations. Who will be next? Many deputies, ministers, mayors, elected officials, must be waking up sweating in the middle of the night. Especially when informed that their names have turned up in the latest edition of the *Canard Enchaîné*, the satirical weekly. There was a time not long ago when the *Canard's* revelations were good to dine out on and a source of mirth in the halls of the National Assembly. Today *le Monde* itself - once concerned only with great political issues and the loftier concerns of the state - reprints these items on its front page and is doing some investigative journalism of its own! To top it all off, Alain Juppé, the prime minister, is being accused of having authorized, while attached to the Finance Department of the city of Paris, the allocation of a municipal apartment to his own son, after having himself lowered the rent by decree! If an official risks being accused of political interference for having shown concern for his family, the Republic is clearly in grave danger.

The infernal machine is off and running, and no one knows who will be able to control it or how far it will go. Until sometime in the 1970s, everything in France was under control. The newspapers had their political allegiances, and were concerned primarily with promoting their party or their faction. Scandals were too mundane for them. Television, despite a certain loosening up during the 1970s, was still closely monitored, as were judges.

Except for the odd extreme and marginal case, the justice system kept its hands off politics. When Robert Boulin, a key minister in the Barre government (and an honest one), was charged in 1979 in connection with a modest property dispute in Ramatuelle, that too was a startling first, an unthinkable occurrence in the political world. The chattering political-media class could only see it as an old-fashioned conspiracy, in this case designed by the Chiraquians to discredit the most Giscardian Gaullist in the government. It couldn't possibly be that Boulin was charged because a 27-year-old judge named Van Ruymbeke decided to apply the letter of the law to a minister just as he would have to an ordinary citizen. Alain Peyrefitte, the Minister of Justice, must have decided to bring him down. No one wondered even for a moment whether a minister had the right to abuse his office, and if Boulin had in fact done so. That was a minor detail, and at worst the minister had been imprudent. The only serious question was, who had desired and plotted his fall.

In fact this was the beginning of the revolt of the little judges, inconceivable then, but widespread today. At the end of the 1970s it meant putting one's career at risk, but since then the judges have found that it is actually a good way to make one's name. As a result charges against ministers have become commonplace,

economic kingpins are in police custody, and preventive detention
- used unfairly as a means of obtaining confessions - threatens half
the French political class. The matter is all the more serious since
it is generally agreed that the amount of money circulating in
political circles literally mushroomed during the 1980s. By some
estimates, Chirac's campaign in 1988 cost 500 million francs,
those of Barre and Mitterrand 300 million. With that kind of float
there is presumably lots to investigate, and political parties and
their various treasurers would doubtless be unable, given the sums
involved, to cover all the donors' tracks. It's not surprising then
that in connection with the Longuet affair, Van Ruymbeke's
attention was caught by *cash* payments of some 32 million francs
to the Republican Party from 1987 to 1991. That adds up to a lot
of money and must involve a large number of intermediaries and
receivers of funds. All the while the immunity enjoyed by the
political class, by the country's elite, since the dawn of time, was
slipping away, doubtless forever.

To its dismay, the *establishment* so dear to right-wing extremist
and National Front leader Jean-Marie Le Pen discovered at the
beginning of summer, 1995, that a brand new prime minister
could be compelled to appear on television news and explain,
supporting evidence in hand, how and at what price he had
allocated an apartment that is the property of the city of Paris, and
what measures he had taken to house a part of his family there
(his son, to be precise). One of these days someone will ask French
high society to reveal what it has done with public money, and to
hand over its pay cheques and its rent receipts. In short, to put its
money on the table, just like in America. Now that *would* be a
nightmare!

3. The Demon Of Literature

Agreed: France is not governed by novelists or professors of
literature. But there is no other country in the world where
culture and matters of the mind play so conspicuous a role
in political and public life.

In the United States, a president or a candidate for that office
has to quote the Bible in order to appeal to the populace and
convince it of his moral probity. He must also like sports, lead an
exemplary family life, and relate to the ordinary citizen in a simple
and natural way. The only exception was that bizarre individual,
Nixon. He recruited a German-Jewish academic to oversee Foreign Affairs, received André Malraux just before setting off for
China, and ostentatiously quaffed fine Bordeaux wines at the
White House. For an American politician who was also a bit
devious and crude this wasn't quite normal. God only knows if
these eccentricities, aided and abetted by Watergate, were not the
true reason for his fall.

If the French president appears on a podium, book in hand,
to seek approval in the eyes of the masses, it's a good bet that
it will not be the Bible. It's Balzac, or Dumas, or Voltaire, or
Laclos, or Jacques Chardonne. As this second millennium
draws to a close, in the age of the information highway, great
literature still rules the roost in the collective unconscious of
the French. Even if the French don't read any more than other
Europeans - in fact a bit less[5] - no political leader is worthy of
their respect if he doesn't have a book to his credit, or at least his
name on a cover. In Paris, concierges and bistro owners defer to a

client who presents himself as a writer. They even go so far as to consider it a lucrative profession, occasionally confusing it with that of a television game show host.

A corollary of this old popular superstition is that there is no public figure in France who has not written - or had written under his name - an essay, a book of reflections, memoirs. At the end of the 1980s, the magazine *Lire* drew up an exhaustive list of French politicians whose names had appeared on the cover of a book, and it boggles the mind! Even quite minor political figures are on the list, including some you would never suspect of having written even 100 lines at a stretch. But to tell the truth, it's not only people with political ambition who have been infected. In this country, every lawyer with a bit of a reputation has committed to paper his career, his life story, his deepest thoughts; two or three of these books are actually worth reading. Scientists too, of course, and some with *real* books; France loves a good dose of philosophizing, and science offers limitless opportunities. Then there are the fashionable surgeons, television hosts, industrialists enamoured of the media, former police chiefs, actors, fashion designers, architects, and a horde of athletes of all kinds. Most of these books are of absolutely no interest, except to their ghostwriters who have (perhaps) been well paid, and to the publishers who hope for a quick hit in the bookstores. But the literary mystique is such that all these "authors" come to believe, quite rapidly, in the value of their books, and to believe, even, that they actually wrote them.

The limit was reached, no doubt, when Valéry Giscard d'Estaing, a former President of the Republic who has never quite given up the idea of occupying that post again, published under his own name a novel worthy of Barbara Cartland or a Harlequin

5   As unbelievable as it may seem, France, with around 13,000 new titles and 30,000 books published each year (a nightmare for bookstores) trails far behind Germany which, even before reunification, published about twice as many titles in a year, and toted up 67,000 in 1993, with a turnover three times as great as that of French publishing (*Le Monde*, February 3, 1995). Reading habits in Great Britain and Germany, as in other northern countries, far outstrip those of France.

romance. He was duly invited to appear on cultural programs of considerable prestige, where he proceeded to discourse on his own writing style and fictional creation, while citing his illustrious predecessors, Montaigne, Flaubert, Maupassant. The novel, called *Le Passage* ("The Passage") does have the virtue of being suitable for any readership, young or old, from the deepest and most puritan depths of the Vendée to the remotest left-wing Paris suburb, and it will scandalize nobody. Only in France could a political figure of the first rank (he would like to think) indulge himself in such a bizarre enterprise and not emerge even more discredited than he was before. It is as though literary France not only honored those (few) figures who can actually write a real book, but was prepared to extend a kind of charitable recognition to the others, the tape-machine writers and Sunday writers, pitiful in their accomplishments, but full of poignant good will.

* * *

De Gaulle may have been a military man, but he was also, incontestably, a writer, whose unique style was widely appreciated for its literary merit. Partly out of respect, and partly to be provocative, he installed André Malraux at his right hand in the cabinet.

Georges Pompidou was from the Auvergne and had worked at Rothschild's bank. He was a most prosaic power-broker, a money man in the peasant tradition, who made a point of expressing his appreciation for modern painting. But he also edited an anthology of French poetry, and came from the education ministry, always a powerful symbol.

Valéry Giscard d'Estaing was certainly the least literary of all the Fifth Republic presidents. And so he was and remains the one most unhealthily obsessed by literature. *Le Passage* is the most recent and the most striking example of this, but it goes way back. On the eve of his election to the presidency, he confided to journalists that if he'd had Flaubert's talent, he would never have gone into politics. No sooner was he declared the winner than Giscard rushed onto Bernard Pivot's literary show, to hold forth for 90 minutes on his passion for literature in general and Guy de

Maupassant in particular. Later he went off and cloistered himself somewhere in Africa, while all the affairs of state ground to a halt, penning *Démocratie Française* (French Democracy), a work about which very little good was said.

Imagine an important political leader in North America, or even northern Europe, who would take two weeks' leave from his responsibilities, in some secret place, on the pretext of setting down on paper his underlying political philosophy. He would be considered ripe for the straitjacket or impeachment. Not surprisingly - unlike the French, who are generally at a loss in that area - German political figures can be very knowledgeable about music, and some, like Helmut Schmidt, even play Schubert well on the piano. But that is a sober, private, discreet activity that does not consume a lot of time, and which Germans value above all else, except perhaps for metaphysics. In Eastern Europe as well - although Communist rule largely falsified the game - one finds a long-standing respect for great writers, poets especially (in that part of the world, Vaclav Havel is in no way incongruous).

But there is no other Western country where literature weighs so heavily in public and political life. Without going back beyond 1958, we can say that all French presidents have cultivated writers. De Gaulle stuck primarily to Malraux, but also took pains to show his respect for Sartre. Pompidou rubbed shoulders more with painters, a group not all that far removed. Giscard seemed not to know anyone in the milieu, which pained him deeply. As a result, he had to issue formal invitations from the Élysée. A memorably funny article in 1978 written by Liliane Sichler described a lunch given by Giscard with, in attendance, Georges Duby and Claude Lévi-Strauss (mute), Bernard Henri-Lévy and Maurice Clavel (chatty), plus two or three other short-lived stars of the literary scene. The conversation was apparently both rambling and listless, despite the valiant efforts of a certain dauntless Lionel Stoléru. It turned out that the writers who had accepted the invitation had done so simply out of long-standing respect for the Prince, or out of vanity, or the naïve idea that they could influence the Prince himself (in the matter of the USSR, the death penalty, etc.), while the Prince-President wanted only to show his mettle, to prove that he too knew how to talk with real intellectuals. It was good for his image as a thinker, and no pictures were taken. I daresay that an American president with the same thought in mind would be more likely to invite Sylvester Stallone or Frank Sinatra, and make sure photographers would be present for the op.

In a style less embarrassing than that of Giscard, Raymond Barre, and Édouard Balladur especially, made it a point of honor to associate with thinkers and writers, who made it a point of honor in return to accept the invitations, and let it be known that they had done so. They said nice things about M. Balladur and M. Barre in print - concerning their intellects, of course. It so happens that the two men, apart from their political status, are well regarded in intellectual circles.

Édouard Balladur, a perfect exemplar of *la bonne société*, with his mysterious origins and his obscure career path, his self-possession and his exquisite television manners, has devoted a lot of time and effort to writing (himself) two or three accomplished works, to which he attaches great importance. Raymond Barre has published little more for the general reader than collections of speeches or occasional texts, but his qualities as an academic - and therefore as an intellectual - have earned him considerable influence and authority. Invited on France-Inter or Pivot's program, he talks most knowledgeably about literature and American movies!

There's no doubt about it, the public image of a French political leader changes radically the day he publishes a book that is endorsed by the Paris intellectual community and its official organs: *Le Monde, Le Nouvel Observateur, Libération, L'Express* and a few others. The extremely brilliant and ambitious Alain Juppé, who for a long time was regarded as Jacques Chirac's errand boy, found himself transfigured overnight when he published *La Tentation de Venise* (The Temptation of Venice), which was praised by critics and thinkers for its literary quality. More modestly, the young centrist François Bayrou seemed suddenly less inconsequential when he brought out an important biography of Henri IV that was considered worthy of notice by experts in the field. Nicolas Sarkozy's biography of Georges Mandel was less well received, but it was not judged beneath contempt. In other words, he scored a (modest) point.

The literary stamp transforms a power-hungry politician into a statesman (or an honest man at the very least, which isn't too bad). Take Edgar Faure for example; his reputation as an amiable and witty individual owes much to the detective novels he wrote for pleasure under the name Edgar Sanday. Then there's Jean-François Deniau, who had already written a novel in the 1960s, and was short-listed for the Goncourt Prize! Since his semi-retirement from politics, he has published a number of well-crafted adventure novels and books of essays. And François Mitterrand, if he doesn't quite merit the title of author (his books are mainly collections of speeches and essays) undeniably has a lovely personal style. And, irrefutably, a genuine passion for literature and writers.

The impact on French political life of the demon of literature shows in the degree to which those generally acknowledged to be "non-literary," or who have confessed to it of their own free will, are handicapped. Consider three examples: Michel Rocard, Jacques Chirac, Laurent Fabius. How many magazine articles have included the lethal little observation that Ricard has never read a novel, hardly any essays, and prefers to bury himself in arid reports teeming with figures? Forthright and honest on this point, Rocard has never tried to pass as a literary type, but that works against him. As for Laurent Fabius, well-meaning friends confirm that he hasn't finished a book in fifteen years, other than, perhaps, a volume of his own speeches. The case of Jacques Chirac is more poignant. Whatever transpires, no one will ever believe that the new president is capable of writing, on his own, a text of any length. Even if Françoise Giroud claims he was the type to hide a collection of poetry behind an issue of Playboy (out of modesty), he's viewed more as a connoisseur of hearty meals, political meetings, TV sports, crude jokes and drinking songs. The problem is that despite all that he insists on publishing. Jacques Chirac is by all accounts a warm and affable man, likable in private, but not the least bit intellectual or cultivated. And it is perhaps the utter lack of regard for him on the part of the intelligentsia that explains why it has taken him so long to climb the last rung on the ladder to power. France wants to be governed by a Prince who, if he is not really a writer himself, is at ease talking about literature, or at the very least has a healthy respect for the written word. On this last point, Giscard went to great lengths to win his spurs. With Chirac (as with Fabius) the horrible doubt persists: has he *ever* actually read a book?

*   *   *

Some may object that it was Jacques Chirac who, after having been written off three months earlier, was finally declared president on May 7, 1995, not the literate and distinguished Balladur, or the socialist professor Lionel Jospin. True. I would only note that, even though he succeeded miraculously in positioning himself on the left to outdistance Balladur, and didn't skimp on populism, Chirac's returns were not all that overwhelming. Especially on the first ballot when he got barely more than 20 percent of the vote, the worst score ever in the opening round for an ultimately victorious presidential candidate. Certainly he did what he had to do: he beat his opponents and got elected. But his obvious virtues of open simplicity - and these are genuine - inspired remarkably little enthusiasm, while Giscard's air of being young, liberal, and *aristocratic* garnered him 33 percent in 1974. It's as though Chirac's brand of simplicity, with its roots in south-central France, didn't really touch the masses. And Jospin did ride to power as prime minister in recent, hastily-called elections whose results - a parliamentary majority for the socialists - were quite egregious to Chirac and his policies.

It will also be pointed out that, at the same time as he was posing as a simple and populist leader, Chirac, or rather his staff, was doing its low-key best to give him an intellectual sheen. He too appeared on television to talk, if I remember correctly, about Pre-Columbian art. Rumors were circulated to the effect that he had a pile of books on his bedside table, each more serious than the last, and that his knowledge of Chinese civilization was considerable. This image-enhancement reached its apogee when, in a televised debate with Jospin, the then mayor of Paris was heard to cite, a bit out of context, the poetry of Lermontov! It must be said that if Chirac's natural simplicity seemed authentic, his exalted cultural and literary pretensions appeared much more forced. You still can't imagine the new president composing, on his own, complex texts, or even spending much time with a book. We'll see in due course how much respect the good people of France will muster for a president who is more instinctive than Machiavellian, more *natural* than cultivated.

4. Cathodic Death Threats

We used to think Soviet communism was eternal. Now we know otherwise. In France, *la bonne société*, which seemed so immutable for so long, is also facing an uncertain future.

The glut of money during the 1980s certainly dealt it a blow. People more accustomed to eating in the kitchen were now dining in a vast family salon graced by gilded panelling: food industry giants, real-estate kings, stock-exchange speculators who were not even elegant or cynically witty. But the temple columns held, more or less.

What is striking about the French economic scene is how solid its traditions and old-boy networks are. At least since the end of the war, banking and industry in France - public or private, it doesn't matter - have been discreetly managed out of the offices of the Minister of Economy and Finance, through the efforts of 200 or 300 senior civil servants, and graduates of the School of Administration and the *École Polytechnique*. They would move back and forth, as a matter of course, from running a large enterprise to a government department and vice versa. They were all soberly-dressed, grey, taciturn fifty and sixty-year-olds. The nationalizations of 1981 made no difference to the tried and true management methods or to the managers themselves. The subsequent denationalizations - in 1986-87, and since 1993 - also changed nothing. Today the same top civil servants shuttle between ministerial offices and the large private and public companies. These are people who never considered upstarts like Bernard

Tapie, the big business buccaneer, one of their own, and who kept their distance from Bouygues, Pineau, Pellerin and other scandal-ridden magnates of their ilk. On this front, *la bonne société* firmly stood its ground.

The most lethal threat may have come from television, whose triumphant expansion during the 1980s affected all sectors, including culture, universities, and science, and shifted centres of gravity. In a few years, *la bonne société* totally lost the absolute control it had wielded over the audiovisual world. It was a foreshadowing of decline, of a transfer of power, perhaps of decay.

During the first twenty years of French television things were quite firmly in hand, even to the detriment of political freedom of speech. Television news and coverage of the domestic political scene was left to the government (rightist and authoritarian by Western standards). Everything else was the affair of the small, middle, and elite intelligentsia, and neither the militant CEOs appointed by the government nor the ministers of information seemed to pay heed to what was taking place on the small screen. As long as it didn't interfere directly in French politics the intelligentsia had free rein, and controlled both culture and the media's overall stance. This included the international arena, where, fortuitously, Gaullist foreign policy could quite easily accommodate reports that were routinely favorable to the non-aligned Third World, and hostile to the United States. Television journalists were able to look themselves in the mirror every morning and feel good about their courageous stands on Latin America or Vietnam, even as they kow-towed daily to the Minister of Information or his throng of administrative assistants.

What really matters however, is that during the 1960s and 70s, French television was, of all the Western television systems, the most cultural, serious, educational, and the least commercial. The impressive historical series that were produced with great care and much talent at the Buttes-Chaumont studios were inspired by the great French literature of the nineteenth century: Balzac, Sue, Dumas, Zola. They embodied History, of course, but social history as well, and the class struggle was implicit in every episode. In the beginning there was only a single channel and so the public had no choice; one evening they even foisted Aeschylus' *The Persians* on the audience during what was not yet called prime time. That was going a bit far. But what was routine at that hour was Molière's *Don Juan*, Barbey d'Aurevilly's *Chanteclaire*, Balzac's *Les Illusions Perdues*, and such.

Even the entertainments were monitored, meted out, contextualized. People had the right to relax, on Saturday night especially, with impeccably French variety shows, but these too had their intellectual pretensions. Among the concessions made to entertainment was the priceless *Au Théâtre Ce Soir* (Tonight at the Theatre), which combined edification (we'll give people a taste for the theatre) with an indulgent attitude toward common folk (we'll only present *simple* plays). The prestige offerings were very cultural and literary, very uplifting. Even popular programming was educational. Until 1980 France was spared the all-American never-ending series, the television tap that's never turned off, the loud, aggressive commercials that pop up every ten minutes, even in the middle of *La Dolce Vita*. French television was virtuous, cultivated, progressive, sometimes brilliant, often dull, and it went to bed very early indeed. But it was not demeaning.

In this climate, which evolved slowly up to the end of the 1970s - with two and a half channels, a bit more competition for viewers, a bit more political independence - the high ground was still held by hosts, some of them fusty and others simply eccentric, who owed nothing to their blow-driers or their sequins. In prime time, the showing of a film would be the occasion for a debate on society or science. The great entertainment was Zola's *Nana*, as filmed at Buttes-Chaumont. As I remember it, there were hours and hours of interview by Jean-Marie Drot with André Malraux. This same Drot, around 1973, produced six hour-long documentaries on Quebec that were shown at 8:30 on Sunday night! The great political debates were considered mass-audience spectacles; the shows began at 8:30 and lasted more than 90 minutes. And so on. Every channel had its own flagship literary broadcast (most of them short-lived) and at first Bernard Pivot, who was to become an icon, had a dubious reputation; he was considered too commercial, too audiovisual. Not cultural enough.

This brand of television imploded, with the socialists' blessing for the most part, around 1985-86. First there was the scandalous assignment of the last two VHF channels to private consortiums, reputed friends of the Socialist Party. (Berlusconi, already! And a few others.) No tenders, no public debate, hardly any attention paid to the costs or to the consequences of this sudden eruption of the commercial into the existing system. One wonders whether Mitterrand was not trying just to block off the last two VHF channels available in order to stop the right from setting up shop there, or if he was not also trying - with a socialist's didactic intent - to create the two most stupid commercial channels in Europe, so as to turn off the good citizens of the left forevermore.

Then, the right, besotted with ultra-liberalism, returned to power in March of 1986, and decided, for strictly ideological reasons, to offer one of the two great public networks as a sacrifice to the Golden Calf. The first thought was to choose *Antenne 2*, doubtless because it was the best channel. In the end it was the earnest *TF1* that was placed on the block. The inflated bureaucratic vessel *FR3*, whose purpose remains obscure despite the gobs of public funds it ingests each year, was left in the hands of the government.

The French, like the Italians, have perhaps never quite understood this quintessentially modern creature that is television, how it behaves over time, how destructive it can be, how the changes it leaves in its wake are often irreversible. It is in countries like Germany or Great Britain, which have fewer cultural pretensions than France, that the broadcasting services have been able to adapt, to negotiate the sharp corners of modernity, without going under completely.

What is remarkable is that neither in 1985, nor under the right in 1986-87, did *la bonne société* seem to sense the danger. Its official organs seem barely to have registered Mitterrand's cavalier cynicism or, the following year, the consequences of destabilizing so drastically public television, brutally dismembered for no good reason. No one seems to have foreseen the scope of the disaster, or the form it would take. As though living in another era, people fretted over a possible political power play by Robert Hersant, and wondered which way Jean-Luc Lagardère was leaning. No one foresaw that the only true threat on the horizon was the ascendancy of the new breed of television personality. And as no one in the country seemed to have taken the time to look at American TV or that of Berlusconi, they apparently weren't even aware that such a thing could exist.

Even when, to everyone's surprise, *good old* Bouygues was handed TF1 in exchange for a fat cheque, still no one worried. Everyone assumed, for example, that he would hang on to funny, irreverent, bright, Michel Polac, with his modest budget and healthy audience. And that he wouldn't upset the delicate airtime balance. How blind we were! Giving Channel 5 to Hersant didn't create any problems where the news was concerned; indeed, that was the only area where the station did well. The combination of Bouygues and Hersant was much more serious. It meant a wholesale rejigging of the French broadcasting landscape, a frantic, minute by minute race for ratings, a leap in programming costs and stars' salaries, and the rapid elimination of any program of any interest whatsoever airing before 11 PM (aside from television news and feature films). There were endless variety shows, game shows imported from the United States, variety acts inside game shows and games inside variety shows, an invasion of sitcoms (especially at the end of the afternoon and in prime time). France now boasts a television service that is as cheap and vulgar as can be found in any Western nation (apart from the United States and Italy). Even its drama is now uninspired. Vaguely literary or cultural shows are either defunct or relegated to the wee hours, sometimes 12:30 AM. The great names in political journalism, who only yesterday were showered with honors and glory, now turn up on Sunday at noon. Bernard Pivot, a distinguished hostage, is the least badly treated: you can see him Friday night, often before 11 o'clock! But given the general climate, his show has lost part of its following and it has to cast a much wider net for its subjects and guests in order to keep its head above water. A strictly literary program that is also something of an event, like his *Apostrophes*, is now unthinkable. And it seems there is no going back.

La bonne société had to all intents and purposes made television in its own image. Despite its deep-seated contempt for this modern gadget, it had turned it into a flawlessly moral adjunct to the ministries of culture and education, and had limited its freedom of action (lights out at 11 o'clock). It violently opposed the introduction of a few pathetic commercials early in the evening, it spoke out against the stupidity of variety shows and of the scheduled films. Even in 1980 or 1982, when French television was still very decent, enlightened spirits were bewailing its general mindlessness (as though they'd never seen foreign TV). But when the real dangers appeared on the horizon - new channels, privatization - no one seemed to see them coming.

The elite probably thought that, even when ceded to the worst commercial interests, television would never be able to get along without them, that writers would remain stars forever, and that Raymond Aron, Le Roy Ladurie and the *Collège de France* would always be welcome at the Rue Cognac-Jay studios. Not in their wildest imaginings - like an old decrepit monarchy that controls only what's immediately adjacent to the palace - could they have predicted that Literature would be represented by Paul-Loup Sulitzer, the businessman and author of cheap novels, and politics by Bernard Tapie, France's answer to Michael Milken. Or that respectable personages would elbow each other out of the way to appear with the Lenos and Lettermans of French TV. Today the world view of *la bonne société* is reduced to appearing on *Arte*, the cable cultural channel, undisturbed by prying eyes, and with no hope of a return or a Restoration.

Unless one believes that television today has no significant impact on society, education and culture, on the way power is wielded, and finally on power itself, one has to conclude that this sudden and widespread shifting of the ground has seriously undermined the position of *la bonne société*.

In her *Journal d'une Parisienne* (Diary of a Parisian), Françoise Giroud recounts a boring upscale dinner party - names beginning with "*de*," diplomats, senior civil servants - where she was one of the guests. It was the cream of society, a bit stiff, not a social climber or nouveau riche in sight. Just as the party was breaking up, the distinguished hostess timidly whispered in her ear: "We were thinking of inviting Patrick Poivre d'Arvor to dinner soon. Do you think he would accept?"

My God, where will snobbery turn next, sighs Françoise Giroud, who has nothing against her talented colleague in the media. Tomorrow PPDA as guest of honor at a dinner in the Faubourg Saint-Germain, and the day after tomorrow, what? In France the question is, have the standards of quality only begun to change? Or has the Old World already been three-quarters interred without its last survivors even being aware of it?

5. In Mickey's Shadow

THE MAGIC KINGDOM DRAWS NIGH: OCTOBER, 1991

Six months prior to the inauguration of EuroDisneyland, just
to behold the work site, the scale models, the offices, even
the *Disneyfolk* themselves, is to be touched by sacred fire.
Before your eyes, the best of all possible worlds is being honed to
the minute and to the centimetre: the 100 percent hygienic
Kingdom of Dreams, the Empire of the Good, of Adventure-
Without-Fear, of Utter and Complete Efficiency, and of Cash-
That-Drops-Scientifically-Into-The-Till. A blessed enclave of the
gods where everyone smiles, where there's no risk of being accosted by hooligans or slipping on greasy paper. And which, bright
and gleaming, will throw open its doors right on time on the day
declared, having hewed religiously to its schedule and its 22 billion
franc budget.

Even the more distant future is writ: after the first park in 1992
with its attractions and its 5,200 hotel rooms, there will be Park
Number Two in 1995, the Hollywood shooting stage, the 13,000
additional hotel rooms, the golf course, the lake, and so on. Of
course, Disney can't see to the end of time, and is content to plan
only up to 2017. But no one at Disney or in the camp of its most
spiteful detractors doubts for an instant that what is inscribed on
the tablets of EuroDisneyland's Law will come to pass. Wars and
political regimes come and go, Disney is forever.

First contact, and the shock of efficiency. It began with the
press office, though there was a slight hitch at the beginning. No

reply to my first fax. Phone call, second fax. The same day, the head of the division - a French native, to boot - was tying himself in apologetic knots: "I don't understand how it could have happened!" He proposed a meeting at some future date, when the press was to be invited in large numbers. It was a bit far off. Five minutes later, I had a firm appointment for ten days hence.

On the appointed day a press attaché was waiting for me in the offices at Noisy-le-Grand, with a Disney car, two helmets, and rubber boots, and we were off to the Disney construction site fifteen kilometres away in the middle of the countryside, near Marne-la-Vallée. My companion spoke French so fluently that it was ten minutes before I realized she was American. Her father is a former (renowned) Vietnam correspondent for the *New York Times*, and her mother writes for the *New Yorker*. She herself worked for more than a year at CBS, where she was production assistant during the Gulf War. So she was neither an innocent, nor a Quaker, nor a Mormon, nor an evangelist, but just an educated citizen who had even lived in Moscow. Strange. Had she succumbed to depression or alcoholism since then? Why else would she have agreed to work for the Kingdom where the Smile never sets?

Eventually I came to understand what at first sight seemed incomprehensible. This young pre-yuppie from the East coast was making no special effort to sell me her product, wasn't flogging the merchandise with dutiful enthusiasm; she just found Disney absolutely fan-tas-tic. She'd visited the Florida park six times when she was a child and had been enchanted by it. When - through some connection - she had been offered this job at Marne-la-Vallée, she hadn't hesitated for a moment. Before coming here she had participated in the great initiatory rite, a whole month at DisneyWorld in Florida, playing every role: hostess, chambermaid, cashier. A dream come true! She smiled at everybody for days on end, chased down lost children, gave directions all day long to people who wanted to know where the pirates were, when was the cowboy parade, how to find Star Wars or the toilets. "It's an incredible experience! You really get the feeling of the place." It was hard to doubt her sincerity.

Our tour, by the way, finished off at the "Disney Space," a kind of show pavilion, where 150,000 visitors had already paid ten francs each to see a publicity film on the park-to-be, to buy Disney products (pins and tee-shirts), and to eat a hot dog. A Parisian press service usually prides itself on its expense claims; even if there's no good professional reason (especially if that is the case), you will be treated to a restaurant meal that costs 500 francs per plate. At the Disney Space you had the choice of a hamburger, a hot dog, or chili con carne served up in a plastic bowl. No wine or beer. The best you could do in the way of vice was to choose "hard" Coca-Cola full of caffeine over the "light" variety. And even at the mass press tour six months before the opening, the hundreds of French journalists found themselves on dry territory, as though Prohibition were still in force.

The eight hundred acres (a fifth the area of Paris) granted to Disney in 1985 are for the moment only a huge work site that it takes a good half-hour to tour by car, and whose entrances are guarded by a private security service in khaki uniforms. Until the opening, the offices will remain far off in a modern building at Noisy-le-Grand. But as soon as you step into them you know that, even in these anonymous and temporary quarters, you are in the world of Disney. Calm and competence. Vague and patient smiles are the order of the day.

A "cast member" - translation: a Disney employee, but properly turned out and labeled - goes nowhere without his plastic oval badge bearing his first name and nothing else. This applies equally to top executives and humble receptionists. During the big celebration on April 12, 1991, even Roy Disney, the heir, and Bob Fitzpatrick, the Euro chief executive, sported their regulation badges, no different from those of ordinary ticket-sellers.

The employment office is on the ground floor of the building. Here the "small jobs" are filled, for hotels, restaurants, and maintenance. The managers, for the most part, are recruited by headhunting agencies. As for the many costumed guides, they will be selected in Paris by Disney scouts, from among out-of-work actors and Club Méditerranée activity leaders.

As they arrive, people stand and wait in a line that forms on the left, marked off by a red rope. A smiling hostess points applicants to a corner where they fill out a detailed questionnaire that probes their life. There must be about fifty aspirants, sitting on padded benches. Every so often a Disney "hiring-person" emerges from a cubicle, softly calls a name, and offers a firm smile and a vigorous handshake to the candidate. This is a first interview, brief and decisive. Those who pass the test will be recalled for a second interview, which most often leads to a serious job offer.

I had barely ventured, hesitantly, into the room (but to the right of the rope, where you're supposed to exit *and not* enter), when the front-line hostess corralled me, gently but firmly, the way you accost drying-out alcoholics and severe schizophrenics in a hospital. "Are you interested in Disney?" (Which means: are you looking for work?) The word "journalist" seemed to cause her some confusion, and occasioned the instant appearance of another "cast member," higher up in the pecking order: a strapping young man, a sort of Pete Sampras without the tennis, doubtless capable of imposing order if need be. "Are you interested in Disney?", he asked in turn. You couldn't tell, from his appearance or the way he talked, whether he was a Frenchman who had lived in the United States or an American who had perfectly mastered French. He was a totally hybrid cultural product, 100 percent EuroDisney. When I asked him how many people were hired on an average day, he smiled at me again: "I'd prefer that a hiring person give you that kind of information."

Although it's some sort of state secret, it turns out that the hiring program is on schedule - it would be strange if it were not in this country with its three million unemployed - but to everyone's surprise there is not an overwhelming crush of candidates. The first day there were 1,100, and since then the turnout has been much smaller.

"The French aren't in a hurry," observed an American manager with just a hint of disapproval. "Not as much as we would have thought, at any rate. It's true that these are mostly low-level jobs that pay decently but no more, and that Marne-la-Vallée is an hour from Paris. But Disney offers good working conditions, you can make a career there. In France, apparently, many people prefer to remain unemployed. I know unemployed executives in the States who would work as receptionists while they waited for something else to turn up."

Another stumbling block to recruiting "locals": the first commandment in the world of Disney is that each employee be there "to serve the public." Happy, smiling, moodless. That doesn't quite describe the merchant or employee that foreign tourists usually encounter in Paris.

Then there's the notorious Disney dress code. No beards, no moustaches for the men. Hair length is monitored. For the women, it's more complicated: three hair colors are acceptable, but no fancy hairdos; heel-heights are prescribed, as well as the maximum diameter for earrings; panty-hose are obligatory year-round. Finally - and this goes for both sexes - no one has his own uniform, because that would open the door to who-knows-what fantasies and individualism. Every evening you turn in your uniform so it can be cleaned according to house procedures, and the next day you pick up another, nice and fresh.

"That's the main problem we have with the French," sighs the same manager: "they're not used to serving the public."

EURODISNEY, THE NEW CITY: APRIL, 1992.

I t's a first for old Europe: next Sunday a new city, authentically synthetic, will be thrown open to the public in the Paris suburbs. This spanking new, perfectly hygienic metropolis already has its 12 thousand employees (themselves squeaky clean), its own station on the express regional transport line (pending the high-speed train station, which will be ready in a few months), its 5,200 hotel rooms, its two autoroute links, and soon, God-willing, its 10 to 11 million annual visitors.

Welcome to EuroDisneyland, the city where Mickey Mouse is prince.

For the greater Paris region, this is one of the biggest instant economic development projects to take shape in the last twenty years. For its few opponents, it's a shameful raiding of State finances and a pandering to the Americans and their moronic underculture. The massive EuroDisney contract, signed in 1985 with various French government agencies, has spawned an overall venture of 22 billion francs.

Budget overruns and delays are routine in France and Europe. The Bastille Opera, whose final cost was eight times the original estimates, is only one example. As for the Channel Tunnel, in 1987 it was to cost 48 billion francs. In October 1991, the revised budget was 80 billion, pending further revisions. Doubling the initial forecast seems to be the best one can hope for. The opening of the tunnel, scheduled for June 15, 1993, was first postponed to the following September, but the Chunnel would only be put to real use (with the high-speed train) in the summer of 1994.

Give Disney the credit it deserves: never has such a huge undertaking been so well managed. They said 22 billion francs, and that' just what it was: 22 billion. They foresaw a first pre-inauguration on April 12, 1991, and it came off perfectly. There was another media day on October 12 to admire Sleeping Beauty's newly completed, sparkling clean castle. It was impeccable.

To keep to the schedule, contracts divided and sub-divided to the nth degree were allotted to different entrepreneurs under very strict conditions, and all the necessary exemptions were obtained from the Employment Ministry regarding night-shifts, weekends, overtime, a 47-hour week, and the right to hire at will in European countries like Portugal that have low wage-scales. None of that was unprecedented for a work site of this nature, but Disney spelled it all out to the last detail. "EuroDisney is an outright American enclave where the government has given up on applying French laws," protested the Communist journalist Gilles Smadja, backed up on this point by the philosopher Alain Finkielkraut, who found the whole project scandalous. But they were voices in the wilderness, as was the High Commission for the French Language, whose objection to the fact that English would to all intents and purposes be the official language of this new city fell on deaf ears. Let's not exaggerate: practical information is available in both languages, and you can go to the bathroom in French. "What people are buying," said one of the Disney people bluntly, "is a little bit of America. So it's in American."

Of the 12,000 or so employees recruited by Disney to perform the essential services at the theme park, a significant (and un- usual) number, at least 25 percent, are not French. Of course, with the Common Market, EuroDisney could hire as many EU nation- als as it wanted. As in most cases where it is essential to speak English, there was an enormous amount of hiring in Holland, Germany, Great Britain, and so on. In the offices and on the site there are many people who speak perfect French, but with a heavy accent. Since the prospect of employment opportunities was crucial to the French decision to lure Disney to the doors of Paris, one might ask if the French authorities were in fact duped into doling out huge subsidies to create jobs, many of which eluded French nationals?

That is the only serious question being discussed here of late. Aside from the odd intellectual - or the Communist Party in full anti-American flight - almost no one in France is dealing with the "cultural" side of the problem. Disney is what it is, which is American, and no one else in Europe would have the means or the credibility to open an amusement park anywhere for 10 million visitors a year - or even to find 10 or 12 billion francs on the European money markets. The EuroDisney complex east of Paris is the equivalent of two large Japanese automobile factories; it is also a "pole of development" in a region that had previously been barren. And at the very least, Disney will be a buyer of services, consumer goods, and so on, with all that implies for indirect employment. So forget culture. In the Parisian intellec- tual community, reactions range from resignation in the face of American might to an almost dotty enthusiasm for the celebrated "Yankee professionalism."

The real question for more astute observers is whether the French authorities have paid much too dearly for Disney. Accord- ing to moderate estimates, the State, the region, the *département*, and so on have shelled out four billion francs. About 800 million went for the extension of the RER transit line. Some 700 million are forecast for the high-speed train line and station. About 900 million more for a very-low-interest loan from the *Caisse de dépôt*, the government funding agency. Add to that two autoroute exits, a police station, the expropriation of local beet farms, etc. And finally, a reduction in Value Added Tax on admissions from 18.6 to 7 percent (the idea is to make it up with the VAT on materials). It's worth noting that at the end of the 1980s, the Astérix theme park - which is open six months a year and attracts a million visitors - did not receive a penny in grants, and even paid for its own autoroute exit.

This subsidization is especially significant, in that Disney was accorded 800 acres of land to develop, at a price close to that of agricultural-use land - and the park that opened on April 12 only covers 240 acres. The rest will come in 1997, the biggest development project in Paris since *La Défense*. All in all, 18,000 hotel rooms, and 700,000 square metres of office space. "Even if EuroDisney were to be a financial disaster, the real-estate added-value accruing to Disney would guarantee it an enormous profit," according to *L'Expansion*.[6]

All this can be explained by the fact that at the time of the negotiation, French authorities were all quaking in their boots at the prospect of Disney's giving up on the project or going else-where. The American firm negotiated masterfully, suggesting that it had two other options, one in the south of London, the other outside Barcelona. This was hardly credible, since both sites were out of the way, but the officials took the bait. Disney represented THE contract for the 1980s, and the authorities were ready to do just about anything for it not to get away.

So it was for the then mayor of Paris, Jacques Chirac, personal friend of EuroDisneyland boss Bob Fitzpatrick, and a great Disneyland and Disneyworld aficionado - he'd been to Anaheim and Orlando a number of times. Laurent Fabius, who was (socialist) prime minister in 1985, had no reservations whatsoever about the project. "Within the government," says one of his former advisors,

---

6   This was at the height of real-estate euphoria in the Paris region. With the slump that continues to prevail today, Disney's prospects in the short or medium term are less bright.

"there was no discussion, no debate, no opposition, despite culture minister Jack Lang's timid objections at the beginning. When the time came to sign the agreement in principle, December 18, 1985, Fabius rushed to put pen to paper before Michel Giraud, president of the Ile-de-France region, had a chance to ink in his name first." To complete the picture, the above-mentioned Gilles Smadja claims that the very literary François Mitterrand lobbied for the project in person during a meeting with Ronald Reagan in 1985. As for Édith Cresson, who was Minister for Foreign Trade in 1985, a much-reproduced picture shows her posing with Mickey, at Disneyworld.

THE HOUR OF GLORY: APRIL 12 1992, 9:30 AM

All the prophecies inscribed in the good book of Disney have come to pass. On the appointed day, at the appointed hour, the pasteboard doors of paradise swung open to reveal the faithful assembled before them, as had been foretold. At the behest of Mickey - and of "Bob" (Fitzpatrick), Disney Europe's CEO, the Followers of the Mouse thronged to the park of Marne-la-Vallée, 32 kilometres east of Paris. Further prophecies concerning EuroDisneyland - unto the year 2017 - are sure to be realized.

The miracle was so eagerly awaited that, for the last two days, it was the sole preoccupation of Paris's various local authorities. As the media reiterated ad nauseam, this was a happening of capital importance, an event both beneficial and potentially catastrophic, liable to sow chaos and panic between Paris and Marne-la-Vallée. On the eve of the event we saw the very obscure Secretary of State for Highway Safety, Georges Sarre, seize the opportunity to sound the alarm on television in person. Yesterday it was the turn of the Paris police chief. He raised the spectre of a relentless tidal wave of families, a great surge of collective madness that would loose its haggard hordes on all the autoroute's fast lanes and slow ramps: 300,000 people? Or 500,000? The lure of the famous mouse was so compelling that it would in a trice empty the capital of its inhabitants. As the infamous CGT, the French pro-communist trade union, had taken advantage of the event to call a rail strike for the same day, everyone would take his car, and there would be 90,000 vehicles that side of Paris, all at the same time. And a Disney parking lot with a capacity of only 12,000. The great dream would turn into a nightmare worthy of Jean-Luc Godard!

In Paris, these days, it has not been Disney madness, but Disney hysteria. Childless myself, I hadn't the slightest notion of the sort of absolute sway Disney held over families of all sorts. Six months ago, a humble taxi-driver (bringing me home from the Astérix theme-park), told me he had already taken his family to the park in Florida, and that he was now waiting impatiently for Marne-la-Vallée to open so he could do it all over again, only more so. A literary friend - a distinguished journalist and biographer, but also the father of two children - told me right off that he'd be going very soon, not for an afternoon, but for a whole week-end! I was dumbfounded by his enthusiasm. In the midst of it all I was informed by one mother that "Disney Parade" (on the FR3 television channel) was a rendezvous never to be missed, that tolerated no lapses, no backsliding. Looking into it, I found that this long weekly program attracts six million viewers every Sunday. And so, even if you grant that two percent of the French abhor EuroDisney, and that some others couldn't care less about it, the vast majority of the population know and love it in their bones. Everyone has been or will go to Disney. Except for the spoilsports, of course.

And so for the media, the opening was an affair of state, a global happening - and the story had legs. If only to criticize it (but oh, so prudently) *Libération* devoted twelve full pages to it just yesterday. Having spent an arm and a leg to buy the rights to broadcast last night's big show (in "mondovision"), the TV network TF1, certain of breaking all ratings records, dedicated its whole evening to that one topic. For the daily newspapers and the weeklies, this was an event comparable to the coming of a new Messiah.

It goes without saying that Disney excels at public relations. Most journalists working in Paris, but also entire regiments from

Amsterdam or London, were duly invited (along with their spouses) to set up shop for three days at Marne-la-Vallée (with two nights in a hotel, worth up to 1,300 francs per night). On the shores of Buena Vista "Lake," between the Newport Hotel (with its pasteboard New England façade and its chic interior) and the New York (with its own comic-strip facade, *Batman* style), the inaugural cocktail party may not have been the height of refinement, but it boasted the greatest concentration of champagne, excellent California cabernet, and diverse delicacies to be seen for many years around Paris.

And everything unfolded like clockwork, of course. Never in my life have I seen so many attendants, so disciplined, so specialized, at an affair of this type. Dozens, hundreds of security people, with walkie-talkies or earphones. Even during the worst crush in the hotels, there was always a smiling hostess. Despite a 24-hour computer breakdown (affecting all the telephones in the Newport hotel rooms) "cast members" were there on the line to transmit articles. Not to mention the countless trash-gatherers, picking up wrappings and other garbage. And the servers. There was no way for a guest to wander off alone or even to slow his pace without being accosted by some bubbly "cast member" assigned to succor any inadvertent wallflower.

But everyone knows all this because in North America "everyone" has already been to Disney. Speaking frankly, EuroDisney is practically the spitting image of what already exists in California, Florida, or Japan. Theme hotels and restaurants where the staff dress (and talk) in conformity with... a theme. Countless boutiques, restaurants and snack-bars. The smallest Coca-Cola comes in a big (for the French) 50-centilitre glass, and the next size up is a full litre. And there is more pop-corn, good old-fashioned hamburgers and very bad pastrami than great cuisine. The 800 acres ceded to Disney no longer constitute part of France, but rather a real plasticized transplant of America. And in the hotels, where the guests are largely foreign, the proportion of non-French personnel seems close to 90 percent - most of whom speak French, but not without difficulty. In the park itself there is more French spoken, but much of the hiring has been done outside France.

Still, one must say in all honesty that, if Euro-Disney's promises are kept, the economic benefits to Marne-la-Vallée will go far beyond the number of immediate jobs. And that, in order to attract six or seven million German, British or Dutch tourists, what was needed was a 100 percent certified American product, designed, manufactured and maintained by Mr. Disney in person. And here it is: the preserve of the American smile.

Scrooge McDuck Lays His Cards On The Table: March 20, 1994

In the midst of the general euphoria, a few mean spirits dared to lay at Disney's door every imaginable sin. Culturally, EuroDisney was a scandalous exercise in mindlessness, and France was being reduced to the status of an American colony. The authorities had subsidized the project far too generously, and more productive jobs could have been created in the same place, for much less money. The Disney corporation was a hard bargainer, paid low salaries, offered no job security, and imposed on its staff regulations worthy of a sect. We had heard it all, even if in the long run this litany of criticisms had provoked little interest in the mainstream media and the population; all anyone knew was that the biggest investment in the last 15 years in the Paris region had created over 10,000 immediate jobs, much indirect employment, and with the wave of a magic wand was going to attract at least 10 million tourists per year. This figure was carved in stone.

However, one thing never entered the minds either of the political authorities or of the project's most vehement detractors: the possibility that this European Disneyland might turn out to be, quite simply, an unsuccesful commercial venture, perhaps even a financial fiasco. That is why the government and the region had accepted virtually all the conditions, some of them extravagant, set by the Americans. You could never pay too much to get EuroDisney because the revenue and profits would be enormous.

Disney's fiercest enemies were those most convinced of its profitability. The very reason they opposed it was that millions of visitors would throng to the park, spend fortunes on stupid purchases, and fill to bursting the silly pasteboard hotels. Disney could only be a factory that manufactured huge profits. The gigantic machine could do no wrong. The perfect emblem of unbridled American capitalism, (along with Reader's Digest and Coca-Cola), Disney was immune to error. It knew how to manage a giant work site in France that met its deadlines and respected its budget absolutely, while outmaneuvering the unions and keeping the mafia at a distance. From the beginning, every prophecy had come true. So would it be with all the others: the opening of a second park, the real estate ventures, the 18,000 hotel rooms. Profits would flow in, and of course the European banks and small investors would be sure of sharing in the wealth - insofar as they were allowed to sit in at the table.

Two years shy of three months after the park's inauguration, everyone is disillusioned, including Mickey's countless European partners. The park is still just as clean, the roller-coasters are still gleaming and the Caribbean Pirates never break down; every year, even, there are not much fewer than the 10 million visitors foreseen in the plan. There is only one small problem. EuroDisneyland is losing an enormous amount of money.

The visitors have come, but the hotels are still half empty, the restaurants do less business than expected, and the ubiquitous souvenirs are not selling well. In 1992-93, the head office chalked up - without batting an eyelash, by the way - a loss of some five billion francs. The EuroDisney stocks that small investors had bought for 72 francs a share - The U.S. Disney Corporation had paid 10 francs for them in 1989 - fell to 27 francs after having climbed to a height of 164 francs just one month after the opening.[7] As for the second phase of the project, which was to include convention centres, film studios, new hotels and a real-estate venture, it has quite simply been shelved, even though in the 1980s it was the kicker that had in no small part helped to

---

7   In 1994, they dropped decisively to under 10 francs.

justify the huge government subsidies and the generous concessions made to Disney.

Disturbing rumors had been circulating for more than a year,
in financial circles at least. Like a splotch in the middle of an
immaculate painting. This was the reason for the steady decline
of the stock since the opening of the park. But the rude awakening
came last November, both for the man-in-the-street and the
hordes of small shareholders; the fairy tale was turning into a
disaster epic. Michael Eisner, the big boss of the Disney Corporation, began talking quite calmly about closing the park. This
would mean the instant liquidation of some 10,000 jobs, perhaps
even hotels torn down, become so many fossils rising out of the
middle of a wasteland. As for the high-speed train station and the
station for the express transit line that the government had
generously bestowed on Mickey, well, there might still be a few
locals to use them. How could it have come to this?

For a start, the great minds of Disney made some whopping
errors in their financial projections. There have been as many
visitors as were predicted, no problem there, but from the start
they have consumed less than expected - perhaps as a result of the
serious recession that has befallen Europe over the last two years.
Above all, visitors didn't stay as long as they were supposed to. It
was assumed that families would spend two or three days sleeping
in the theme park's hotels, and then would make a side-trip to
Paris. The opposite happened. Many people visiting Paris took the
opportunity to spend just a single day at EuroDisney. This world
was upside down. Could Paris be more tempting, and - dare we
use the word? - more important a destination than Walt Disney's
newest and most sparkling park?

Might Mickey's little band, who seemed to know everything
there was to know about business, after all have been just a bunch
of amateurs? Or was their business acumen even more astute than
we realized? When the idea of closing the park was floated last
November, everyone began to do their sums. In direct grants,
Disney had received some four billion francs from the French
government, a figure that even *L'Expansion*, an extremely down-
to-earth business magazine, found pretty extravagant. But more

to the point: thanks to an unusually baroque financial arrangement, Disney USA managed to complete this gigantic project
while barely dipping into its own pockets. Most of the financing
was assured by sixty or so French and European banks. Last
November it was calculated that closing the park would cost
Disney-U.S.A. about two billion francs, and the banking consor-
tium about ten times as much. Disney might even come out a
winner in the long run, because it had arranged to be paid billions
of francs in "consulting" fees, plus other miscellaneous revenues.
Its biggest risk in the event of a sudden shutdown would be to its
image. The real financial blow would be to the European bankers
- who confess, today, that they opened up limitless lines of credit
on the strength of Disney's charmed name.

As a result, although the recovery plan devised early this week
in Paris obliges the Disney head office to fork out three billion
francs in cash, it still involves the banks on an equal basis; so as
not to lose everything, they throw three billion more into the kitty
and forgo 18 months of interest. In short, the rescue is being
financed by the natives themselves, who thought at first that they
had stumbled on a gold mine. Mickey was a financial wizard and
he had agreed to share his profits with the Europeans. Two years
later, they've discovered that they're in fact dealing with Scrooge
McDuck. And Scrooge gave them a good lesson in finance: even
when he loses, it's the others who pay.[8]

---

8   In the summer of 1995, with a little more than nine million visitors,
     EuroDisney showed its first profits, thanks to lower prices for hotel rooms,
     special packages, reduced personnel (at the cost of a few food wrappers left
     on the ground - "just like at Astérix," according to the nasty unionists)...
     and the introduction of alcoholic beverages, even in the middle of the day.
     The ambitious plans for new parks and hotels seem to have been
     abandoned. And so EuroDisney is certain to survive, but without its sheen.
     The myth of infallibility has been compromised. What remain are 600 acres
     of development land that for the moment are untouched. Perhaps one day
     a good financial analyst will tell us what this undertaking really cost the
     State, and how much it profited the mother-house.

6. *Tomorrow We'll Dream In American*

L et's look on the bright side: France is still the least Americanized country in Europe. In Germany, American films monopolize 90 percent of box-office receipts. In Holland, English-language films are shown in English on television, and some Amsterdam bookstores stock almost as many American paperbacks as books in Dutch. From Italy to Sweden, the number of bands that record directly in American are legion. From east to west and from north to south in Europe, the juggernaut of American mass culture is working overtime, spewing out its look-alike television series, its "top 50," its latest incarnation of *Police Academy*. You can spend a whole week in Frankfurt, Amsterdam or Copenhagen in an environment that is almost exclusively American. (Italy is a special case: its magnificent cinema has disappeared, its television is one of the most vulgar in Europe, it has been Americanized to the nth degree, and yet it's still *very* Italian. Doubtless that's because its native culture is so far from Anglo-Saxon, and so is less easily assimilated.)[9]

---

9   240 million tickets to movies were sold in Italy in 1980 - that was in the days when you could still find old neighborhood or village movie-houses, with news and advertisements, sometimes even variety acts or strip-tease artists, as in Fellini-Roma. Italy had more filmgoers than any other country in Europe, and its Seventh Art was, along with that of the French, the only one to hold its own next to the American giant. Since then, Berlusconi - and other plagues - have come along, and now only 80 million tickets are sold yearly in Italy, most to American movies shown in ultra-commercial

By comparison, France isn't doing too badly. It's the last country in Europe to boast a national film industry, with from 100 to 150 features produced each year, that garner 30 to 35 percent of box-office receipts. Similarly, the French music industry controls about 40 percent of the recording market.

Some French political or cultural officials may find reason to rejoice in these figures. In fact, what they point to and imply is an utter collapse of French production in the area of mass culture, which constitutes the daily diet of the ordinary Frenchman and of young people in the suburbs. The young watch American television series, go to American films, and other than the odd bit of French raï or rap, only listen to American music. And there's no likelihood that things will change in the foreseeable future. This train has left the station.

Despite my irreproachable sense of professional responsibility, I never tune in to the most popular FM stations. I only hear the popular rock-music radio station *NRJ* when I wander into a clothing boutique in Les Halles, and I don't even know where to find *Fun* or *Skyrock* on the dial. I've seen neither *Police Academy 1* nor *Police Academy 8*; until recently I'd never heard of Whoopi Goldberg; I can't identify Prince on the radio, and I only know Bud Spencer by his photos. I find EuroDisney inordinately ugly and depressing, and I would never eat a fast-food hamburger, not as a matter of principle, but because I'm suspicious of industrially-produced ground beef.

French young people, starting with those in the working-class suburbs, now do all of that - and know only that. Their day to day *culture* consists almost entirely of low-grade American products. Their universe is not of course that of Tom Waits or Jarmusch, not even, really, of Spielberg or Coppola (except occasionally by accident). The lives of French youths are permeated with heroes and personages that are utterly foreign to me, and that have no

---

chains. And Italians stay home and watch television. Italian cinema has practically disappeared, except for a few bright lights who do not even come close to filling the shoes of Fellini or Visconti.

connection with their own background, surroundings, or society.[10]

It's not just that the huge Hollywood blockbusters like Batman, Star Wars, or Raiders of the Lost Ark pull in huge profits in Paris. After all, only the Americans have the money and perhaps the genius to create these space stations of the film world. And it's not surprising that Walt Disney, with his puritanism and syrupy uplift, but his consummate professionalism, has cornered the market on animation and every Christmas, like clockwork, produces another commercial success. But how to explain that adolescents in the suburbs of Brest, Toulouse or Clermont-Ferrand - who neither speak nor understand English - throng to the movie theatres to acclaim the newest performance of Bud Spencer? Or that Whoopi Goldberg and Eddie Murphy are an integral part of their private world? It's very mysterious. These idols are not even praised to the skies by the media (other than the *youth* media, perhaps, for which I don't qualify), nor are they promoted by the big television networks. But they are now part and parcel of the *youth* culture, which flourishes outside the standard promotional circuits. School kids and college students know Whoopi the way their elders know Woody.

And so when I looked into the attendance figures for films in France in 1992, I found that *Sister Act* was in third place, *Bodyguard* (with Kevin Costner) was in fourth, *War Games* was in seventh, and the ineffable *Home Alone II* in eighth. If *Police Academy* or an Eddie Murphy film had been in release that year, they would have figured in the top ten.

In 1982, French films attracted 110 million spectators, and American films, 62 million. In 1991 there were 70 million entries for American films... and only 36 million for French films. In ten

---

10   In a recent television sketch Robert Hue, the new general-secretary of the French Communist Party, meets with young people in a suburban housing development, where of course no one has ever heard of him. "We have broken with Stalin," he declares, trying to get them on his side. "It's pronounced Stallone, not Stalin!", they all shout at once.

years, the French film industry lost two-thirds of its audience. Ten to fifteen productions each year succeed: the films of Bertrand Blier, of Jean-Jacques Annaud, *Cyrano de Bergerac* or the surprising *All the Mornings of the World*. And excellent filmmakers such as Sautet, Pialat, Tavernier still cling to the status they enjoyed ten or fifteen years ago, with respectable box-office success in the category of quality or art films.

In 1991, the figures spoke loud and clear. The ten big winners for the year were ALL American, from *Dancing With Wolves* (6.8 million spectators in France) to *Look Who's Talking Too* (1.7 million). The most successful French film came eleventh. Admittedly, it was an unusually bad year, with not a single big French box-office hit. But the trend is inexorable.

The time seems to have passed when the French film industry could count on a few big box-office stars who guaranteed a film's success. In those days, a decent film starring Louis de Funès was automatically a big grosser. Jean-Paul Belmondo regularly pulled in a million filmgoers in Paris, as long as his vehicle was reasonably well-crafted. On a somewhat higher plane, Alain Delon or Catherine Deneuve were thoroughly bankable, and could ensure a film a very respectable audience. There was an important commercial or popular cinema that fed the machine, kept the distributors busy, and filled a vast network of theatres, which is essential to the health of the industry.

Today, among the actors, there are no safe bets, other perhaps than Gérard Depardieu or Isabelle Adjani, and even there, only on condition that they appear in quality productions with big budgets. On the other hand, there have been films hitched to that powerful locomotive, Depardieu, that flopped completely. Belmondo has been virtually absent from the screen for the last five years. The *Casanova* for which Delon was paid six million francs was a box-office disaster. Today neither Lelouch, nor Chabrol, nor Resnais, nor any of the others can count on a respectable turnout in the theatres. A good film with Michel Serrault may be successful, but there's no guarantee. Films with variety stars like Patrick Bruel or Johnny Hallyday went nowhere. The few films that make it are either big quality productions with budgets over 100 million francs (*Cyrano, The Lover*), or the occasional production with no stars that comes as a complete surprise, but turns out to be timely: there was *Une Époque Formidable* by Gérard Jugnot, *The Visitors*, and *Un Indien dans la Ville*. But these are the exceptions that prove the rule, and no one has a recipe for them. What is more, there is no sign of any kind of renaissance.

Where music is concerned the situation is not much better, but it is different and more complex. On the one hand, the public's alienation from French songs is much less marked than for the cinema; in 1992 French records accounted for 39.9 percent of the sales, which was something of a miracle considering the publicity machine behind American music. This means there is still some cultural room to maneuver here, and the public truly wants to buy in French, whether it be Bruel, Cabrel, Goldmann, Sardou or Céline Dion. On the other hand, this same French music is being sabotaged by the media, television, and above all radio.

On France-Inter, the quality public radio network, the proportion of Anglo-Saxon music on regular programs is two or three times as high as on Radio-Canada, the Quebec equivalent. In prime-time hours the American share must be 40 or 50 percent.

But France-Inter - and the two other general audience networks, Europe 1 and RTL - are the small trees that hide the forest. The three FM networks together attract about as many listeners as the three biggest general-audience stations. NRJ is heard by an average 4.2 million listeners. Just behind it, the Skyrock network and Fun-Radio have an additional six million fans, all between 15 and 30 years of age.

These three FM stations are almost entirely musical: the top 50 and pop, round and round, 24 hours a day. Here are the percentages of French music they broadcast in October of 1992 (including the middle of the night): 7.8 percent on NRJ, 6 percent on Skyrock, 4.9 percent on Fun. These figures include, of course (or rather consist entirely of) the big French sellers such as Bruel, Goldmann, and Roch Voisine. On the FM band, if you want French music, you'll find it for the most part on a station that was named prophetically: Radio-*Nostalgia*!

It's an understatement to say that the FM stations don't exactly encourage French production. They don't even program - or barely- the big French sellers like François Cabrel, or the month's biggest French hits. "We don't care about record sales," say the station directors: "We broadcast what our public wants, period." And it goes without saying that no one in France would even consider a quota system for music on the radio; that would be an infringement of creative freedom and freedom of expression.

Under the circumstances it's no surprise that Vanessa Paradis, the French Lolita with a voice like a kitten caught in a door, recorded her last album in the United States, entirely in English (it includes, by the way, a very pretty song). And that lesser known singers are following her example. Not only does a French hit stand little chance of making it in Germany or Italy, but it will do better in France if the lyrics are in American.

We may still only be near the top of this cultural slippery slope, because it's clear that the day-to-day culture or sub-culture in which young people (and sometimes our own generation) are immersed is in large part made in the USA. On television there is practically no French series, soap opera or sitcom that has succeeded with the general public.[11] The grannies from Marseille love *Santa Barbara*, the young people watch *Malibu Beach* or *The Cosby Show*, and deep in the hinterland the countless TV mags put second-rate American actors and actresses on their covers. (There is one notable exception: *Hélène et les garçons* (*Helen and the Boys*), whose low-end production values and design are so slavishly American that sometimes you think you're seeing a dubbed program.)

So why bother with scruples? Jean-Jacques Annaud shot Duras's *The Lover* in English (even if the action takes place during the French colonial period in Vietnam). Polanski shot *Bitter Moon*

---

11   There is something fascinating about the inability of the French to create and produce non-historical popular television series (soap operas or sitcoms) that will attract an audience and, with whatever degree of talent, deal with their own time.

in English, a film based on a Pascal Bruckner novel whose characters are quintessentially Parisian.

One of these days the French language may resemble, perhaps, one of those folkloric dialects you use at home to converse with ancient relatives who have fallen behind the times. We'll sing in American, shoot films in American, write scientific articles in American (this is already the case), publish our novels in American, do business and work in that language. On occasional nostalgic evenings we'll play old scratched 33s of Barbara, Goldmann or Alain Souchon. But after turning out the light, we'll dream in American.

Of course, I'm getting ahead of myself. There are still lots of singers who sing in French. And directors who are happy to film in French. They are often the most talented and the least commercial. By the same token, we have not yet reached the point where writers feel they must write directly in English (as is the case in the small northern European countries) in order to reach the vast American audience directly. In short the elite culture, quality culture, is still for the moment totally national. But what will it be like in ten or twenty years, when it is completely surrounded by a mass culture that has become entirely Americanized?

There is certainly no simple, European solution to this problem. But what makes it worse is that very few people in France - other than a small number of old cultural nationalists no longer in fashion - are paying any attention to it or seem to realize that like lemmings, we are all heading, quite happily, straight for the precipice.

IV:
The Portrait Gallery

I. The Devils

The Divine Marquis and the Patron Saint of the Luberon

What is surprising about the Marquis de Sade is not so much that certain professional French feminists denounce his odious habits and his morbid influence on Parisian literary circles, but that there are so few of these anti-sadian resisters (it's true that in this country feminism, even at its peak, was a modest matter, never interfered with sexual morality, and never lapsed at all into puritanism).

In fact, among the intelligentsia, almost the only women to take umbrage at the divine Marquis's turpitudes are Madame Yvette Roudy, Minister for the Rights of Women between 1981 and 1986, and the historian Élisabeth Badinter.

"In treating Sade as a great writer," Madame Roudy tells us, "Parisian intellectuals have legitimized all sorts of pornographic and misogynist aberrations." For Élisabeth Badinter, the monstrous Sade is an outright precursor of Nazism (this thesis has apparently made some inroads, and has turned up more than once in university dissertations). Of course, we are talking here about a writer who glorified torture and excused murder after himself having indulged in hard-core debauchery with prostitutes, and apparently his wife. However, one wonders if these points of view are pertinent. After all, whether in the west or around the world, pornography has never needed the Marquis de Sade to prosper and proliferate, not even in its *sado-maso* manifestations. And many consumers of porn probably don't know his work at all. As for his affinities with Nazism, they are a bit far-fetched. Sade was undoubtedly a true sexual pervert, but he never worked up his fantasies into a political program. Insofar as he took an interest in politics, it was to profess liberal ideas. We can certainly consider him vile and assert that his literary genius extenuates nothing, but need we for all that grant his work the status of a prophetic text when it is more of an individual case history and a historical curiosity?

The problem is not with the Marquis de Sade himself, whom nobody really reads for purposes of titillation, but rather with the elaborate cult devoted to him in Paris literary circles. And on the left.

Intellectuals of both sexes consider the Marquis to be a great literary genius, an "exquisite" writer, a prophet for all revolutions, and, finally, the dark star of "absolute freedom." Just dare to utter the word *morality* in a Parisian salon when referring to the author of the *120 Days of Sodom*, and you expose yourself as a hopeless fuddy-duddy whom the women present will shun like the plague all evening long.

When the principal works of Donatien-Alphonse-François, Marquis de Sade, were finally published around 1950 after a century and a half of "purgatory," it was no purveyor of pornography who was responsible, but rather the distinguished publisher (and trouble-maker) Jean-Jacques Pauvert. The beginning of the 1990s marked a second minor rebirth for Sade, when he was admitted into the literary pantheon of the Pléiade editions (with his writings on Bible paper, which does seem like a prophecy come true). Then, at the end of 1991, there appeared two works of very different dimensions, which made for a kind of Sadian autumn, good for rainy days in Normandy with a fire in the grate.

One was an appealing epistolary novel, *Je Vous Salue Marquis* (Hail, Marquis), written under the pseudonym Justine Saint-Ange. The other was a remarkable and fascinating book by the historian Maurice Lever, who claimed to have written the first real biography, based on archival research and the study of documents never before published. All of which inspired Paris's chief Sadian, Phillipe Sollers, to consecrate half of the front page of *Le Monde*'s literary magazine to the Marquis, who is one of his idols along with Laclos and the Cardinal de Retz. Lever's book was one of the major events of the literary season.

"Justine Saint-Ange's" novel was a pretty concoction: a correspondence between an imaginary twelve-year-old adolescent girl(!) and the hero of her dreams, Donatien-Alphonse-François in person (the narrator allows as how she had originally hesitated between Machiavelli and Roch Voisine as correspondents). The author seemed to have read his books - the most sulfurous ones at any rate - and to have found therein an appealing echo of childhood Edens with their secret games. The novel was in fact dedicated "to Sade when he was a little boy - and to all the depraved children."

This fantasy in letters, full of amusing literary in-jokes, was not even one of those mock-products generated so often in Paris by a busy editor perched on the shoulders of a talented ghost-writer. It was "Justine's" first novel, and she had written it because "she had been inspired to do so"— and because she had just discovered Sade, "a writer of genius, an utterly free spirit". "Justine," it turned out, was a young woman in her thirties who had studied political science and graduated from the *École Nationale d'Administration*, and who had formerly applied herself to professions much more serious than literature. Very well turned-out, tall, thin, blonde, and rather pretty, she was also the devoted mother of an eight-year-old girl. Four years younger than her heroine, all the same.

Did she plan to set her daughter to reading *The Philosophy in the Boudoir* at any time soon, so that she might also correspond with the Marquis at the age of twelve? The diplomaed and licentious mother was perfectly at ease with the question: "I'll wait until she discovers Sade on her own in the library, and let her make up her own mind. It's up to her to tell the difference between imagination at play and what is real."

"At the age of thirteen?"

"Why not thirteen? Anyway, she has lots of time. Sade will still be a classic two centuries from now."

LOUIS-BERNARD ROBITAILLE

As for the historian Maurice Lever, when you meet him he makes it clear from the outset that he considers Sade's major writings to be absolute masterpieces - beginning with the *120 Days* - and bridles with indignation at the slightest implication that there may be a link with Nazism or the practice of torture. "Sadism always existed, long before a German psychiatrist called it that at the turn of the century when he brought out the unpublished manuscript of the *120 Days* and presented it as a case history. And the Marquis cannot be held responsible for the way his name was used for 150 years. His writing was an act of creative freedom and has nothing to do with a program of political extermination like *Mein Kampf.*"

In any event, the real life of Donatien-Alphonse-François far outstrips any banal novelistic fiction; it's more like a comic book for adults. With the glaucous spectacle of his family's chateau near Avignon looming in the background, the fellow has more in common with Dracula than the Countess of Ségur, even if the Comtesse had nothing against spanking little girls.

It was a very old, very noble family, but in decline. Sade's father was a libertine, gambler, ambassador by profession, and a minor writer, with close connections to the Condé family. Sade in his youth was young man of means: governesses, studies with the Jesuits at Louis-le-Grand in Paris. As an heir, D.A.F., twenty years old in 1760, was just the sort one would associate with the end of a line, and he was a common enough product in this twilight of the old order. As much a gambler as his father and even more debauched, an inveterate sodomite and habitué of the brothels, Sade in this markedly decadent period, was a noted libertine at a very young age, which must mean that he deserved the reputation.

Having made an advantageous marriage he persisted in his escapades, which appalled his wife's family and soon set them against him, along with the police of Prime Minister Maupeou, who wanted to make examples of these dissolute young men. A first prison term resulted from his sessions with prostitutes, modelled on the black mass (the whip, hot wax on wounds), and a few years later came a new and heavier sentence. But Sade had flown the coop. It was his own mother-in-law who maneuvered him into jail, and then asked the king for a warrant of imprisonment under

158

royal seal (common practice for noble families who wanted to rein in their recalcitrant offspring). And so the divine Marquis found himself at Vincennes, and then the Bastille where he would rot from the age of 37 to 51. Those fourteen years of incarceration gave him the leisure to monitor his incidents of masturbation (he called them *prestiges*) with a certain precision: he counted 6,536, most between 1777 and 1780. And in the intervals between *prestiges* he wrote his most violent sexual texts. His imprisonment came to an end only with the Revolution in 1789, and the taking of the Bastille. But however liberal his ideas, Donatien was still a noble, an ex-aristocrat. He was picked up during the Terror in 1793, and spent another ten months in prison. He escaped the guillotine - by the skin of his teeth - by buying off the guards every time the tumbrels rumbled too near.

Freed after the fall of Robespierre in 1794, he tried to make a career as a real writer, struggled in vain to have one of his 25 sentimental stage plays produced, while at the same time publishing his pornographic works anonymously and in secret, in the climate created by the debauched years of the Directory. Then Bonaparte's accession to power brought morality back into vogue. Sade, who had become something of a celebrity in the realm of vice, was shut up in an asylum in Charenton for *libertine dementia*. There he spent the last eleven years of his life engaged in endless philosophical and erotomaniacal conversations with the director, and putting on his plays with the help of the other inmates.

We can't really say that in his case vice was rewarded, since the good marquis spent some 28 years of his life behind bars, which is a lot for a well born heir who was certainly no choirboy, but who was more of a tempest in a teapot than a dangerous criminal. But look at the evidence: despite the vicissitudes of his long incarcerations, perversion kept him going to the ripe old age of 74. Does a penchant for *prestiges* lead to the fountain of youth?

Today there are still distant descendants of the Marquis to be found, and they are proud to bear his illustrious name. As for the ancient familial lands of Saumane, they are in the heart of the Luberon, vacation country long cherished by the left-wing Parisian intelligentsia. Just a coincidence, of course.

Celine, the Evil Genius

Parisian intellectuals venerate Céline and consider him the greatest French novelist of the century along with Marcel Proust. But they've always had a small problem with him: how to deal with the fact that this artist of genius was *also* a fanatical anti-Semite right up to his death, an avowed Nazi (or close to it) until the Germans were defeated, in short a bastard of the first water.

We've just seen how the Parisian intelligentsia, since the 1950s, have come to venerate another monster of genius, in the person of the Marquis de Sade. It's as though at regular intervals they fall prey to a fatal attraction for Beelzebub, at least when he is reincarnated as a great writer. Of course, where the divine Marquis is concerned, his followers can indulge in a little intellectual snobbery without running any real risks; after two centuries, Sade's sulfurous profanations have become virtual classics. They've all been declared revolutionary, *and everyone is happy.*

Things have always been more awkward with Céline. On the one hand his creative genius is dazzling and less debatable than that of Sade. On the other, the baseness of Doctor Louis Destouches (Céline's real name) is so recent and so tangible that no one can turn his back on it or chalk it up to creative freedom or simple derangement.

Born on May 27, 1894, Céline died in 1961, not all that long ago. To the end he persisted in his hateful ravings against humanity in general and Jews in particular. He recanted nothing of what he had said or done during the 1930s and under the German occupation.

We can give him credit for persevering in his abominations (as did the Marquis de Sade during his twenty-odd years of imprisonment). But it doesn't make things easy for his many admirers. They have to try to save the day with a series of maneuverings and omissions: his virulent anti-Semitic tracts from the end of the 1930s (such as *Bagatelles Pour un Massacre*) are simply not mentioned, or are treated as lunatic ravings unconnected to his *real* work; his contributions to the ultra-extremist collaborationist press are not counted, and his tributes to Hitler are glossed over. I even heard the writer Bernard-Henri Lévy, some time ago, speak of Céline's *revolutionary anti-Semitism* - as though it were all only a metaphor, a figure of speech that really referred to something else. One way or another, the crucial question is dodged: what are we to make of great masterpieces inseparable from a body of work steeped in racism and anti-Semitism?

Philippe Alméras, the writer's most recent biographer, gives a blunt and simple answer: "What does it matter? Excuse me if I come across as a total cynic, but Céline was both a great genius and a true Nazi partisan, philosophically at least. But there's no connection between the two." This is a novel way of dismissing the problem, and offers little comfort to Céline loyalists.

But what they especially dislike is that Phillipe Alméras's book totally discredits the patchwork of extenuating circumstances that had been feebly constructed around the author of *Journey to the End of Night*.

Louis Destouche's childhood was not particularly miserable. He was the only child in a family of reasonably well-off small shopkeepers. As banal as that. If there was not much emphasis on schooling, it was less from lack of money than from simple ignorance, not unusual in the French lower middle class. All the same, he was sent abroad to boarding school to learn German and English.

A lieutenant in the cavalry in 1914, he in fact experienced the hell of World War I for only a few months. Toward the end of October 1914, he was wounded (in the arm), invalided out, and excused from military service for the rest of his life. Contrary to legend - a legend Céline himself cultivated - he was never wounded in the head, never trepanned. If he was prone to delirium, its source must be sought elsewhere.

When not quite 35 years old, Louis Destouches was a strapping six-footer in perfect health. He was presumably attractive to women, as he had his share of amorous adventures, including three marriages and a seven-year liaison with an American dancer, Elizabeth Craig.

Toward the end of World War I, he had neither a job nor any prospects. No matter. He married his second wife, Édith Follet, daughter of a distinguished surgeon in Rennes who made sure the couple lived a comfortable life while Louis studied medicine. Barely had he set himself up in practice when he divorced his wife, writing her a charming letter: "I would rather kill myself than go on living with you. I detest marriage, I abhor it, I spit on it." Édith Follet brought up their daughter (who is still alive) almost entirely on her own.

Even if he was not on easy street, Doctor Destouches prospered quite nicely after 1925. He travelled to the United States, and worked for international organizations. Contrary to one's picture of him in his last years at Meudon in the Paris suburbs, where he lived (deliberately) like a *clochard*, he never lacked for money and even earned a lot of it, between the appearance of *Journey to the End of Night* in 1934 (it was a best-seller) and his escape to Germany in May 1944. On his 1951 return to Paris from Denmark, where he had taken refuge to escape retribution, Gallimard still offered him the less-than-modest advance of a million francs in today's money, against future works. Even if he was no grand bourgeois born with a silver spoon in his mouth, Louis-Ferdinand Céline never came close to being the exploited pariah and outcast his books suggest. He deliberately cultivated this image almost from the day *Journey* appeared, at a time when he was being widely celebrated, and he did so with even greater enthusiasm, and morbidity, on his return from Denmark. It was as though he had spent the better part of his life in misery and isolation.

What is most extraordinary when one reads this biography of Céline is that we do not always understand what lies behind his work and its stylistic sizzle. Setting aside two texts written prior to the 1920s, L'Église and Semmelweis, the discreet Doctor Destouches was from the very beginning, with the first book he finished and published - *Le Voyage* (*The Journey*), in 1934 - an apocalyptic writer, a fulminator. And the books that followed were, without exception, even more violent, and, if one can use such a word, satanic. In the midst of this sea of pessimism and universal loathing, according to Alméras, anti-Semitism and biological racism held a fundamental place. As simple as that. Amid all the chaos that enveloped France and the West in the years between the wars, Louis-Ferdinand singled out, as a mortal danger to his native land, the mixing of blood between "the fair-haired northerners and the little fuzzies." His letters leave no room for doubt: Céline was a violently obsessive racist. With the passing of time the obsession became increasingly hysterical. He did his arithmetic, lined up names, added up "Jews and Jew-lovers," and concluded they constituted half the population of France.

Ingloriously, he escaped the bloodiest reprisals in 1944. In May, even before the Allies landed in Normandy, he was on the very first train spiriting collaborators out of France into Germany. Had he remained in Paris he would certainly have been executed, like Brasillach, another writer and Nazi sympathizer. Before him, in fact.

Exiled in Denmark, a wanted man under house arrest resisting extradition any way he could, he managed to hold out until 1951, by which time memories of war and liberation had been thrust into the background by the intensification of the Cold War. And when he returned to France in 1951, completely amnestied, he let it be known - not openly, perhaps, but in letters - that he regretted none of his past opinions or his public denunciations of the Jews under the Occupation. In a 1952 letter concerning an article on the war by the German writer Jünger, he takes the author delicately to task for having "jerked off mightily to please the yids." Just one of his courtesies. Even in his last public statements - in interviews with the magazine L'Express and on television after 1957 - he presented himself as a victim of persecution, someone whose only crime was to oppose a war against Germany (understood: conducted in the name of Jews), and who ended up as the target of some sort of world-wide conspiracy (in other words, Jewish).

What was the *real* source of these ravings, that went so far beyond the garden-variety anti-Semitism in France at the turn of the century, or even the official racism of collaborationist politicians? Alméras recalls that during his trip to the United States in 1925, Céline was much impressed by the anti-Jewish crusade orchestrated by Henry Ford in Detroit. Perhaps he was also influenced by various "scientific" theories on race in vogue during the 1930s. But the anti-Semitic rage of Louis-Ferdinand Céline remains a mystery. His diatribes and his calls for bloodletting during the Occupation, particularly odious and sinister in that context, cannot even be explained in terms of political expediency or careerism. Céline wasn't acting under orders, and, if he relished his role as a prophet and scourge, he was never an official collaborator, did not court Otto Abetz, the German ambassador, and held Pétain in contempt - he wasn't Nazi enough for Céline's tastes.

That he may - for whatever reason - have possessed a genuine streak of madness (which brings us back to the Marquis de Sade) doesn't set anything right or make for any viable extenuating circumstances. But it does deepen the mystery, where both the man and the writer are concerned. As does the indisputable tenderness he showed his cat Bébert, which accompanied Monsieur and Madame Céline in their flight through a Germany in ruins, under bombs, shared their Danish exile, and returned with its masters to die a quiet death in Meudon.

2. *The Bizarre*

The Untouchable Monsieur Boulet

For a distinguished graduate of the School of Oriental Languages in Paris, who has already lived several lives - "in the skin of a Chinaman" for a year, more recently as a beggar in Benares, India - Marc Boulet is not what you would expect. And he seems oddly young, with his hair in what's close to a brush cut and a large upturned schnozz in his street urchin's face.

The truth is that Boulet is only 34 years old, and embarked on his globetrotting adventures when he was very young. And although his various undertakings deserve to be taken seriously, they sometimes seem almost like gags, or like silly wagers you agree to after having drunk too much at a party.

His recently published account, *Dans la Peau d'un Intouchable* (In the Skin of an Untouchable), tells the story of his most recent adventure: how he lived for ten weeks the life led by some 130 million Indians, indigent for the most part, and *always* totally ostracized by the rest of the population. From October to the end of December he was a beggar and an untouchable in the sacred city of Benares. Begging for a few rupees a day along with the lepers and the lame gave him enough money to buy food from the street vendors. He slept on sidewalks or in train stations. At the doors of temples he gathered up food the priests tossed on the ground so as to avoid any risk of contact with the sub-humans.

Although his research in the field is motivated by serious intellectual and anthropological interests, Marc Boulet clearly has a long-standing fondness for deception and disguise. "It's not so much that," he tells me, "it's more that you can't understand a situation that's foreign to you unless you blend into the group in question." But it's obvious that nothing gives him more pleasure in his travels than to bring off his disguises without a hitch, never to be unmasked.

Leading a clandestine existence in China in 1986-87, he carried forged Chinese papers and invented for himself a "Turkish" persona from the Chinese outlands. That explained his "long nose" and the fact that his Chinese was not perfect. To turn himself into an Indian, he made his hair almost woolly, and made a careful study of Hindi (using dime-store or pornographic novels, to learn street language). Once again, he gave himself distant roots, as a Mundâ, from a small aboriginal tribe of a million individuals. Once again, that served to explain his imperfect mastery of the language. And it worked! He speaks of the exploit with no small pride.

From the age of twenty, Marc Boulet has spent his time changing his skin. Influenced by an old anarchist French tradition, he has often taken an interest in Communist regimes without actually supporting them. In 1982, on assignment for a newspaper, he assumed the identity of a student of psychoanalysis ("It's a field where you can say whatever you want without fear of contradiction"), and joined a small group of French Communist experts on a working trip to the U.S.S.R. It was a good way to learn about psychiatric prison-asylums.

China was his pièce-de-résistance: a year and a half of living on the margins of society while masquerading as Chinese. In the end he married a young Chinese woman he had met in the course of his adventure. He returned to China two years later to write a book on the cultural and political subtleties of the cuisine, and had a long interview with the former personal chef of Chairman Mao. He returned one more time, but on this occasion he played at being a very rich French businessman interested in investing his millions in the region of Canton, while his wife played the interpreter: "I was offered everything: the chance to build a Disneyland on the site of a leprosarium, old Tupolev passenger planes for regional airlines, deals of all kinds." Boulet has fun.

Between trips, he applies himself to the Korean and Albanian languages: "What interested me in the two cases is the fact that the same population was living under two diametrically opposed regimes: ultra-communist North Korea versus South Korea, dictatorial Albania versus the Albanian population in the Yugoslav province of Kosovo. I wanted to see if this split had influenced the languages, if the vocabulary was the same!"

He was never able to set foot in North Korea, but he had two stints in Tirana on French government fellowships, the first during the rule of Albanian strongman Enver Hoxha, the second after his death. "I was an official foreign personage, I had a car and a chauffeur. And that in an extremely poor country, where you met people in Tirana going barefoot. It was the most police-ridden, sinister country I'd ever seen. No Albanian dared even speak to me, it was forbidden to talk to a foreigner, there were boxes or boards for denouncing people at the entrances to every building."

A freelance journalist for a variety of French publications, with three books to his credit, Marc Boulet now boasts an impressive professional title: Albanian interpreter for the French Ministry of Foreign Affairs. But the contacts between Paris and Tirana are still very occasional, and that leaves Boulet lots of free time, to spend a year studying India and its caste system, for example.

"I decided to become an untouchable in a large Indian city in order to learn about human misery at its most abject, not misery caused by a war or a famine, but organized, enduring misery built into the system."

Monsieur Boulet's approach is nothing if not scientific.

His skin colored, his hair tinted and curled, dressed in rags, he lost himself in the city of Benares, and discovered that one could survive indefinitely under this system - though in wretchedness. Begging actively for half of each day, he was able to earn the ten rupees he needed, not enough certainly to buy a bottle of mineral water or Pepsi-Cola, but sufficient to purchase, at least, the anonymous (and sometimes, he says, delicious) street food. And even, from time to time, a movie in a grimy popular cinema, or some cheap alcohol.

Experts in India and Hinduism will probably learn nothing new from Marc Boulet's book. For the rest of us however, who have only heard vaguely about the caste system, there are surprises in store.

The caste system is essentially Hindu, and so primarily religious, but "the system is much weaker where Hinduism has been established in other countries. On the other hand Indian Islam is steeped in it." Thus the phenomenon is both religious and national. And unbelievably rigid, even today, and even in bourgeois financial and intellectual circles.

If you factor in all the sub-divisions and distinctions, the number of castes - classified by profession, and other identifying characteristics - comes to between two and three thousand. But if one sticks to the basics, the classifications are much simpler.

There are first the four *varna*, or traditional orders, grouping together the humans born of the Creator. At the top are the *Brahmans*, (from the name of *Brahma*, the Creator). Just below are the Warriors. Still lower are the Merchants. The first are born from the mouth, the second from the arms, the third from the thighs of Brahma. Whatever their inequalities, these castes are all aryan and superior. Below them swarm the innumerable hordes of *shudras*, the servants, born from the feet of the Creator.

There is yet a fifth human group, that was not even brought into the world by the Creator, and whose distant origins are perhaps foreign. The untouchables - or *chandâl* - are the "dirty *shudras*," whose jobs have traditionally been the degrading ones (cobblers, sweepers, launderers, undertakers), and whose customs have been judged unclean. They drink alcohol, they eat pork - some will even go so far as to eat cow meat!

The caste system was officially abolished by Gandhi, in 1947. In practice, almost nothing has changed. "Not only do the untouchables make up the vast majority of the poorest classes - maintenance workers in the city, farm laborers in the countryside - but they are treated like animals, they can be beaten. It's a bit like the Blacks in the United States during the 1930s or the 1950s."

The time is past when the untouchable had to have a pot of dirt suspended from his neck because he was forbidden to soil the earth with his spit, and he is now allowed into all public spaces, whether train stations, schools or restaurants. But the segregation is still in place, the most incongruous proof being that parliament still has quotas of untouchable deputies, and ministerial posts that are reserved for them. "A Brahman or a Warrior would never enter the house of an untouchable, even if he were rich," says Marc Boulet. "He would never eat food an untouchable had touched. I had a friend who sold newspapers, he was poor and dirty. But he was a Brahman, and even an untouchable who had become rich and powerful, he held in contempt. In some wealthy neighborhoods in big cities, the castes sometimes mingle. But if there is a rich cobbler nearby who has become successful, everyone singles him out."

With the eye of a professional Candide, Boulet is content to record what he sees. He first spent several months in India "in the skin of a white man" to get his bearings. His next-door neighbor was a scientist, modern and liberal. He never uttered the word *untouchable*, but instead drew on an official and "polite" vocabulary: he spoke *of children of God* or, better still, of *classified castes*(!). When the Frenchman persisted with his questioning, he tried to change the subject. But he made it clear that, while he had nothing against such people, he systematically avoided rubbing shoulders with them, finding himself in the same house with them, or breaking bread with them.

"What with modernization and the changes occurring in society, we see a certain number of departures from the norm, but they are rare. In the police forces and the army, the three dominant castes intermingle. At the university, the Warriors have been known to fraternize with the Merchants. But these are exceptions. For the most part, each sticks to his own kind."

In the course of his Indian wanderings, Marc Boulet came to realize that this colossal society is shot through with dozens, with hundreds of invisible barriers, most of them unbreachable. Among the untouchables themselves there are strict hierarchies, there are streets in the shanty-towns that separate the territory of the palm-wine bottlers from that of the cobblers. And if an enterprising foreigner manages to land an invitation to a cobbler's house for a celebratory meal, he had better not do as our author did, and inadvertently touch the meat, which is bad enough, but what is worse, with his left hand (unclean)! The whole banquet could come close to being tossed into the garbage! And he will see that for these untouchables, outcasts of society, a foreigner is someone inferior even to themselves. He is the essence of unclean.

Although attached to the French Foreign Office, Boulet is not particularly diplomatic. He adores China, but goes on to say that "the Chinese, whom we mistakenly consider to be polite, shun, scorn, and despise the foreigner, the white devil, this barbarous creature who is the source of all their woes, they who are the heirs of the oldest civilization in the world."

As for Hinduism, he doesn't mince his words: "Westerners think that Indians are tolerant. In fact, their religion teaches them utter indifference toward others; as a Hindu, one has obligations only to oneself. To be well reincarnated after death, one must live the life of a perfect Brahman, or Warrior, depending on the caste into which one was born. And avoid the unclean. But, unlike the Christian, Jewish or Muslim religions, Hinduism does not promote the notion of charity or compassion. A Hindu's duty is to behave well vis-à-vis himself. But if you're dying in the street right in front of his eyes, he doesn't give a damn."

Lord of the Ants

Is there life after *The Ants?*

That's the question a very odd young man is asking himself today in Paris. Bernard Werber, 32, was for years an unsung science journalist in the French capital, but in 1991 he published his first novel, which became one of the biggest best-sellers on the literary scene.

His science-fiction novel (although he dislikes that label) is called *Les Fourmis* (The Ants). It was rejected, in the best tradition, by a host of Paris publishers. Accepted by Albin Michel, it sold 150,000 copies in its original French edition, and at least twice as many in paperback. Translated into something like fifteen languages, *The Ants* has become a best-seller in, just to cite one example, South Korea. Suddenly American publishers have begun to show an interest. Canal Plus has bought the film rights, for a computer-animation version. At the age of 29, Werber, who until then had lived from his earnings as a freelance journalist, became a successful author, living high off the hog as a novelist.

He says proudly that it took him "twelve years" to write and rewrite *The Ants*. It took him only one year to bring out, in 1992, a sequel to this entomological saga, *Le Jour des Fourmis* (The Day of the Ants). It's not that he was in a rush to capitalize on the unbelievable success of the first book. It's just that Bernard Weber had decided from the outset to build a trilogy around these little beasties (about which we know little, although there are a billion billion of them on the earth). "The number three is rich with possibilities," adds Werber, a partisan of the esoteric and of ancient philosophy, with appropriate seriousness.

His *Fourmis No. 2 - Le Retour* (The Ants 2 - The Return) was another triumph. And now in January of this year, the young Werber (who looks ten years younger than his age) has gone off in another direction and brought out a new, mind-boggling work of fiction, *Les Thanatonautes* (450 pages), a detailed and utterly persuasive account of the first exploratory expeditions in 2062 - and the organized tours that followed - to the Continent of the Dead.

His first little snag on this literary road: the latest novel is doing less well than the two earlier ones. But it's all relative. France's bookstores have already sold some 50,000 copies, and sales in Quebec, as in Switzerland and Belgium, have been phenomenal. Many celebrated French novelists would be very happy to do so well. But Werber, who published his first book without any expectation of popular success, is now somewhat let down by what he considers an inferior performance. "I never planned to spend the rest of my life writing novels about ants - or grasshoppers - I just want to write novels. And now I'm wondering if the public is going to stay with me when I turn to other subjects. Or is it the idea of death that's scaring people off, in France at least?" This is the man who saw himself "liberated" once and for all from having to write just to make ends meet, and set free to devote every morning from eight to twelve-thirty inventing stories that would both give him enormous pleasure and put bread on the table.

I found him at home at the end of the Canal Saint-Martin, in a small, new, rather untidy apartment whose bay windows and balcony look out on the trees lining the Loire Quai, where there is practically no traffic.

Werber came to the door in what looked like jogging pants. In a cocktail glass, he offered me a little Diet Coke, decaffeinated and totally flat. The account of his literary tribulations was interrupted a little later by some muffled cries. "This is my most recent creation," he said, reappearing with a ten-day-old baby named Jonathan just like the hero of *The Ants*. With all the enthusiasm of a beginner he got busy giving the baby its bottle, at the same time explaining to me how he had retyped his first novel's manuscript A HUNDRED TIMES.

As a child he'd been fascinated by ants, whose comings and goings he had monitored tirelessly while on summer vacation with his grandparents. But he had also, and above all, been bitten by the bug of fiction writing.

"I was sixteen years old, and I was ill at ease, as one often is at that age. I began to write as an escape. I told myself that if I could create a world that was sufficiently intricate and precise, I would come home to myself every time I sat down with a pen and paper. Whenever I felt bad, I wrote. In short, it was a kind of schizophrenia."

At about 20, he took a journalism course, "which led me nowhere." On the other hand, when he was 21, he won a prize for a science article on the ants of Africa, which opened doors, as a science writer, to several magazines.

"I did one piece per week. That left me time to work on my novel. I'm quite a perfectionist, very concerned with detail - and I type very quickly, 30 pages a day (!) - so I did a hundred successive versions. I kept improving it, a bit like the artisans working on cathedrals in the Middle Ages. For me, the book was to be my single work and to include everything I knew at the time, about writing, biology, history and philosophy. If I hadn't found a publisher after six years of trying, I would have gone on refining it indefinitely. When I reread it today I see flaws that I could have remedied, but everything I knew about the world at the age of 28 is there." No less.

Bernard Werber is an odd bird, difficult to classify. Reviewers and journalists call him a "scientist" or "entomologist" because of the range of his knowledge. But he has no science degree, and is quite happy to possess "the passion for knowledge" in all its forms. Some French critics who read him without knowing him thought he was American, because science-fiction is a genre that hardly exists in France, and is looked down upon.

In fact, the fellow is something like a true eccentric. Classical literature is not his thing: "Chateaubriand, Proust, they're not for me." He has of course devoured the great classics of science-fiction. But not them alone. He also adores that "genius of playfulness" Georges Pérec, Rabelais ("he's fantastic!"), Poe, Kafka, and Flaubert's most unreadable novel, *Salammbô*: "What a story! What battles! It's real Schwarzenegger!" Add to those an absolute priority, the great texts of antiquity: the Egyptian Book of the Dead, the Kabbalah. And a touchstone in fiction, Tolkien's *The Lord of the Rings*. As for *Foucault's Pendulum* by Umberto Eco, "I see myself as belonging to that kind of great tradition, even if I find Eco too learned, too erudite. I want to be read by everyone, including children."

In its final version, the manuscript of *The Ants* came to a modest 1,500 pages. On the advice of his publisher he cut it by two-thirds: "I took out dialogue and description..."

What remained was the essence, that is, the structure. "Reading Agatha Christie, I realized that a story's structure is like the architecture of a house; every clue is like a pillar. So I decided to build my novel like a cathedral - because that's the most beautiful of houses. You know that cathedrals in the Middle Ages were all designed with Solomon's Temple in mind, and that the temple expressed in architecture the formula for the Philosopher's Stone."

In response to his first two novels, he received mountains of letters from adepts in the new ant-religion. "Someone told me that he had read the first one 17 times, and had found new meanings every time out. I like the idea that there are hidden secrets. And I designed the story as a kind of labyrinth, beginning with the end, so that no one can figure it out as he is reading."

In France, land of Descartes, science-fiction and everything like it is automatically classified as sub-literature. Publishers don't want it (unless it's translated from the English), and critics ignore it. As for scientists, it gives them heartburn. For ten years Werber made the rounds of publishers, all of whom found his story bizarre and unpublishable. Albin Michel finally brought it out, but played the ant card to the hilt and didn't bother mentioning that the author was French. If he were to be taken for American, so much the better!

Werber is amusing and original, so one appearance on Bernard Rapp's literary TV show was enough to spark some action and then a tidal wave in the bookstores. None of that changed the attitude of the established literary critics. Given the scope of the phenomenon, a few papers deigned to print some articles on this strange writer and his pet subject, but almost no critic treated the book as just a novel, unlike the reaction in Quebec or Belgium, where these "unclassifiable" books, at the crossroads of science, religion and history, were praised to the skies by the established critics. Jacques Folch-Ribas, in Montreal's daily *La Presse,* wrote of the first: "Science-fiction, mystery, metaphysics? All of that. This novel is like no other." The total novel, as it were.

In France, still no respect. And now this third novel that did not dominate the best-seller lists, like the other two! Bernard Werber, adept of so many Eastern philosophies, is not the sort to complain, he's just a bit bewildered. "It's like a letter that hasn't arrived at its destination." For the moment he hasn't started another novel, he's biding his time. These days he's merely writing a new short story every day, five to fifteen pages in length, and dropping it into a drawer with all the others. At about one o'clock he goes for lunch with some scientist-pals who are just as eccentric as he is, and with whom he exchanges bizarre information and outlandish ideas. In the afternoon he does research, strolls about and talks to people. Or goes home to give Jonathan his bottle.

A Mercenary in Bosnia

There's no reason not to believe what he says. Because under the circumstances there's no reason why he should invent such "details." And so he killed, himself, half a dozen enemy Serbs - including a lone member of the militia whom he didn't want to risk taking alive. He personally executed two fighters who had just been taken prisoner - so they wouldn't be tortured by his own men, because the day before, these same Serbs had massacred five Croat families in the village, and nailed one of their German-Croat "friends," a certain Millo, to a barn door while he was still alive.

From December 1991 to February 1993, Gaston Besson was a volunteer for the Croats, first in the Croatian war, then in Herzegovina. Others would call him a mercenary - but these are mercenaries who operate below the poverty line, who get arms, a uniform, and about a hundred dollars a month in devalued dinars. Plus the princely sum of $300 when they go on "leave" in Zagreb.

Slightly wounded four times - mortar or shell explosions, ten days in the hospital - Besson returned to Paris last February, and was seriously injured in a car accident. His kneecap was fractured, and he'll be limping for a year. When I met him at his publisher's in Saint-Germain, he was walking with crutches. He had perhaps lost weight, and his moustache was gone. Overnight, the "killer" reverted to a young man barely 26 years old, very dark eyes, about my size, which would make him something like 5'8" and 145 pounds, shoes included. By the end of his stint in Bosnia, he was commanding a hundred men.

Up to 500 Western volunteers have fought alongside the Croat forces since the beginning of the war. There were many more on the side of the Muslims: Afghans, Azeris, perhaps 3,000 in all. And Russian nationalists supporting the Serbs.

"The westerners fell into three categories," says Besson. "First the idealists, those who were there because they believed in what they were doing. Sometimes they were people who had never even done military service, teachers, employees of one sort or another. In my group there were three Frenchmen from the extreme right, but also a former Trotskyist. There was a British Laborite, another who was a Conservative; they spent all their time arguing with each other.

"The second group included former professional soldiers, for whom war is like a drug. Many Anglo-Saxons. I had three English-Canadians who had just deserted from the Foreign Legion.

"And the third: adventurers ready for anything, who found themselves there because that's where the action was, and who got attached to these young people with no experience who were fighting against ten-to-one odds. But without exception, once there, people forgot the reasons they had come. There was no more politics, nothing was rational."

Besson belongs to the third category. Born in Mexico of French parents who apparently travelled widely, he was a "grave-robber and gold-hunter" in Colombia at the age of 16, along with his older brother. He did his military service at 18. Then he found himself successively in Surinam and Burma among the local guerillas: "But it wasn't really war. There were many calm periods, there were women, it was exotic, there was nature."

Still with his brother, he sold television news reports shot in inaccessible places: Burma, Laos, Cambodia. "But with both the guerillas and the reporting we always chose our side not really according to ideology, but more by instinct: always on the side of the losers, those who were one against ten." He arrived in Croatia in 1991 as a photographer in Vinkovci, which was being besieged by the Federal Serb army.

"It was just after the fall of Vukovar, closer to the Serb frontier. It felt like the end of the world. There wasn't even any more room to retreat. The refugee columns were entering the city. In the trenches there were bureaucrats, students, office workers who often had never even held a weapon, and who were fighting against the tanks and artillery of the Federal army, the third biggest in Europe. I didn't know anything more about war than the others.

I felt like an idiot with my camera. I ended up in the trenches with a Kalashnikov. The uniform, the ID card and all that, that came afterwards when there was a bit of calm, when we could reorganize."

How did he become a military "leader" at the age of 24 or 25? "It's simple. If you last a year and a half, it happens all by itself. Everyone else around you has been killed or wounded. Those who survive find themselves covered in glory, they bring luck, you follow them. I had a commander, Selenic, who was made major at the age of 22. He'd become mad for war. Before the war he was a hippie who wore his hair long and dreamed of Woodstock."

At first, after returning to Paris, Besson could not talk about any of his experiences. Only the stupid automobile accident enabled him gradually to emerge from the walking nightmare, the "trance state" in which he had lived for 18 months.

"War, real war, is long, grey, ugly and sad. People die beside you. Corpses don't matter. The worst are the wounded, the ones who scream. Why do you stay? It's absurd, but it's easier to desert an army that's winning than an army that's losing. And against the Serbs, that's all you did, lose and retreat. The Serbs were never very combative. They had tanks and artillery and they fired, without losing many men. When we had too many dead and wounded, we retreated a hundred metres. That's how you conquer territory, a hundred metres as a time. Everyone was full of holes, we'd all been wounded at one time or another. We went back to Zagreb and then we returned to the front. You know it when you're there, there's something not right in your head, you're suicidal. And at the same time it seems reasonable, normal. There's a powerful rush when you go into combat. It's horrible and very beautiful at the same time. There are moments of extraordinary joy when things have gone well, when you haven't lost any men, when you've taken three streets or a hill. Fear? There isn't any. Here is where I'm afraid. It's like I'm being choked, here."

In this savage triangular war, where everyone looks the same and talks the same language, the whole problem is knowing who you're dealing with. One day Besson and a companion found themselves at a Croat control point, down on the ground, guns at their temples. They had been taken for Muslims. At other times they headed out to fight with three armbands that they kept changing. The enemy on the other side put on the same colors to try to pass as Croats!

And then, quite simply, "there were horrible things that went on. Fortunately, most of the time, the victims were corpses." Were the wounded killed? Of course. "The wounded are killed in every war. We had neither hospitals nor any kind of infrastructure for our own wounded. So if there was a Serb on the ground with a bullet in his belly, it was the logic of war. We didn't take prisoners either, because that meant running the risk of being shot yourself. Of course there were exceptions, guys that came out of a farm-house, their hands in the air, when it was all over. We gave them coffee, sometimes we chatted amiably. It was crazy."

Will Gaston Besson go off again - when, as he says, "the second Croatian war begins, and it will be soon, to reconquer Krajina and Slavonia"? For the moment he says no, but without much conviction. The horror fascinates him, doubtless. And then Besson - like others mad for war - is a fatalist: "The atrocities you see in ex-Yugoslavia could be happening in any country, once war has begun. Look at France or Canada, where there are laws, where there's democracy - there is still violence, murder, rape, gangsters. Imagine what it's like in a country where there is no more law, where total anarchy holds sway."

3. Irregulars

Visions of Adjani

When a big-budget French film comes out in Montreal, the distributor is happy to offer you an interview with the leading player. Or rather he offers it, according to mysterious criteria, to one outlet only, as the actor has signed for only *one* interview - usually for television, but there are exceptions to the rule. If it's a star - and sometimes even if it's not a star - there's often no interview at all. The actor in question knew nothing about it, had other engagements, had not agreed to it. Or else an appointment laboriously arrived at through the good offices of five secretaries, impresarios and press attachés results in a "conversation" eight minutes long in the company of two chauffeurs and three bodyguards, while other journalists line up outside the door of the hotel suite. The star already has memorized stock answers for all the following questions: Why this film? What was it like working with the director Trucmuche, and the actor Tronchemolle? And so on. In short, it's an exercise that brings you face to face with the humbleness of your lot in life and the modesty of your profession.

As the occasion here was the premiere of *Camille Claudel* and an interview with Isabel Adjani, I was prepared for the worst. Adjani doesn't just avoid journalists, like Catherine Deneuve - she also has a dangerous reputation, and one hell of a track record. A "secret" liaison with Warren Beatty, with all the paparazzi in the world at their heels. Knock-down drag-out battles with such-

and-such an actor, such-and-such a director; the play closes abruptly, the shoot goes from crisis to crisis. She appears, she disappears. She is photographed in Algiers talking with students opposed to the regime. The rumor mill, generous as always, has her afflicted with Aids. Where is she hiding today? What is she doing? She was seen in New York, or in Marrakech, or in the Pacific. Adjani is a walking enigma in the spotlight's glare; her life feeds the fantasies of a nation.

For *Camille Claudel*, unlike her usual practice, she gave interviews to many of the major media outlets, thereby guaranteeing the film excellent promotion. There's a reason for that. *Camille* is the film she wanted to do above all others; she was its co-producer, and its director was Bruno Nuyttens, her ex-"husband," and father of her son. Suddenly she was talking for the first time to various journalists about her (late) Algerian father, about the rumor mill, about what it was like to be a star. That doesn't exactly mean, of course, that she had taken on the rustic simplicity and good humor of a staunch Norman farm wife.

Anyway, the day before the interview, my go-between seemed to have lost all trace of her. "I can't confirm the place or the time," she said frankly, "because I don't know where she is." Simple as that. And perfectly normal. For me this interview was as unreal and evanescent as Adjani's spectral apparition in *Barocco*. I called my contact back three or four times, things got less amicable, and I decided there was no point in pursuing the matter.

A few hours later, to my astonishment, there was a message on my answering machine: "This is Isabelle Adjani, can you call me back to set a time for our meeting?" A voice a bit childlike, a bit solemn, both assured and shy. Should I add: troubling? I called back and was put straight through. Where should we meet? "At a hotel bar, perhaps?" She suggested the Ritz, I proposed the Lutétia, perhaps just to seem knowing, or to feel out my client. She agreed to the Lutétia, but then it occurred to me that the Ritz would be better. "Are you sure about the Ritz?" she said, with no sign of impatience. "At a quarter past three, then." Not three or three-thirty. A quarter past.

I entered this peaceable kingdom - one of the rare spots in Paris that is really sheltered from noise. The bar was deserted, and even the barman seemed to have vanished. *She* was telephoning at the bar, black skirt, black hair, red pullover and panty-hose, red lipstick. A clean, crisp image, that might have been cut out with a razor blade.

I apologized for my lateness - two minutes exactly.

"That's very, very serious," she joked, swivelling slightly in my direction. No watchdog or press secretary in view. The Ritz is not the kind of place where chic clients at nearby tables are going to rush up to ask for your autograph. A little later we'd be joined by a few very discreet customers, and a pleasant harpist would take up her post. But it was nothing like a public place. We talked quietly about film and life, as though it were the most natural thing in the world. Only once did reality intrude. At a certain point there was a noise like a camera shutter, from somewhere behind us. Mademoiselle Adjani, for a nano-second, became a panther poised for action. Aside from that, nothing, no tension, not the least trace of anxiety. She ordered a glass of cold grapefruit juice, which she didn't touch, then calmly consumed two slightly over-ripe bananas that she'd brought in her purse. Two hours later, a woman friend who had telephoned arrived to join her. But there was no rush. The star had all the time in the world.

There was much talk, of course, of *Camille Claudel*. But also of her spectacular career, about which she speaks with utter detachment, amusement even, as though it had all happened to someone else.

She was a sixteen-year-old high-school girl in the suburbs with nothing remarkable in her life except for the fact that her father was Algerian and her mother German. Enamoured of the theatre like many young people, she put on Molière's *Les Fourberies de Scapin* at her school, but also, at the age of 13 and 14, played small roles in two limited-release films. A precocious beginning, but it seemed not to be leading anywhere. She worked for her baccalaureate, and there was no thought of theatre school.

When Robert Hossein spotted her sitting on the steps of the Paris Conservatory, it was a matter of pure chance. She was neither a student nor a candidate, she had simply come to watch a competition. Captivated by her beauty, but something more as well, Hossein hired her for his theatre in Reims to perform in a play by Lorca. Also in the play was a member of the Comédie-Française, Annie Ducaux. And the Comédie-Française was looking for someone to play Agnès in Molière's *School for Wives*.

"It was all," she said calmly, peeling her banana, "such a series of unbelievable coincidences. It happened so easily that it was hard to take for those who go through the Conservatory and are ready to die to get into the Comédie-Française. It was all so quick that I didn't have time to dream about anything. I was at Reims, I went to school during the day, I performed in the evening. After Reims, I was introduced to Pierre Dux, the manager of the Théâtre Français, and he hired me. And I stayed at the Comédie-Française from 1972 to 1974."

She was 16 when she joined, 18 when she left, time enough to play *School for Wives* and Giraudoux's *Ondine*. And to acquire - instantly - her reputation as a "little prodigy." During the same period she starred with Lino Ventura in an amiable, unpretentious comedy by Pinoteau, *La Gifle* (The Slap), which broke all box-office records. Curiously, though she is extremely hard on both her own films and those of others, *La Gifle* left her with only "fond memories. It was an amusement, an entertainment. I was 17, and the carefree young person in the film was, in fact, me. As I was then, in any case. It was a good time in my life." Similarly, she who for the most part has played only tragic roles looks back with pleasure on the (excellent) comedy of Rappenau, *Tout feu tout flamme*, in which she was later to perform alongside Yves Montand.

And then there was her first great film: *Adèle H* by Truffaut, where at 18 she portrayed the daughter (capricious, then mad) of Victor Hugo. At that point she left the Théâtre Français forever, and the theatre as well.

She'll go back to it one day, certainly. If the great directors, Chéreau or Vitez, make her offers. "It's true that in the theatre there is physical and temporal continuity. That's very attractive." She'll go back, "but in the public, subsidized theatre, where people don't just think about making money."

Because in the interim she did return once. "It was terrible," she says mysteriously, as though she'd been a victim of fate, or of some horrible curse. It was 1983, and the play was Strindberg's *Miss Julie* at the Théâtre Édouard-VII.

"Two years earlier, when I went there to see a show, I'd had this awful feeling, and I told myself I must never set foot inside, I must never play there. And then like an idiot I fell into the trap. My father had just died and I needed to go back to my roots. For me my roots are the theatre."

The director was also part of her "roots": Jean-Paul Rousillon, whom she'd known at the Comédie-Française. Everything went wrong. "Rousillon wasn't up to it. Two weeks before the opening he walked out. I should have done the same, but the theatre director begged me to stay for the sake of the public."

"It was a miserable experience. Never mind Niels Arestrup, who played the male lead - he's a monster. I suppose some actors think that to do this job you have to be a real bastard. He was playing a macho role, and he kept on playing it offstage, and it got bigger and bigger. Onstage he would have killed me if he could, he would have beaten me within an inch of my life. He threw his boots in my face, he broke bottles. It got so bad, it was as though he were trying to wipe out the enemy. Ultimately it was a profound spiritual and mystical experience. But two or three experiences like that, and you're dead."

"They only cared about the money. Every night they showed me the box-office receipts. I walked right past the theatre director, disdainful, my head in the air, and I ripped up the sheet without reading it. They killed me. I ended up a wreck. I fell ill after twenty performances. I swore never again to work in a private theatre: I'd rather be a salesgirl in a 5-and-10."

Precocious as a child, Isabelle Adjani now claims not to be obsessed with her career, never to plan ahead. "When you come right down to it," she says, "I'm someone who doesn't like to work all that much. I like doing nothing, just being quiet." Not for her a film a year. Besides, as someone who's cornered most of the good roles in recent years for leading ladies, she's seen them become increasingly rare.

"You know, I don't get that many exciting offers. Sometimes it's a good script, but with no director. Often the project falls through. It's rare to find a good story, a good role, and the right director all at the same time. To decide to do a film is to take a chance on something that doesn't yet exist."

Although Mme. Adjani's track record is nothing to sneeze at - more than one masterpiece and many good films - she's a harsh judge, to say the least. Strangely, no film meets with her approval, perhaps because the shoots often left her with unpleasant memories. Or maybe she just likes to dramatize.

She doesn't like André Téchiné's *The Bronte Sisters*, nor does she seem to think very highly of Isabelle Huppert and Marie-France Pisier. Where James Ivory's magnificent *Quartet* is concerned, she doesn't mince words: "I much preferred the novel." Téchiné's *Barocco* - with Depardieu - "came too soon" in her career. In short, she's not easy to satisfy. She'll even reproach herself, bitterly, for having undertaken certain films: "*Antonietta*, for example, by Carlos Saura. You don't know it? Just as well. I thought I couldn't stoop any lower than that, that nothing could be more commercial. But I was wrong, it got even worse along the way. It was a horrible shoot. A horrible director. A horrible flop. I saw it coming, but I said to myself, I have to work, I need the money."

She made one film in the States as well, Ishtar with none other than Warren Beatty and Dustin Hoffman. "The director had made three low-budget films a long time before. She was overwhelmed by all the money, this huge machine - totally lost, out of her mind. A disaster."

It happens that Isabelle Adjani speaks fluent English, practically accentless. And her first language, by her mother, is German. Which means she could work just as easily in the U.S. or in Germany. She reveres Wim Wenders for *Wings of Desire*, just as she respects Alain Resnais: "They each have their own world that springs from the imagination. They may think of me one day, but you don't force yourself into their universe."

Perhaps most great actors, by definition, float somewhere up above the world around them, touching down here and there to inhabit the characters they portray. Isabelle Adjani is doubly detached: "My parents were immigrants in France. I feel I'm French to the extent that I live here, but my roots aren't that deep. I think of myself as airborne."

And so she turned up at student meetings in Algiers, wearing dark glasses and sitting in the back, during the worst moments of police repression when there were pro-democracy demonstrations in the streets.

"I had never been. Because he'd not participated in the war, I suppose, and had experienced independence as a terrible rupture, my father never said a word about Algeria. He refused to let my mother raise me as a Catholic, but I never knew Islam either, or the Muslim world. Algeria was all in my head."

"I can't give you a rational explanation for that trip. I'd been revolted by the scenes of violence I'd seen on television. I went there as a Frenchwoman - not as a native, which I am not. But at the same time I knew that, being half Algerian, I was one of the few to be accepted there (she adds, provocatively and in an ironic tone of voice: *I had the added virtue in their eyes of not being Jewish*). I went first just to see. And then, at the university I got caught up in the movement and I became involved. And I'm very glad I did. I suppose I was known there - the official association for Algerians in France had urged me to go on a number of occasions, and I had always refused."

And now? Eight weeks after the premiere of *Camille* - which, with 600,000 tickets sold in Paris, is a very big success - the film is still her sole concern. After opening in Quebec, it will be released in the United States. A three-hour film with sub-titles is not usually a resounding commercial success in the Mid-West. But an "intellectual" success in the big cities is possible, that's still not bad.

"We have to play the French and European card to the limit," she says, "there's no point in trying to pretend that it's an American film."

"So you'll be there for the New York opening to promote the film? And you'll say to yourself, Inshallah?"

"Inshallah, as you say."

And she taps the wooden table at the Ritz three times with both hands, as a hedge against fate.

4. The Illustrious Nomads

Michel Legrand: Umbrellas and Oscars

He's not a movie actor. He doesn't have his own show on TV. He's one of the most celebrated French artists in his country, and in Hollywood, not to mention the world, but he is not much in the limelight.

Sixty-two years old, glasses on the end of his nose, dressed in an anorak with Adidas on his feet, perched on his scooter to zip around Paris, he's like an eternal adolescent, and no one pays him any attention. He pilots his own plane to go to Italy or England, but he doesn't invite photographers. He's always refused to lend himself to a biography or a volume of memoirs. In short, for 35 years he's shunned anything showy, while securing himself one of the most brilliant careers in France.

His name: Michel Legrand, musician by profession. Even if by some unlikely chance you don't know him, you know his music; it's impossible not to have hummed it at one time or another. *The Umbrellas of Cherbourg* (1964): it was his idea to make a film that would be sung from beginning to end, unique in the history of cinema. A masterpiece that fits no category, a cult film, a story in pastel hues or a rose-water melodrama-tragedy, what you will. *Umbrellas* went around the world.

Legrand has composed original scores for 250 films: half the French New Wave, dozens of American productions. Along the way, he has casually picked up three Oscars: for *The Thomas Crown Affair*, *The Summer of 42*, and *Yentl*, a musical written for Barbra Streisand.

When I met him, he had just finished Paul Mazursky's new film, *The Pickle*. Plus an American LP for Nana Mouskouri, where he had taken great classics of film music and re-arranged them, mixing the original sound-track with the singer's voice. Plus an album of his own hits (*Windmills of your Mind* and others) sung by Johnny Mathis, with new orchestrations. Plus a duo jazz album with Stéphane Grapelli.

Not to mention the *small* projects bubbling away. Michel Legrand has bought the rights to a best-seller by Patrick Cauvin, *L'Amour Aveugle* (*Blind Love*), and is preparing its musical adaptation (using a totally new technique, he says) with actors Jon Voigt and Nastassia Kinski. He has another project for a feature with Marcello Mastroianni, where he would both compose and direct - he has already directed two films.

What else? With the young novelist Didier van Cauwelaert, he's working on a comic opera based on Marcel Aymé's *The Walker-Through-Walls*. With his friend Erik Orsenna, who won the Prix Goncourt in 1987, he has finally started to prepare a big musical for the Paris stage, harking back to the success of *Irma la Douce*, which is still, he allows in all modesty, the landmark show. ("*Starmania?*," he murmurs vaguely, "it was pleasant, but there was no real story or subject, it was a revue.")

The first problem for a journalist, with Legrand, is just to get hold of him. Not that he hides out. On the contrary - he gives the impression, in Paris, that he's everywhere at once. On the radio I hear him talking about stress, explaining how he got over his fear of flying: "I learned to pilot a plane, and I bought myself a private jet." Three days later, again on the radio, he takes part in a show on the cinema, where he tells stories about his career in Hollywood. Ten days later, on television this time, I see the one-hour profile directed by his friend François Reichenbach.

So he must be easy to find. Not so. He has no agent or publicist, just an ordinary secretary who takes care of his schedule and his mail, makes appointments, and tries (in a car) to catch up with his scooter as he flits from one meeting in Paris to another. I fall back on the record companies, which always have media people, only to find to my horror that Michel Legrand has recorded for

practically *every* label in town! Songs, jazz, film music, arrangements! I try Polygram first. I couldn't have chosen better, because
he has just released a record for them with Stéphane Grapelli.

They tell me what I ought to have known from the start. To
find Michel Legrand at home, in his beautiful house in the
suburbs west of Paris, all you have to do is telephone - here's the
number - and ask for his secretary.

The secretary answers as predicted, and says: "That's perfect,
he's going to the Montreal Jazz Festival this summer, he loves
Montreal." Meanwhile, where to see him? "Nothing simpler, he's
playing four nights next week at a jazz club in Montparnasse. You
can catch him at 11 o'clock at the break."

At 11 o'clock at the club in question there are 300 people packed
in like sardines. It could be a subway platform at rush hour during
a strike. On a handkerchief-sized stage, *he* is at the piano, backed
by three musicians. Glasses still on the end of his nose, Adidas,
sleeves rolled up, tie undone. The same air of concentration - or
absence. At the break, he goes - of course! - to sit with his wife and
friends, after tendering me a vague "We'll get together later."

It's Thursday night. "Come to his house on Monday," says his
secretary, appropriately consoling behind smoked glasses. Only to
inform me by phone the next day that unfortunately, it's now off.
Legrand is in charge of the music for the Césars, the film awards,
and that will take up two whole days. And then? "He's going to
Los Angeles for two weeks." Suddenly, an inspiration: "There's
only one solution: *you* invite us to lunch on Wednesday. At
Fouquet's. It's practical and it's not expensive." (In fact, it's the
most famous show-biz eatery on the Champs-Élysées, and not the
least expensive.)

At the appointed hour at Fouquet's the secretary arrived by car,
followed ten minutes later by Michel Legrand, who seems to have
passed our way entirely by chance, with his anorak and his motor-
cycle helmet. He looks vaguely into the middle distance and
embraces a friend without breaking his trance. His natural air of
distraction doubtless serves him well when he wants to avoid
unwelcome encounters or dumb conversations.

Michel Legrand is a disconcerting interviewee. At times he's extremely cooperative, enthusiastic, letting you in on secrets or making up stories, and then he stops short, buries himself in his plate, asks his secretary for the mail he is to sign, gets upset over a small detail, makes a scene, asks about the next appointment. A moment later he has a rush of adrenaline when he realizes that I don't know his career inside out. "Why, you haven't prepared!" Right away I decide he's a difficult character.

At least he levels with you from the start. "I'm all colors," he says, and he rattles them off. "Black because I play jazz. Green because I'm a doubter. Blue because I get tired. Red because I get angry. I've got white skin, and my heart's red and yellow."

"Are you ill-tempered?"

"No, no, no (without conviction). I'm a charming fellow," he says, glumly.

At that point he looks straight ahead and sees a photo of Raimu up on the wall: "I loved Raimu. They say he was a pain in the ass to work with. A real dog. The other actors hated him."

Michel Legrand is a lively and imaginative raconteur, but he doesn't take well to being questioned. "My past is of no interest to anyone. What's most important in my career is what I'm doing now and what I'll do tomorrow. Publishers wanted to make me tell the story of my life. I always refused, and I have no intention of changing my mind now. It's of no interest."

In the dictionaries of jazz or music, he is invariably referred to as the son of Raymond Legrand, a very popular post-war conductor. Is that where his vocation comes from? "A family of musicians? Are you talking about a family of musicians? My father left my mother when I was three years old! He went out to get some matches and never came back! I had a hard childhood. We walked to save on subway tickets. That drove me nuts all through my childhood. We lived in the suburbs because we didn't have the money to live in Paris. Still, we managed to eat every day."

After 250 films, some enormous international successes, enviable invitations to every country in the world, you'd think all that would be far behind him. But perhaps this distant past explains Legrand's incredible addiction to work.

"I almost never go to the theatre or the cinema. I don't have

LOUIS-BERNARD ROBITAILLE

time. You know, music takes a long time to write. There are billions of notes to get right. I spend my life at home writing and transcribing. I work a lot at night because I'm always behind schedule, because I have to deliver the next morning or in the afternoon. I find it technically very easy to compose. But I have to be driven by an assignment, or more than one. So I'm always short of time."

"But you have an ideal life, you choose what you want to do, between Paris and Hollywood."

"Don't believe it. Sure, I earn a good living. But that's not what counts. It's hard. I don't do what I want. Even right after the success of *Umbrellas*, we had enormous difficulties, Jacques Demy and myself, getting the *Desmoiselles de Rochefort* produced. Even now, every project is a struggle!"

Quite an outburst from someone who, after all, was highly successful from a very early age. Born in 1932, he attended the Conservatory and then studied with Nadia Boulanger. "I knew I would do music, one way or another. I was a great pianist, but I knew I would never be a concert artist. I got nervous, and I always lost my cool in front of a jury, so I failed my exams. I threw my lot in with the writing group, and decided I would be a composer."

At the age of 20, in 1952, he did the arrangements for a Dizzy Gillespie recording - then five years later, in 1957, he brought out his own jazz record with a big orchestra. From the word go, he tried everything: jazz, orchestration, film music. He wouldn't write songs until the beginning of the 60s.

It all sped up in 1958. Well known in the music world if not to the public, he did the score for a shock-documentary by François Reichenbach, *L'Amérique Insolite*, which was a huge hit and became a landmark film in France and the United States.

"That got me right into the New Wave. For a few years Georges Delerue and I did almost all the films. I did Demy, Varda, Godard. Delerue did Truffaut and the others. One year we scored 15 or 18 films."

This period came to a close with the adventure of *Umbrellas*.

"Jacques Demy came to me at the end of 1962 with a very dark script about a love affair shattered by the Algerian war. And he

190

wanted to shoot it in black and white. I don't know why, but I suddenly had the idea of doing the whole thing through song. It was totally crazy, but Demy went along with it. I wrote the music in three months. He wrote the words, then I composed, sometimes the other way round. We made the deliberate decision to start with a very banal scene, in the garage, with very jazzy music, to force the audience to accept the concept.

"Demy and I were already well known, but it took us a year to find a producer - and even then we had a paltry budget, it was a threepenny opera. I remember doing the rounds. We hadn't enough money for a demo, so I stood up in front of the producer and sang the lyrics myself. I can still remember the snoring."

The budget was very tight, there were technical problems: "We wanted real singers. We thought first of Sylvie Vartan. After a few tries we gave up. Then we decided to do the sound track first, and have the actors dub - but they attended the recording session to get the feel of it."

The rest is history. The film was a huge success, both in France and abroad. It received three Oscar nominations, including, of course, for music. It lost out all three times (the music Oscar went to another *Frenchy*, Maurice Jarre, for *Doctor Zhivago*.)

By 1966, Legrand needed a change. He picked up his family and moved them all to Hollywood, not an easy place to crack even when you land there with a certain reputation.

"I was lucky. Right after I arrived I did the music for a totally mindless comedy with Dean Martin. Then another comedy with I don't remember who. And suddenly, the third film: Norman Jewison had asked for Henry Mancini for *The Thomas Crown Affair*. Mancini didn't have the time, but he said, there's this young Frenchman, etc. So I told Jewison I could compose all the music prior to editing. And he bought the idea."

That was the first Oscar for Legrand, who would go on to win two more.

But he only stayed three years in Hollywood: "Now when I work there, I stay in a hotel. I realized that I couldn't live in Los Angeles, it's a way of life that's foreign to me. I've also tried London and Rome. Couldn't do it. I can only live in Paris."

Or more exactly, near Paris. He has a magnificent house in the suburbs west of the city, in the middle of a park. "I can't live in Paris any more either, or in the city, because of the neighbors. I have what you call in music, perfect pitch. When I compose, if I hear just one note, I can't get it out of my head. I need total silence."

Since he resettled in Paris for good, his routine is both varied and unchanging. Legrand divides his time between his worktable ("I compose right onto the paper, I hear what I write"), his scooter to run into Paris, and the Boeings that take him to the United States. Or elsewhere in the world.

Producer Denis Héroux remembers their collaboration on *Atlantic City* for Louis Malle: "Suddenly we thought of him for the music, and it worked out - he's hardly ever free, you know. Michel is incredible. When he works on a project, he's so enthusiastic that you'd think it was his very first. And at the same time, he's a true professional. When you show him the film, he can tell you what kind of music it needs, with a small or large orchestra. Even if he's expensive, you always know what the music budget will be. God knows, that's precious!"

Alain Simard, a variety producer in Montreal, recalls the first Montreal Jazz Festival, when Michel Legrand was paired with Ginette Reno: "It was a great moment." Seven or eight years later, Legrand's face suddenly lights up: "I have a wonderful memory of that, Ginette Reno is sublime! It was great fun! She's a real jazz singer. As good as Judy Garland!" Then, after a moment's thought: "It's too bad her choice of songs leaves something to be desired - and I'm not saying that because she doesn't call on me!"

For 20, 25, 35 years, he's been doing everything, and the beat goes on: jazz, songs, television, films of all sorts. Which doesn't mean he'll take on anything at all. More than twenty years after *Umbrellas*, his friend Jacques Demy came up with another script for a film in song, *Une Chambre en ville* (Dominique Sanda, Michel Piccoli). "I read it, I didn't like it, for me it didn't hold together. I hopped in my plane, I went to see Demy in Noirmoutier to explain why I didn't like the subject, to tell him I wouldn't be at my best. He did the film with someone else, and I still don't like it."

On the other hand, what he likes about the cinema is that it forces him to write every kind of music. "I've always had a lot of fun. I've done jazz, ballads, sentimental airs, Elizabethan music. I did Yiddish music for *Yentl*. I even became a specialist - I did Israeli music for the series on Golda Meir with Ingrid Bergman. Finally my American agent asked me, "Listen, how were you able to write that music, are you Jewish?"

"What do you think?"

"I think you're Jewish."

"In that case, I'm Jewish!"

In the same vein - with a touch of contempt - he explains how it is that he scaled the heights in Hollywood (along with Maurice Jarre and Georges Delerue). "A producer asked me to do the music for a film on Billie Holliday, *Lady Sings the Blues*, starring Diana Ross. I said why me, when the music is typically American and black? The producer replied, because you're the only one who does *really American* music!"

When he attended the Conservatory he didn't want to choose this or that, he wanted to do all kinds of music. Besides, he likes them all. When he composes, total silence. But outside work he listens to everything, and keeps up with what's being done. He loves Vanessa Paradis and Wagner ("though he could do with a bit of editing"), Dutilleux and Mozart. He doesn't like Boulez as a person, but he respects *Le Marteau Sans Maître*. John Cage is "a fraud," but "as soon as a musician writes three notes, I'm interested."

So has he tried his hand at all kinds of music? "All? No, I'd like to have tried my hand at a thousand different styles! And I will!"

But might not the music world be suspicious of someone who does "too many" things at once? Will the coteries - of jazz or contemporary music, for instance - still respect you when you're exploring other, more "popular" genres?

Michel Legrand replies, as he gets up to leave for his next appointment: "It's true, we love coteries in France, we pigeonhole people even more than in the United States. There are people who say, but who does this Legrand who dabbles in everything think he is anyway, what gives him the *right*? Well, those people in their little boxes, they can go to hell. Those little cliques bore me stiff."

Louis Malle, Gentleman Traveller

L ouis Malle, when I met him, was "spinning his wheels a bit," by his own admission. He had finally abandoned the script he'd been working on for the last six months. Should he return to the United States, where he had worked for ten years, sometimes very successfully? "Well, not if I have to work in the *studio* system!" Instead, while he waited for inspiration, he would take off for Russia with his camera and two or three technicians, to shoot a documentary. He had already made fifteen or so over the years, in India, in the United States, during the Tour de France. At 61, Malle, who had never done anything just for the money (commercials, television), was probably the only director of his reputation committed to this - if not minor, certainly Spartan - genre.[1]

Louis Malle didn't give many interviews. Our bargain was struck only through the intercession of a mutual acquaintance. We were to meet in the offices of his production house (run by his brother Vincent), the *Nouvelles Éditions de Films*. The premises, on the Rue du Louvre near Les Halles, were modest and low-key, and the furniture was about the same as in 1958. He himself exuded the unassuming, natural elegance native to good French families, where one wears with the same assurance a tuxedo or (good quality) cords.

"You know, I've got nothing much to tell you," he said, shuffling his papers. "I really don't have a film in the works." He got up, went to have a word with his assistant in the next office, and came back: "Are you related to Luc Robitaille?" A film technician? "No, a hockey player with the Los Angeles Kings. He's my daughter Chloé's idol. She spends all her time in front of the television set watching these characters beating up on each other. It's terrifying. Well, I guess she'll grow out of it."

---

1   He ended up changing not his mind, but his focus, and shot "off the cuff," as it were, the rehearsals for a New York play, a version of Uncle Vania, with his old comrade-in-arms from My Dinner with André, André Gregory.

Ten minutes later he remembers that he has to telephone his wife, the American actress Candice Bergen whom he married in 1980, and with whom he had the said Chloé, then ten years old. (He was married once before; later, in 1971, he had a son with a German actress, then a daughter with the Canadian actress Alexandra Stewart in Paris in 1974.) "There's a nine-hour time difference between here and Los Angeles," he says, "I have to phone now before she goes to work."

Louis Malle must have been one of the rare Frenchmen to speak English with practically no accent. Some of his intonations were even vaguely American, and every once in a while his anglicisms seemed to startle even him.

For months he had isolated himself in his magnificent house in the Lot region near Cahors, where he was writing the script for a third film about the Occupation, specifically July 1944. As has happened with many of his films - for which he has written most of the scripts - he eventually bogged down and called on the services of his old friend Jean-Claude Carrière, the most prestigious film writer on the Paris scene.

Together they took the story apart, put it back together again. In vain. "It wasn't working. I had one foot in *Lacombe Lucien*, the other in *Au Revoir les Enfants*. But not as good. The supreme luxury I've always afforded myself is that of not doing a film unless I really believe in it."

Suddenly he became very busy. Without a film shoot to offer as an excuse, he began accepting the invitations he was sent for retrospectives of his films in Strasbourg, Berlin, around Paris, elsewhere in Europe. "I was alarmed to discover that I could spend the better part of the year opening this sort of retrospectives, in South Africa, in Australia. It's very nice, it's flattering, but it's a bit like going to your own funeral, and the truth is I hate looking at my old films. When you're done with one, you know, with all those months of editing, you've seen it about 250 times."

It's hard to know whether Louis Malle looked on it as a gift of the gods or a burden - probably both - but he had been privileged since birth. In the foggy little town of Thumières where he was born in 1932, his father ran THE sugar factory and his mother was a Béghin, one of the great names in French capitalism. As in a distant dream, Malle still remembered having seen the red flags of the Popular Front unfurled outside the family home when he was four years old. When he was eight there was the Occupation, and Thumières, where his father remained, was cut off from the rest of France. His mother and the six children were in Paris and he remembered it as a very free life. He would spend his afternoons selling portraits of Pétain for charity! In 1942, along with an older brother, he was sent to a boarding school run by the Carmelites in Fontainebleau. It was there that, in 1944, following a denunciation, the Gestapo arrived to arrest two Jewish adolescents who had been in hiding, including a classmate with whom Louis Malle had been good friends. It was a cruel episode that it would take him forty years to exorcise, with his film *Au Revoir les Enfants*, which is a faithful account of the actual events.

The bourgeois home in which he grew up was very comfortable and very conservative, but not too confining. As his brothers were all poor students, Louis was singled out to take over the family business. Big disappointment: he began by failing the entrance competition for the Polytechnique, and then, at the risk of giving his mother a heart attack, declared that while pursuing his studies at the faculty of Political Science, he would attend IDHEC, the French film school.

He excelled in film from the very beginning. After one year at the school, Jacques Cousteau offered him a job as cameraman.

Since that time, he had done only what appealed to him: the documentaries already mentioned, comedies with big stars, dramas with unknown players. The results have been uneven; there have been some great successes, no utter failures. A brilliant career to say the least, but it has earned him an ambivalent reputation among committed filmgoers.

The French prefer things to be logical and cartesian. A director who insists on jumping from one subject, genre, or mood to another, tends to be frowned upon, or even to be regarded as something of a hack. This clearly irritated Malle: "I don't understand why I'm asked that question. Of course, there are French filmmakers who make the same film over and over - and some do it very well indeed, like Eric Rohmer. I never wanted to do that, above all I didn't want to make 'Louis Malle films.' I wanted to try my hand at all the genres: comedies, melodramas, adventure films. Do people criticize John Huston for having made films as different as *The Dead* and *African Queen*?"

Malle often made critics uncomfortable, because he was never where they expected to find him. He was considered part of the French New Wave, because he was about the same age as Truffaut, Chabrol, Godard, and the rest. As he put it, "It's true we all loved Bresson and Renoir, we wanted a *cinéma d'auteur*, and we refused to compromise. And within two or three years, there appeared on the scene a dozen filmmakers, the most brilliant generation in French film history."

But while most of the others went on with their activism at the *Cahiers du Cinéma*, Louis Malle, the youngest of the group, "was directing fish" for Captain Cousteau. In 1956, that won him, as co-director of *World of Silence*, both the Palme d'Or at Cannes and an Oscar for best documentary in Hollywood.

He was the first to direct a feature film, *Ascenseur pour l'Échafaud* (Elevator to the Gallows). Its mood was Bressonian, it provided Jeanne Moreau with her first big role, it had original music by Miles Davis and dialogue by Roger Nimier - the credits did not go unnoticed. Then came *The Lovers*, a romantic film through and through, and a box-office triumph. "At the age of 26," he remembered, "I was more famous than I've ever been since." Immediately he decided to cover his tracks with *Zazie dans le Métro*, a zany fantasy that kept people away in droves.

If we had to give Malle a label, it would be that of gentleman. A gentleman traveller, a kind of Phileas Fogg of French cinema, from a good family, wealthy, eccentric, and attached to tradition. Above all unpredictable. When small-budget films with unknowns were all the rage, he shot *Viva Maria*, a superproduction, in Mexico. Then he spent two years making a series of documentaries on India.

Lacombe Lucien (1974), a film about collaboration during World War II that caused a sensation, put him back in the first rank of French directors. He took the opportunity to leave for the

United States, where he remained for ten years. It was thought that he had become an American filmmaker - and it almost came true with *Atlantic City* in 1980 - but in 1987 he was back with *Au Revoir les Enfants* (Goodbye Children) and *Milou en Mai* (May Fools), his two films most steeped in France, and perhaps his most personal. Then a new film, this time Anglo-European, *Damage*, with Juliette Binoche and Jeremy Irons.

So it went with Louis Malle, who saw it as a point of honor "never to make the same film twice in a row."

But with only one exception, Malle always co-authored his scripts. In dealing with producers he was utterly intractable where the choice of actors is concerned, or the final cut. For *Damage*, "I had a choice of three famous American actresses who would have done a lot to sell the film in the United States, but I decided it would be Juliette Binoche."

Pretty Baby (1978) was a small-budget film (three million dollars). He retained total control, and refused to show the producers rushes on a regular basis. In terms of the American system his behavior was outrageous. The film was successful, but was restricted to the "intellectual" distribution circuit (New York, Boston, college campuses). "Make no mistake," he says, "neither Altman, nor Cassavetes, nor even Woody Allen have been given access to the big commercial circuit. Altman and Allen do very nicely, but they're completely marginal."

Atlantic City - which was perceived, all in all, as a real American film - won five nominations for major Oscars in 1981. But it too was shut out of the big commercial circuits. "When I got the nominations, about which I had no illusions, I met with the Paramount distributors. They had two million dollars at stake for my film, and fifty million for Warren Beatty's *Reds*. I asked, does that mean you're going to spend 25 times as much money in the Oscar campaign on *Reds*? They laughed. For them, for *Atlantic City* to win, as it wasn't a mainstream commercial film, would have been a disaster."

True to form, he followed it up with *My Dinner with André*, a no-budget film without a plot that consisted of a conversation at a restaurant table, 111 minutes long, between two New York theatre people. It was a cult film in New York and in intellectual circles. At the same time he worked with John Guare (who had written the script for *Atlantic City*) on a project that would perhaps - on his own terms - open the doors to him, of the System.

"It was a very violent, very disturbing, comedy-satire on political corruption. The major studios were interested. Why? Because John Belushi would play the leading role, and he was the star of the moment, after *The Blues Brothers*. With him on side, the studios would have bought the telephone directory! And he had completely won me over. I was in France on family business and we'd already given a first draft of the script to *Columbia*, when Guare phoned me. Belushi, fool that he was, had just died of an overdose! I knew the project was finished. I tried for a while to get it back on the rails. But without Belushi it was a lost cause."

A producer who had been after him for years to do a remake of *Pigeon*, an Italian comedy by Monicelli, was able to catch him off balance. "I agreed to take a look at it, though I was far from being convinced. I got one finger caught in the gears, then an arm, and that was it. The script wasn't working, we rewrote it. It didn't help. We started to shoot anyway. Every day I asked myself, what am I doing here? Then the producer who got me into it in the first place was replaced; his successor didn't believe in the project. It was called *Crackers*, and it was a horrible flop from beginning to end. No one saw it anyway, it never made it into the theatres. Which is just as well, because it's a total failure, and the fault was mine. I knew I shouldn't have done it and I did it all the same, for the wrong reasons."

Malle had left for the United States because he was afraid that if he stayed in France he'd become "a regional filmmaker." In the States he hadn't really believed that he'd ever be seen as a true blue American. "Besides," he says, "My vantage point was always that of an outsider in my American films." Perhaps, despite himself, he did harbor certain illusions about the feasibility of doing his films inside the sacred System. Finally, after a few more documentaries - for PBS and HBO - he returned in 1987 to France, where he directed his two most personal and most deeply French films. And, in a bitter twist of fate, it was *Au Revoir les Enfants* that brought him to Hollywood yet again, but through the back door: a nomination for the Oscar for best foreign film. This is the Oscar for cinema's Third World, regularly conferred on obscure European films with no commercial future. Even this (false) recognition was ultimately refused him. "That failure really hurt him at the time," says someone close to him.

Was that the last straw for Malle in the United States? His American experience did seem to have left a bad taste in his mouth. "I am the first to say that the cinema, ungainly and costly as it is, is an art of compromise. You never get everything you want, you have to know how to be reasonable. But in the studio system, you have to accept that the *executives* control the casting, that they see the rushes before the director, that they have the last word in the editing. For me that's unthinkable, and I've never gone along with it. And over the last ten years it's become worse than ever. Even Scorsese has to make a pot-boiler from time to time, just to keep going. Of course you could say that Hollywood has always been like that, with diabolical, dictatorial producers. I agree that the Goldwyns and the Zanucks were real monsters, but at least they loved movies!"

Already in 1966, the young and brilliant director had held out some hopes for America with *Viva Maria*. The film had been a sensation in Europe, Bardot was a celebrity even in the United States, and the comedy was set in Mexico, in the United States' back yard. And so the film was launched like an American product, and was dubbed instead of sub-titled: "The dubbing was bad, but no worse than that of American films in Europe." The film bombed. "The general public and the distributors reject films in their original version, and then the critics shoot down on sight European films that, on rare occasions, come to them dubbed."

French films have their designated niche in the United States "on the two or three streets in Manhattan where you find all the art houses," says the producer Toscan du Plantier, bluntly ironic. Did Louis Malle think in 1976 that all you had to do to clear this hurdle was to shoot in American? Of course not. But with *Atlantic City* he almost became the exception to the rule, and came close to making an American career like Milos Forman or Roman Polanski.

It was not to be. Louis Malle, a true gentleman with extensive knowledge of the vast world in which he lived, did not go so far as to show surprise. But, despite his elegant fatalism, one had a sense that there were times when he looked back on his lost illusions - and lost opportunities - with a certain regret. Lost forever? Before he reached sixty, he already had a few warning signs where his health was concerned. There was still a project awaiting him in the United States on the life of Marlene Dietrich. But was it the great film of which he dreamed? And why let himself be sucked back into the studios' infernal machine since he no longer had any faith in it? Finally, death caught up with the dream-maker when he passed away, of cancer, in 1995.

5. Serene Perfection

Take a country with a thousand years of history, including a century and a half of hegemony over Europe. Bestow on it one of the two or three great international capitals. It would be remarkable if it did not, at regular intervals, produce, if not masterpieces, at least consummate creations, flawless jewels. In a pejorative sense, one talks of *articles de Paris*, or "Paris goods." The implication is that such objects are perfect in style and execution, even if the inspiration leaves something to be desired.

But in literature - which is its chosen domain - France has not for many years produced the great novel or play that might be said to define its age.[2] What we do find in today's high quality writing is such exquisite craftsmanship that one sometimes wonders if it is not a hereditary gift - unless the authors have quite simply been spurred on by the daunting example of all those forerunners to whom France owes its literary glory.

Of the hundreds of novels published each year in Paris, many are of no great interest, but almost all are impeccably crafted. In Paris the knack is there, whether it be for a well turned-out literary confection, or a modest beef and carrots served up as the noonday special in a bistro on Boulevard Henri IV, or for a pair of shoes

---

2   There are sometimes great essays - for instance the most recent book by François Furet, Le Passé d'une Illusion (The Past of an Illusion) - but by definition these are not the books that attract the most attention.

made to measure at Hermès, or for a dinner at the Grand Véfour.

This serene perfection holds true, conspicuously, for Parisian journalism. It's a matter of form, more than content. The first rank of the French press is made up of people who write French well, intelligently, sometimes even with humility, without seeking to attract undue attention to themselves: Claude Imbert, Jean-François Revel, Jean-Claude Casanova, André Fontaine. Whether they write daily or weekly, their intellectual mentors are themselves serene, their talents discreet, their writings often profound; Fernand Braudel could be considered the patron saint of this brotherhood, and Raymond Aron a kindred spirit. Even among those most in the public eye, Jean Daniel, Jacques Julliard, Philippe Meyer, Franz-Olivier Giesbert and some others, there are many fine wordsmiths. What perhaps makes Paris a hub of modern civilization is the fact that common, everyday products like daily newspapers and beef with carrots are routinely turned out to perfection.[3]

---

3   There are those who might think I've left something out here: the "brilliant young man," a central and enduring player in the Paris landscape for at least a century and a half (Rastignac, Musset, Benjamin Constant, etc.) who today for various reasons (including the rise of television), dominates the political-intellectual scene. He sometimes seems a reincarnation of one of his illustrious predecessors: Régis Debray as a Jansenist D'Artagnan, Phillipe Sollers as Diderot, Bernard-Henri Lévy as Musset-Baudelaire-Malraux, Jacques Attali as Cagliostro. These eternally young men, who have utterly banished from the scene all competitors who lack the requisite "look," have this in common: they all became very famous in their early twenties. They are fearsome on the public stage, and create at lightning speed, and are everywhere at once. But they have more virtuosity than serene perfection, which requires a calmer approach.

LOUIS-BERNARD ROBITAILLE

Deneuve the Immaculate

Catherine Deneuve is a consummate modern incarnation of French perfection. In the tradition of Gallimard's white book covers, the writing of Marguerite Duras, the virtuosity of a Charles Trenet or the style of Yves Saint-Laurent. Not a single error or flaw.

Perfection, of course, of her features, with their steadfast limpidity. It's a perfection that is never labored, that is imbued with intelligence and culture. Perfection, above all, of her musical voice, which with a slight effortless inflection shifts from coldness to amusement, from polite indifference to animation, from spontaneous laughter to boredom. She says, just like that, "Ah, you think so?", and you hear the angels sing. Natural perfection, and perfectly authentic. It's the kind one inherits in the happy families of good Parisian society, and that is cultivated in the course of a successful life and career. It is no surprise that Bunuel, at an important juncture, made her his actress of choice. If his intent was to profane purity, who could better embody its elusive traits than Catherine Deneuve? If he had known her a little earlier he might have cast her as Viridiana.

There is no doubt about her success. Except perhaps at the very beginning of her career, when she was acting for Roger Vadim, Madame Deneuve has to her credit no bad film or bad role, even if of course the great roles have not always come in great films. She has, unlike many current stars, worked for the greatest directors: Bunuel, Truffaut. She has become, to all intents and purposes, the one star of French cinema, even if she finds the idea "ridiculous. There are no stars in France." She has conducted her personal life in perfect freedom, not hiding anything, but not allowing the media any access to her private affairs, either. Shuffle all you want through the back issues of *Paris-Match*, you won't *anything*!

"It hasn't happened," she says, "quite simply because I said no. There are actors who didn't want to or didn't know how to resist. When a film came out pressure was applied, and they weren't

204

always able to refuse. I never wanted to make compromises of that sort." And indeed she never gave in, except perhaps when Polanski asked her to pose for "suggestive" pictures in *Playboy*, to help promote *Repulsion*. But that was in the beginning, in the 60s. For twenty years, Madame Deneuve has been one of those celebrities who almost never gives interviews. Just a few words into a microphone on the way out of a screening at Cannes. Or an appearance on Bernard Pivot's cultural program, *Bouillon de Culture*, for the launching of *Indochine*. When she talks to the media - for a minute or an hour - it's with complete naturalness, as if she was with colleagues or friends. But the opportunity arises as rarely as possible: "I don't mind talking about a film I've just shot, because that's important, and I've always done it. But not one interview after another. And I'm not interested in giving speeches or going on about noble causes, or even the cinema in general. Today everything is out of hand. You're asked about so many things that it's discouraging. You have to have an opinion on everything. No one just does what he knows best!"

As Catherine Deneuve is nothing if not professional, she now gives *one* interview for each major country where her most recent film is being released. So it was for *Indochine*. And for *Ma Saison Préférée* (My Favorite Season), one of André Téchiné's loveliest films, where she plays the role of a woman in her forties, separated and in a state of crisis.

On my way to our rendezvous at the Hôtel Lutétia - one of her favorite spots - I vaguely expected to find her surrounded by secretary-bodyguards. In fact I passed her in the street without at first recognizing her. Dressed in slacks, a blouse, flat shoes, with glasses and handbag, she was lightly made-up and looked busy. Much shorter in person than she appears on the screen. An all-purpose outfit - at first you don't notice her, then it takes a few seconds before you realize who she is. It's the only way to walk around Paris undisturbed if your name is Catherine Deneuve.

Afraid she was just about to vanish, I accosted her. "Ah, the interview's with you?" she said, perfectly matter-of-fact. "Go to the bar, I'll be there in five minutes."

The hotel bar is inherently discreet, but what is also true is that although people glance at her out of the corners of their eyes, not everyone turns and looks when she walks by, as would be the case for other stars. She seems not to care one way or another if people look at her or not, stare at her or not.

She was right on time for the interview. The agreement I'd made with her secretary stipulated that it last no longer than thirty minutes. We went to forty. Then, in the same perfectly pitched voice, as though to apologize (but not really): "I have to leave you. Do you have any other questions? Because I must leave, I have an appointment." I did indeed have another question (and a half) to which she replied patiently, but in few words. Charm, unfailing naturalness, a very definite authority, but always exercised with exquisite courtesy: all of that is Deneuve.

When I brought up the names of Bunuel or Truffaut, she only said with unanswerable gentleness: "That's so long ago. I have no wish to linger over what is past. They were marvellous people that I loved dearly, but I've been asked about them so often that I can only reply by rote, so there's really no point. I've said it all too many times, and I don't want to talk about it any more." On the cinema itself, she prefers to avoid "generalities that are of no interest." Even if she loves Coppola, Scorsese, great directors. On the closing of the American market to European films, she considers herself a "fatalist": "For America, European cinema is very far away. Not only the cinema, but Europe itself." She has, from time to time, been called on to "defend" French cinema in the United States, "but I've never been an ambassador for anything at all. I'm free, I'm my own boss!" (smile). The same thing for politics: "I vote like everyone else, I talk things over with my friends, but I don't see why I should take public positions. I did once for Amnesty International. That's very important." And in fact, she is one of those French public figures whom you really cannot pigeonhole politically.

She made no pretense: if she was there, it was to talk about Téchiné's film. She has already shot two features with him. "Téchiné is a real "auteur" - not at all fashionable, as you say - a very sensitive man who comes from the provinces, who has his own world." Her leading man, Daniel Auteuil, "is an extraordinary actor, very subtle. We enjoyed ourselves a lot during the shooting, he's very playful. And mysterious at the same time."

What strikes one in her role is that this time she is not a character who comes out on top, like the bourgeois temptresses or "femmes fatales" she could have played.

"Me, bourgeois? But everyone is bourgeois today! We live in cities, we have cars, houses. There are no more peasants, there's no aristocracy. Naturally, the signs are more visible in some cases than in others. But I don't see myself like that at all. None of the characters that I've played are like me, it would make me very uneasy to play myself. I've done all sorts of things, which is normal for an actor; there are films where I'm the victim, others where I'm the executioner, still others where I'm just going along for the ride."

"The heroine in Téchiné's film is certainly lost, but the point is that she learns to know herself and to get her bearings. A turning point in my career?" She laughs. "They've been talking about my significant turning points for the last ten years! No, I've played very different roles, and I have already been 'lost' already in *La Reine Blanche* (The White Queen). Should I worry about my *image*? I don't think I have the same image for everyone. Of course, actors do get typed and are more believable in certain roles. But I've never thought in those terms. I work with creators, with people I want to work with. It's happened that I've refused good projects because I thought they weren't right for me. But good scripts are already so rare."

And in fact, seven or eight years ago, she shot - with Gérard Depardieu - the first film of an absolute unknown, *Drôle d'Endroit pour une Rencontre* (A Strange Place for a Meeting). "You could see right away that despite its flaws, it was a wonderful script. Depardieu, who was already the most sought after actor in France, was absolutely determined to do it. No one is swamped with tempting offers, and I'm no exception; a good project is something it takes time to develop. I shoot on average a film and a half per year. But it would be hard for me to do much more than that. Only Depardieu shoots all year long, but it's because he's offered all the best projects."

That she's seen as a star only makes her shrug her shoulders. "That label doesn't apply to European cinema. Even in the United States it's a status that has nothing to do with career, with craft. On the one hand you do this job, on the other you deal, successfully or not, with this image that's been superimposed on you. In our day only very famous rock singers belong to this category, with all that implies of glamour, sexiness, surging crowds, mystery, passion."

Catherine Deneuve became an actress "a bit by chance, when I was 16. So of course it was not a deeply felt, irresistible vocation. It was fun, more than anything else; a way to escape reality, and cut short my studies. To be listened to, admired. There's nothing unusual about that, everybody wants to make films!"

Curiously, she has never, in all her career, come near the theatre - even to dabble in it - as though, out of a combination of prudence and modesty, she never wanted to face that acid test. "I've always been apprehensive. And I still find enough interesting challenges in the cinema. I don't know. It would have to be an ambitious new work, or the chance to play an important role from the repertoire in a new way."

"And so if Patrice Chéreau were to offer you a great role?"

"You're starting at the top! Oh, of course, a great director, with a great subject, and a great role - but I'm not saying yes! You need time for the theatre, you need a year set aside."

And of course, Catherine Deneuve knows that she hasn't, will never have a whole year in reserve. Even if interesting projects are not thick on the ground, she is one of those rare actresses in French cinema who gets first refusal on the great roles. She doesn't feign modesty to the point of professing surprise at this. She is just very happy that it is so. Serenely happy. And she doesn't ask for anything more.

Echenoz, a Modern Classic

Had the austere Éditions de Minuit not won the Prix Goncourt twice in the last ten years, and were the famous prize not first and foremost publisher-influenced, with the jackpot earmarked for the trio of Gallimard, Grasset and Le Seuil, and a few consolation prizes allotted to the others now and then, Jean Echenoz would be the favorite this autumn for his fifth novel, *Nous Trois* (We Three), which quickly established itself as THE novel of the 1992 literary season.

Of course, Echenoz is a "formalist" (or a non-naturalist) and that genre is not what the Academy prefers. But in every other respect he fulfils the criteria Michel Tournier was happy to restate for us: "A novelist in full command of his talents, in his early 40s, with three novels behind him." Not only that, he now has a public that is both loyal and large in number - for a "difficult" author, at any rate. Ten days after appearing in the bookstores, *Nous Trois* was in fourth position on the best-seller list of *L'Express*.

Jean Echenoz, at 48, has something else going for him. He's very close to being what one might call the novelist of his generation (or, let's say, of the 90s). A cultural touchstone, a bit like Godard in the 60s.

His first novel, *Le Méridien de Greenwich* (Greenwich Meridian) in 1979, sold a grand total of 600 copies (or was it 400). Echenoz today is still perfectly happy with it, and rightly so. At the most he will agree, like Mozart before the Austro-Hungarian emperor after the premiere of *The Abduction from the Seraglio*, that the work had "a few two many notes." Since then he's trimmed his manuscripts much more severely. But let's not get mired in details. The first novel Echenoz wrote, over two years in the writing and published at the end of the 70s, was already good, and possessed the virtues of those that would follow.

Cherokee, a novel by an "unknown" won the Prix Médicis, a literary prize often awarded to obscure writers, especially if they're published by Les Éditions de Minuit. He sold about 10,000 copies of this oblique tribute to the detective novel. But he already had a loyal following. *Cherokee* became a cult novel for the happy few.

With *L'Équipée Malaise*, (Double Indemnity) Jean Echenoz became someone to reckon with. A chorus of praise from the critics, his first invitation to appear on Bernard Pivot's literary television show, *Apostrophes* (a consecration in itself), and impressive sales for the genre: 30,000 copies. And then *Lac* virtually established him as a writer for the general public; it's not often that Minuit has a novel that lingers on the best-seller list, and sells over 100,000 copies. Nor is it often that that a new novelist makes such a breakthrough without writing in the newspapers or using them to provoke controversy or selling film rights or appearing on television or even making the Paris "scene." A few years ago Echenoz was declared one of the flagship writers of the new generation, along with a small number of others who were writing articulately about the emptiness of the times, the weightless or trifling insignificance of things. With *Lac*, and today *Nous Trois*, he has broken from the pack and is well on his way to attaining that privileged status where you are regarded as a very special writer (in the same league as Gracq, Roussel, Malcolm Lowry), and where your books are eagerly snapped up in bookstores. It happened to Duras and Le Clézio, but only after twenty or thirty years of what were virtually limited editions. [4]

I had met him ten years earlier, in the wake of his Prix Médicis. I saw him again the other day, at the launching of *Nous Trois*. For that first interview in 1983, after a brief consultation in the offices of his publisher, we opted for his favorite café, the Tabac Saint-Claude, just down the street: perfectly situated, well-kept without being chic, central but discreet. Echenoz, a creature of the city, is a connoisseur of cafés and the ins and outs of Paris streets.

Another weighty deliberation on where to meet this time,

---

4   Echenoz is available in English, translated by Mark Polizzotti: *Big Blondes* (New Press, 1997),*Cherokee*(1994), *Double Jeopardy*(1994)(University of Nebraska Press), *Lac* (David R Godine, 1997).

between a resident of the Buttes Chaumont (him) and a native of the Bastille. We agreed on his choice, the Clown Bar, near the Cirque d'Hiver, one of the magic spots (for initiates) in Paris. Echenoz was there on time, in front of the café, which was closed as it turned out it's only open for lunch. The fallback was an old café, recently renovated (but in the old style) on the Boulevard du Temple. He seemed to appreciate it for what it was, like a wine-lover tasting, not a great vintage, but an honest regional wine. He had walked all the way from Buttes-Chaumont, half an hour on foot, along the Canal Saint-Martin and through the little streets, not too clean and to most eyes boring, that border on the Place de la République.

Echenoz still adores the Paris neighborhoods with their thousands of secrets: this sign, that little shop, a dead-end, an empty square, an aging bistro with its horseshoe-shaped counter. For him the big city is inseparable from a passion for jazz, cigarettes, coffee, alcohol, late-night discussions that never end. He had and still has the greyish complexion of someone who hardly ever sees the sun, a slightly rumpled, adolescent air, a casual, timeless elegance (Burberry's + 501 + Arrow + loafers) - the brands have changed but the style remains the same. And he has that penchant for tinted glasses (blue lenses) common among nighthawks.

"But no, I have nothing against the country," he protests, as always when someone tries to pigeonhole him, this time as a denizen of the city. "I like the countryside. I can even manage to stay there now 36 hours at a stretch. Of course, at the seaside I can easily last a week." Clearly this is not a novelist of rural life. In 1983 he claimed that outside of Paris, Marseille was the only city with enough mystery for him to consider it as the setting for a book. One of his bravura pieces in *Nous Trois* consists of an eight-second earthquake - which takes thirty pages of the novel - in Marseilles. More recently he has begun to discover, and developed a fascination for, the other Western city of the fantastic, New York.

Echenoz does not really come from the city. What makes him a man of his time is that he is from everywhere and nowhere. His social origins are equally confused. According to official documents, he's a native of Orange. He even lived in the south of

France for the first twenty years of his life.

"But you can't talk about southern roots," he says. "My mother's family came from Marseilles. But my father, who was a doctor, came from Paris, and his family from Nantes. When I was young he practiced in Marseilles, Aix-en-Provence... In short, we were a nomadic family - even if I'm still attached to Marseilles."

In 1970, in his twenties, he settled in Paris "to follow a woman - doubtless to study as well." He never left. The 70s were political years, almost to the exclusion of everything else. And so Echenoz got involved in politics, like just about everyone. He was on the extreme left, of course.

"I worked to put bread on the table, I changed jobs all the time (copy editor in a press agency, proofreader). In those years, it was as though the novel didn't exist. All that counted were essays, texts, Deleuze's *Anti-Oedipus*, Marcuse. Or popular genres like detective fiction, with political content. I wrote small things, just for me, at night, without reworking them or showing them to anyone. For pleasure. And then I turned 30, and I told myself I had to write and finish a real novel. I worked two years on *Greenwich Meridian*, and there it was. That was in 1979."

Echenoz had his style and tone right from the start; it came naturally to him. And he belongs to a rare species: one of the few new writers published each year by the very exclusive Éditions de Minuit. He's even become their star novelist, but without ever having tried to join a school or a coterie.

"The *nouveau roman*? I don't know exactly what that means, because I never really read them. I loved Robbe-Grillet's *Les Gommes* (The Erasers), and that's all. And I have no theories concerning my own novels. I write spontaneously, to have fun, to surprise myself. Not that it comes right away, of course; I rewrite five or six times. Most often, the first draft is awful; when I reread it I get depressed, I'm ashamed. And then I rewrite it. But not from any theoretical point of view."

Unlike many Parisian writers who are a product of their milieu, of Parisianism and its successive fads, Echenoz had a very eclectic apprenticeship. At home there were many books and he read voraciously, everything in sight, except for what was prescribed for him at school. "I'm very glad not to have read most of the great classics when I was 15 or 18; Flaubert was a tremendous revelation for me when I discovered him at the age of 30. Had I been younger, I wouldn't have appreciated him. Now I'm discovering Chateaubriand, and I'm entranced. And a bit of Balzac."

Tucked away in Echenoz's brain is a great variety of writers, who took up residence there at different times: Alexandre Dumas, Edgar Allen Poe, Joyce, Dashiell Hammett, Kafka, Malcolm Lowry. A bit of everything, really, except for the naturalistic or psychological novel ("Does the psychological novel really exist? I don't know what it is.") But there is no one key novel, no author who is his guiding light.

One exception perhaps: Flaubert. By pure coincidence, the café where we find ourselves, Boulevard du Temple, is almost right across the street from the building where, I'm told, Flaubert kept an apartment in Paris for many years. "There was an apartment for rent in that building - maybe it was Flaubert's - and I was briefly tempted to rent it, just like that, as a kind of game."

The precision and spareness of the writing, the cold distance from his characters - Echenoz doesn't mind seeing himself as a descendant of Flaubert (he also reveres Mallarmé, the austere writer par excellence). But his love for Flaubert came late, after a chance encounter at the age of 30, and had nothing to do with his adherence to any fashion or school. Echenoz has never thought in terms of systems of punctuation or narration, of technique. Clearly his detached, ironic accounts of present-day characters who seem to have sprung from detective novels are quite simply what he himself found appealing. And so he doffed his hat to that genre, then to the adventure novel, and finally to the spy novel (*Cherokee* to *Lac*).

"With *Nous Trois*, I wanted to do a novel-novel in the first degree, and no longer lean on a particular genre." For two years the title of the manuscript was *Le Mal des Transports* (Travel Sickness). The novel's hero, Meyer - "He could be you or me" - is a Paris ad-man who goes on vacation and meets a young woman on the freeway whose car is going up in flames. He experiences the earthquake in Marseille, and ends up on a space shuttle.

Business as usual, one might say: in this fin-de-siècle, we see the Berlin Wall come down, then drink a glass of whisky (or milk, as the case may be); we do three orbits in space or have it off with a bleached blonde in the bed of a two-star hotel. It all comes down *almost* to the same thing. And there's nothing very sublime about it - or very serious either. In the West, the century is closing out on a note of widespread and placid equivalence. And Echenoz has fun telling himself all about it.

Giroud, *Grande Dame* and Honest Man

Madame Françoise Giroud cannot, perhaps, claim the international renown of an Oriana Fallaci, the fearless Italian interviewer. She's never possessed the power of a Beuve-Méry, a Jean Daniel, or some other notables. Still, she writes very well indeed, sometimes with the genius and limpidity of a Françoise Sagan, without being or taking herself for a great author. She has not *made* post-war French history. And she has even experienced a few failures, both in politics and journalism. But if you put end to end her family history, her personal and professional growth, her gift for the journalistic turn of phrase, the modesty with which she has exercised power and exerted influence in Paris, not to mention her peerless natural elegance, one might say that she is the incarnation of a certain grand-bourgeois-intellectual perfection. In its Parisian guise.

I don't know whether Madame Giroud was a *great* editor-in-chief, whether at *Elle*, which she co-founded, or later at *L'Express*, which she ran jointly with Jean-Jacques Servan-Schreiber. She was greatly respected, at any rate, and never lapsed into megalomania or took herself for a weekly prophet, a common trap for those who become media celebrities in Paris. Even if she knew her own worth, she doesn't give the impression of ever having been, let us say, pretentious. In Paris that's tantamount to heroism - or extreme wisdom.

Les Leçons Particulières, published in 1990, provides further proof of this thoroughgoing grace. (The title plays on two meanings of *particulières*: the lessons are both private and special.) Others, who have lived lives less full, impose on us thousand-page memoirs. Madame Giroud has always, with great tact, kept things short. Her book runs to barely 260 pages. And she deftly, obliquely, alludes to the inevitable question: why write her memoirs now? The answer is hard to believe when you see the author either in person or on television. She was born in 1916, and everyone is mortal. Her book begins, in fact, with an account of the recent death of the man with whom she was living. He had throat cancer, and was asking for assistance to die. The first sentence: "That night, it was difficult for him to speak."

A few pages later, just in passing: "Today I walk heavily, my sight is dim, my back stiff, my arms soft, my hearing bad, I can no longer recall the shape of my body when the firmness of its flesh and the delicacy of its curves still endowed it with the grace of youth. I have forgotten myself. To age is abject."

Asked later about these words, she almost apologizes for being so gloomy, always with the same smile: "I'm describing the situation, that's all. I'm totally indifferent to the idea of my disappearance and death. And old age is a transition one is forced to make. It's degrading, that's all."

Madame Giroud, who was close to Jean Renoir, Pierre Mendès-France, François Mauriac and François Mitterrand, and whose dinner parties were the most exclusive in Paris, was born in Istanbul of a Sephardic mother from Spain, and a certain Monsieur Gourdji, born in Baghdad, who seems to have had a greater gift for adventure than for family life. Françoise Giroud soon found herself an "immigrant" in Paris, along with her mother and her older sister. It is not clear what became of her father, although he did remain in the picture long enough to cry out, when she was born: "What a misfortune! It's not a boy!"

At the age of 16 she began to work as a stenographer. She was beautiful and intelligent, and luck came her way. Suddenly there she was in the film studios at Boulogne, where she met Jouvet, Renoir, Michel Simon, and the rest, and learned more about life: "It was an appalling milieu. Rotten with sexism and harassment. The assistant directors treated the female extras like cattle. Anyone who protested was put on a black list. Pigs sat at the wheels of Packard sedans."

With supreme pessimism, the woman who in 1974 would become Minister for the Rights of Women in France writes, "They and their kind did not make me hate men, who are, let me make clear, quite nice overall, when not under the dominion of that obsessive appendix attached to the lower abdomen. What they did do was make me feel sympathy for women."

This wholehearted, smiling pessimism is typical of Giroud. She was and remains a reformer - in society, and for women - but she has no illusions. Talking of her youth, she says neatly, "What's horrible about poverty is that there's no reason it should ever stop." But she doesn't dwell on her difficult beginnings. To have class, for her, one must first refuse to indulge in self-pity. In the same way, we are told briefly and in passing that she was arrested by the Germans in the summer of 1944 for her work in the Resistance. Her sister was sent to Ravensbruck but she escaped that fate, and was held for "only" a few weeks in Fresnes.

The former brains behind *Elle* and *L'Express*, confidante of French political leaders, woman of influence and celebrated dinner hostess, could have filled a volume the size of a phone book with the "indiscretions" to which she has been privy. In fact there are no revelations about anyone. The only indiscretions - on which she does not elaborate - concern herself: a nervous breakdown at the age of 40 after having been "walked out on," her analysis with Lacan, her difficult youth, and the accidental death of a son whom at first she had not wanted. There are a few comments on her political misadventures, including her exclusion from the Giscard government in 1977 at the same time as her dismissal from *L'Express*.

Madame Giroud takes stock of her very full life, of those "private lessons" she received from great men and others, in a little book whose style is free of pretension, and in which sparkle, here and there, a few real gems. All this in a vein of mitigated intimacy.

* * *

216

Everything Françoise Giroud does is done with style. Whether she's writing or talking, Madame Giroud is limpidity itself, and it's hard to know whether this is an innate or an acquired gift.

The *grande dame* is also what was referred to in seventeenth century France as an *honnête homme*, or honest man, that is to say someone who, while not necessarily a genius, is truly cultured, wise, modest, and aware of his limitations. All of which endows him with a certain perfection in his range.

In the 1950s, Françoise Giroud was a highly regarded presence on the Paris scene. She was known, without being a star. Curiously, it's when her career seemed to have ended that she took flight. In 1977, Giscard d'Estaing summarily cut short, after two years, her ministerial tenure as Secretary of State for Women's Rights and then for Culture, following some unfortunate reversals in municipal elections. On her return to "civilian life," she learned that she was no longer editor of *L'Express*. The road to celebrity began there.

She became a modest television critic at the *Nouvel Observateur*, and it was a revelation. Her simple and controlled style, her short sentences that murdered with a smile, what she calls her "inability to run on," established her as a model for print journalism.

And above all, she started to write books. She had no oracular pretensions here, either. But *La Comédie du Pouvoir* (The Comedy of Power), about her experiences in government, is one of the most amusing and instructive accounts of its kind. Her novel *Le Bon Plaisir* (Good Pleasure) is a rattling good story. Leaving aside her biographies, and also *Men and Women*, her dialogues under the olive tree with Bernard-Henri Lévy, we come to *Leçons Particulières*, which is one of the most exquisite memoirs to appear in recent years.

Journal d'une Parisienne (Diary of a Parisian) is in the same vein, even if, as might be expected, the form of a daily diary entails a certain number of longueurs and digressions. Obedient to her moods, and without ever wearying us, she walks us through the year of 1993.

This *Diary* was commissioned by the publisher Le Seuil, and she did it "because I cannot stop myself from working; I'm less bored when I work than when I'm enjoying myself." Nor did she ponder for long the question of whether her daily reflections were worthy of publication; it's a bit like official honors and decorations, which she has always accepted - with a pinch of self-deprecating irony - because it would be even more pretentious to make an issue of refusing them. In the diary there is always, between the lines, a sense of the futility of things - and of herself - but the author never stoops to ridicule; (French) political life may harbor all the vices known to man, and it is sometimes absurd, but it's worthwhile working at it in the hope that it might succeed, and to avoid even worse things happening.

And so she kept her diary day by day, thoughtfully but without false modesty. It includes some lovely reflections on the passing of time, and on her two-year-old great-granddaughter "whom I will never know when she is twenty." She has a weakness for Bernard-Henri Lévy, which is understandable as he has become a close friend. And she draws a fair bit of blood, this way and that, before you're even aware of what she's done. Talking of Jean-Jacques Servan-Schreiber, one of the important men in her life but who was always a bit over-excited, she writes, after one of his scandalous declarations: "Now what's the fellow up to this time?" Balladur does well on television, but she is much surprised, because he has "neither charm nor talent."

I see her briefly at her home, as much to get a feel for her surroundings as anything else. Madame Giroud, who prides herself on always answering letters from readers, also graciously accepts requests for interviews. And so she receives me in her magnificent apartment in La Tour-Maubourg (a ten-foot ceiling, modern paintings on the walls). Although she was not born into the bourgeoisie, she is unquestionably one of the paragons of Parisian "bonne société," which tilts moderately (but sincerely) to the left and prefers to live in the Faubourg Saint-Germain.

The face is the same as on television; it remains amazingly young. The body follows behind with a bit more difficulty, and its owner (who makes the occasional reference to her difficulties) walks like someone with back problems. That's another reason not to draw out the interview, while she has given so many that she has "the impression I'm putting on an old scratched record." But, she adds later, "I always complain about being called on from near and far - but what if I no longer was?" So she plays the game, polite but undemonstrative.

And then she, who swears by brevity, becomes frankly terse: "Do I regret my experiences in politics? Why no, what a bizarre idea!" She is pessimistic about this "fin-de-siècle," of course. Governments are helpless to deal with unemployment. Populists and demagogues such as Bernard Tapie and Berlusconi "whom I put in the same bag" are on the rise. And then there is the gravest political sin: "the absence of courage, the courage that would help us shake up this old country, and take the risks and make the painful reforms it needs."

American feminists would doubtless see Madame Giroud as a thoroughgoing traitor. She neither likes nor shares their sexual puritanism or their entrenched aggressiveness. Above all, she deplores the increasingly hostile and unhealthy relations between men and women in the United States.

This does not stop her from noting - and regretting, with no illusions - that "politics in France is one of those areas where almost nothing has changed over the last forty years. Here, men continue to see politics as a sacred calling for themselves, and don't let women in. The only ones who have made careers for themselves - Édith Cresson, Simone Veil and myself - did so by virtue of the Prince, and not through the ballot box or a normal career in the ranks of a party. It's very unhealthy."

Françoise Giroud still doesn't think that's the end of the world, or that one should undertake a war of extermination against men. She deplores the situation, period.

And in this vast salon with its sumptuous furnishings, she remembers the story of a political figure, a woman, who once stood at the podium of the National Assembly while the deputies shouted up at her, as if they were watching an exotic dancer, "Take it off!" She brings out her wide, serene smile, but a bit mechanically: "Take it off! Wonderful, no?"

V.
The Canucks and
The Yanks

Discovering the Other Solitude

Spread across two pages of the *Nouvel Observateur*, the Paris intelligentsia's favorite magazine, last September was the striking photo of a 79-year-old colossus with a long white beard, the (left) eye all the more piercing in that the other was hidden by the opaque lens of his glasses. The title of the article was "Visit with a Remarkable Man," an allusion to the French title (*Un Homme Remarquable*) of his most recent novel to appear in that language: *What's Bred in the Bone*. What is most remarkable in all this is that the journalist flew all the way to Toronto to interview the great man, an honor usually reserved for the likes of Kurt Vonnegut or Norman Mailer. Three weeks later the same bearded giant adorned the front page of *Le Monde*'s book supplement, with an admiring text by the American novelist John Irving.

This "singular individual" is Robertson Davies, and he is introduced to us as "the greatest novelist in English-speaking Canada." He had already been highly praised in an earlier issue of the *Nouvel Observateur* by the critic and writer Frédéric Vitoux, who is a power to reckon with on the Paris literary scene: "*What's Bred in the Bone* has a power to enchant that sweeps all before it. It's a magical novel worthy of Nabokov." For *Lire*, Bernard Pivot's magazine, Davies's book "has the sumptuousness and depth of Thomas Mann." This is only a sampling of the feature reviews in prominent publications.

My interest was piqued all the more in that I had never read Robertson Davies, nor heard his name mentioned in Paris. And suddenly he's been declared a great man! What is also intriguing is that at the very same time two other English-Canadian novels were released in Paris: *Swann: A Mystery*, by Carol Shields, and *A Casual Brutality* by Neil Bissoondath, a novelist with Indo-Jamaican roots who writes in English and lives in Quebec.

While she did not receive the royal treatment accorded Robertson Davies, Carol Shields still got a lot of press, including a full page in *L'Express*. Published by Calmann-Lévy, Ms. Shields had the benefit of an efficient publicity department, and "visible" displays in bookstores, already a luxury. As for the Bissoondath, which came out at the end of September with the small but very well regarded Phébus Editions, I saw a stack of them in an airport bookstore, a sure sign of good distribution.

Three English-Canadian novels for September 1992, backed up by good publishers, prominent in the media, available in the bookstores. Then there was *Solomon Gursky Was Here* by Mordecai Richler, successfully launched in the spring by Calmann-Lévy, much talked about in the newspapers ("My Kabbalah in Canada," punned *Libération*). You begin to wonder if, just like that, English-Canadian novelists have become more popular in Paris than their counterparts from Quebec.

This autumn the evidence was clear. Unless I'm mistaken, there was only one Quebec novel in view, Francine Noël's *Nous Avons Tous Découvert l'Amérique*, with Actes Sud. But despite the beautiful design of its books, Actes Sud, which puts out more titles than one might suspect, can only really "defend" its most celebrated authors, such as Nina Berberova and Théodore Monod. Many books, including those from Quebec, are invisible in the bookstores and the media.

All this might have been only a fleeting coincidence. But in fact, if you consult the file recently put together at the Canadian Cultural Centre, you find that at least a dozen English-Canadian writers have been published in Paris in recent years. What is more, most of them have been "well" published, by important houses or influential editors.

For 1991, there is *Lives of the Saints*, the first novel by an Italian-Canadian from Toronto, Nino Ricci. Ricci is published by Denoël, but what is significant is that it's in the new collection of foreign literature edited by Marie-Pierre Bay. Bay is one of the heavyweights in Paris publishing, having edited the *"Cabinet Cosmopolite"* series at Stock - and when she left, took along "her" authors. A protégé of Madame Bay will at the very least be taken seriously in Paris by the critics. And Ricci was highly praised, and at length, in papers as difficult to crack as *Le Canard Enchaîné* and *Le Monde*, where he was allotted half a page.

Also in 1991, the *Éditions de l'Olivier* published *Running in the Family* by the Sri-Lankan-born Canadian, Michael Ondaatje, which was accorded a feature review in *Libération*, and more. As for Mavis Gallant, who has lived in Paris since the 1950s, she has seen most of her work published in Paris, either at the (small) Éditions Tierce, or at Fayard. Last June, *Libération's* book supplement devoted half its space to her.

I won't go on indefinitely. Suffice it to say that Margaret Atwood is with Laffont, Alice Munro with Albin Michel. John Saul has successfully published four novels in ten years, and if he changes publishers it's usually because he follows his editor, Olivier Cohen. It's this same Cohen who has persisted in publishing Robertson Davies for the last ten years. A discreet but influential figure in the Paris book world.

Similarly, a journalist and novelist from Vancouver, L.R. Wright, is being published in the new "prestige" detective series at Le Seuil. It too is in good hands, those of Robert Pépin, well-known for his translations of Vonnegut.

There are a number of different ways you can be published in Paris. You can find yourself with a very large house that does nothing for you: no distribution in the bookstores, no reviews. You can have a devoted publisher, but one too small to get anywhere near the bookstores or the press; for example, the Editions du Félin, who published two novels by Francine d'Amour simultaneously and did the best they could, but to no avail. And finally there is what we might call the inner circle, where you get privileged treatment, including a (real) publisher, a real publicity machine and real distribution in the bookstores.

Most of the above-mentioned English-Canadian novelists have just that. They have good and influential connections, including the publisher Maurice Nadeau and the literary agent Michèle Lapautre, who specializes in Anglo-Saxon literature in Paris.

I'm not sure that Quebec novelists, for the most part, have been as fortunate. Réjean Ducharme, Anne Hébert, Antonine Maillet, doubtless Michel Tremblay, are all part of the charmed circle; Robert Lalonde, Marie-Claire Blais, Jacques Godbout, are treated respectably, but no more.

Asked about this phenomenon, Olivier Cohen or Michèle Lapautre have no ready-made explanation; they appreciate each writer for what he has to offer, without asking themselves whether his qualities are specifically "Canadian." Olivier Cohen, for his part, finds that there are at least three overall trends in this literature: there is the North-American vein that includes, notably, Davies; the classic English tradition (Mavis Gallant, John Saul); and the "post-colonial" wave that gave us Naipaul and Rushdie, but also Ondaatje and Bissoondath. We find the same sort of analysis in feature articles by Paris critics, who compare one novelist to Rushdie, another to Conrad, and yet another to Catherine Mansfield. Which is a way of saying that if English-Canadian literature has been successful in Paris, it's not because it's first and foremost Canadian in any narrow sense, but because it is a participant, in its own way, in this vast nebula of modern Anglo-Saxon literature, where Australians and South Africans happily co-exist.

And that is preferable, apparently, to being identified as a Swiss, Belgian or Quebec novelist. A country cousin, in other words, whom one adores, but who is still provincial.

The Complete Exile

I magine that, for thirty years, a writer of Anne Hébert's stature had been living in Paris and we'd forgotten all about her. An Anne Hébert who had continued to publish in France, honored and respected in literary circles, though without achieving great commercial success. Who in short had become a modern classic, but unremembered on the shores of the St. Lawrence.

Such is the story of Mavis Gallant. But it's more complicated than that. Recognized now in her native land, more or less reconciled with it, she has recently spent a year as writer in residence at the University of Toronto. Her collection of "Canadian" short stories, *Home Truths*, which in 1982 won her the Governor General's Award, is to appear in French with Boréal Editions in Montreal. But this homecoming - still an uneasy one - follows on 30 years of exile. Having settled in Europe and then permanently in Paris, she set foot on Canadian soil only twice between 1950 and 1963. What is more, had she not made her home in Paris she would have followed her star in New York, with the *New Yorker* no less, where over the years, she has published almost a hundred stories. Although her books are now co-published in Canada (and in Great Britain), her loyal publisher is also in New York: Random House. She published nothing in Canada before 1975. That's cutting one's ties in the extreme. And yet Mavis Gallant never became a French citizen or an American writer. "Even if Canada were to disappear, I'd still be a Canadian," she says flatly. One way or another, *Canadianness* is implicit in most of her work - one play, two novels and five collections of stories. There are stories set in Canada itself, during the time of her youth - these are assembled in *Home Truths* - but there are also tales set in Europe whose protagonist is frequently a young English-Canadian (or American) woman. The Canadian malaise is one of the touchstones of her work, a genuine illness that she cannot shake even after 30 years of absence. If Quebec writers have at times been at war with their country, there are few examples of such hostility on the part of a writer toward his or her native land; Ms. Gallant's "home truths," as they apply to (English-speaking) Canada, however civil their expression, are rarely flattering. Whether in her introduction to *Home Truths*, in a long interview accorded *Canadian Fiction Magazine* in 1977, or in conversations for this article, the theme recurs, almost obsessively. Gallant's version: Canadians are totally humorless, have ashen complexions and wear poor quality shoes; though they're not actually illiterate they write little; and when they read fiction they think it all happened "for real." In the Toronto of her childhood, people were "unbearably sad." As for Canadians in London around 1950, they were ashamed of their nationality and tried to pass as British. "Fundamental to the English-Canadian character," she says finally, "is envy and jealousy." I could go on, but it's already clear that the author of *Home Truths* is extremely hard on her country. The judgments she makes - all the while claiming that she does not want to be too critical, "since I no longer live in Canada" - couldn't win her many friends in Toronto or Vancouver. "Don't make me say awful things, I don't want to have problems in Canada," she says.

Reading her prose, one could get the wrong impression. Mavis Gallant is a great stylist. "I write very slowly, I revise a lot, I spend much of my time changing one word, a punctuation mark," she says. Few dramatic effects, little violence or adventure. Finely drawn, her characters inhabit a quiet world, ordinary, almost banal: no heros, no tragic victims. One might almost picture the author as being serene. In fact, beneath an almost icy, almost too perfect surface, the same wounds, the same familiar demons, turn up over and over again. Mavis Gallant's universe is peopled, as if by chance, by refugees, displaced persons who wander from here to there, uncertain of where they belong, who and what they are. There are also - above all, perhaps - young women who are overly naïve, victimized by men who are not really monsters, only egotistical, empty and coarse. There are children whose parents are absent, indifferent to them. There are also young North Americans who are a bit lost in Europe, helpless in the face of an old culture, a cynicism they do not comprehend. Nothing horrible occurs, only disappointments, wounds that heal badly, bewilderment, boredom, anxiety. The brilliance of the style, its soberness, its discretion, can create a misunderstanding. In truth, this universe is not gay, it is not happy. But, as we say when talking of humor, there is in Mavis Gallant a kind of "courteousness born of despair," as though a certain everyday unhappiness were inescapable and it would be pointless and unseemly to dwell on the sordid details. It's no surprise that the two writers she most often rereads are Proust and Chekhov.

You will have guessed that she is hypersensitive, easily hurt by real life, society, men. With only one drug to assuage her pain: writing. When you ask her how many hours she works each day, she is indignant: "But I work all the time, it's not a discipline, it's my life! I've never remarried, I have no children. So there's no question. It's what I think about all day long." There are things she loves: Paris, cities. She's interested - at one time she was passionate about it - in politics. But of course, all that is her raw material. She is indifferent to or bored by everything foreign to literature. She doesn't like the country, or games, she has no sense of ownership. Her exclusive passion is not exempt from a certain misanthropy: "People don't leave each other alone as much as they should. It's important to me that I not be disturbed."

Need I state that to meet Mavis Gallant is not a simple matter? Not just because she's protective of her work schedule and private life, though in a situation like hers where her time is her own, it's important not to let yourself be overwhelmed by all sorts of demands. There is no need for us to get together the very next day. The appointment is put off for two weeks.

No, above all she is extremely wary. On the telephone she sounds a bit exasperated: "Do you read English? Because if not there's no point in our seeing each other. Every time I've given an interview, my words have come back to me all upside down, it made no sense." Where shall we do the interview? "Not where I live. I've decided never to give interviews here any more." After two hours of conversation, sometimes tense, sometimes relaxed: "The next time you'll come to my place," as though I'd just passed an exam. Then, just as she's touching on politics: "I say that, but I don't even know what you're thinking, you could be on the extreme right for all I know." (*Natürlich!* And I also collect Nazi insignia!)

Almost in passing, this admission, spoken as though she were indifferent to what she is saying: "I don't want to play the little orphan girl, but I swear I would not relive my youth for anything in the world." Her father, who died young, would be an enduring absence, but also a focal point for her imagination. He was an artist, a painter. His commitment was absolute, but unfortunately he had little talent. "My memory of that has stayed with me," she says. "I've never doubted my passion for writing, but I've always been afraid not to have talent, or to have it no more." We know almost nothing about her mother, but the little we learn does not put her in a very good light. After living in convents in Montreal, being shunted from one place to another, Mavis found herself in Toronto between the ages of eleven and thirteen, then in New York. Why all this moving about? "For family reasons. My mother had remarried, I reminded her of her past, I was in the way." Ms. Gallant insists that she's already said all there is to say on the subject: "But my biography exists! It's the story of Linnet Muir, this young girl from Montreal." See *Home Truths*, then, if you want to know about her childhood, but you have to be able to pick out fact from fiction.

Her memories of Montreal are on the whole positive ones. But not of Toronto. "In Canada, people are anything but carefree," she says. "The Toronto I knew was like Belfast. The people were preoccupied and morose, provincial. Since then a lot has changed, I like it there, I'm quite happy with the year over there, there's no comparison." The disaffection has not totally disappeared, however: "Even now I see small young women - Toronto journalists -

all the same, little round eyes, short blonde hair, thin, pretty... they scare me. Horrors." Even the English spoken in Toronto displeases her: "People all talk with the same mid-western accent, whereas in Montreal, before the war, we spoke the most attractive English. Before television came along and flattened everything out."

The way out of her Toronto adolescence was New York. Freedom and wonderment. "The young girl who is reborn in New York is me. People smiled at me in the street. For the first time in my life, I heard people laughing in the movie theaters."

In her memory, the Montreal she rediscovered at the age of 18 was just as magical. It was the 1940s. "It was a very gay city, with lots of trees, and cosmopolitan, full of European refugees. I had an apartment in the centre of town, on Mackay Street, opposite what is now that horrible Concordia University. I feel like crying when I see that."

What do you do when you're 18, you want to be a writer, and you already have to earn your living? You knock on the door of a newspaper. In this case it was the *Montreal Standard*, since disappeared. She was told she was too young. She went back when she was 21 and was immediately hired. The editors were young, and from the start she was given important stories. "Aside from the sports reporters who'd learned French in the streets, I was one of the rare really bilingual journalists. So I was very soon given most of the stories in the francophone world: unions, politics, and so on."

The young Mavis Gallant loved politics, which means to say she was a leftist. "I went to cover the workers' strikes, then I went back to the paper and collected money for the strikers. Eventually I was barred from the picket lines. How can I explain? I don't know what your ideas are, I know that today they're rewriting history, making folkloric television series about Duplessis (Quebec's authoritarian premier in the forties and fifties). A Quebec writer I met recently even claimed he brought electricity to Quebec! But in fact those were very hard times. No union freedom. And that Padlock Law[1] that was always used against poor people, never the bourgeois!"

"On the other hand, it's true, I found something fascinating in

Duplessis. It was the old corporatist conservatism (not Fascism as some have said), hand in hand with the big capitalists - and the Church as well, of course! He was far from stupid. He was Salazar. He only read newspapers. He read them and dropped them, one after the other. I remember, he had no refinement. And you had to see how he chewed out the journalists; he wasn't really serious, you felt he worked himself up on purpose. Once he caught sight of me in a press conference. I was young, rather pretty, with long hair. I had thought of proposing to the paper that I do a profile of him - personal, not political. It seems that he agreed but finally it never happened. I'd have liked that! Just for the experience. What a sly man! What a crocodile! He had small eyes, and that fold at the corner of the eye that you see in Germans. What was fascinating was that you knew nothing about his sex life. But his tastes, the way he lived - he drank profusely and then he stopped completely. He didn't like money that much. And I believe his piety was all political."

Mavis Gallant was baptized a Protestant, but what with the trials and tribulations of her childhood, she found herself in a Catholic convent. She cannot talk about Duplessis without thinking of religion: "The Catholicism of that time was so different that you should give it another name. It instilled so much fear in me that it was many years before I could see religious objects as works of art. For me they were symbols of power, cruelty, obscurantism. It's horrible, the masochism that was implanted in little girls, the taste for suffering. That came out of a certain old France. Think of Saint Theresa of Lisieux, that little five-year old girl who accused herself fifty times a day of having committed imaginary sins! I remember those confessionals where an adult man listened quietly to little girls. He'd never have thought of saying, just leave them alone! Even today that seems extraordinary to me. All that's ancient history, it was all swept away at the beginning of the 1960s."

---

1   The law permitted police to padlock any house that was being used to produce or distribute loosely-defined "communist propaganda".

Mavis Gallant mentions - without going into details - that she was married. Not for long, because at 27, she was already divorced. "It doesn't count, it's of no importance," she says. All that remains is the name. What did count were her - difficult? - relationships with men. "Problems between anglophones and francophones didn't exist in 1950 in the newspaper world. We all had fun together, we went to *Brokers* or *Chez Son Père*, we spent time in the bars. The problem that did affect me was the relationship between men and women."

A Press Club was set up, in the British style, for Montreal journalists. The males voted to exclude their female colleagues, and it was a shock. *"They don't like us!"* It was a bitter pill. "They didn't like us! Except of course to chase after us, to ask things of us, or to have someone there in the kitchen at home. And this realization hit me hard, it changed my life."

Of course, if their female colleagues were allowed into the Press Club, "their wives would come too, and that would be a disaster. Their wives lived in Notre Dame de Grace, in Westmount. When there was a party, they put on their little pearls, their little earrings, and they said things like: *You find him funny but he's not like that at home* or *You're not going to tell that old story again.* All that had a big impact on me. At the paper women and men were the best buddies in the world, but if by chance a woman was complimented by a minister, everyone whispered: what's going on between them? I told myself, God can do with me what he will, but I'll never be the little woman, the wifey from the other side of Outremont."

(And her comments on the novelist Anthony Burgess, whom she'd just met at a conference in Angers, did they too stem from her conflictual feelings about men? "He detests short stories and boasts about it. What was he on about? All right, he'd been drinking. But why be so aggressive? He's brilliant and prosperous. He certainly *was* a good-looking man. I think finally I was very disagreeable with him...")

Mavis Gallant was a perfect candidate for expatriation. Almost no family ties, and divorced to boot. "What decided me was the paper's creating a pension fund. I said, if I stay I'm finished, I'll be waiting to retire. That was out of the question. I had to leave before

I was thirty. At the age of twenty-seven I'd already covered everything imaginable on the paper; the rest would be all repetition."

She had always wanted to leave. Why Europe? She was impassioned by the tragic events of the war; fascism, the Nazi camps. And then Europe, for someone who only wanted to be a writer, was culture. And it was far. There was also the Korean War, that threatened to degenerate into a world conflict. On this subject she is eloquent: "If there were another war, I wouldn't want to find myself trapped behind closed borders! I'd have to be outside!"

As though to rule out any possibility of her beating a retreat, she burned her bridges behind her. If she had "always written," she had not yet been published, other than in a mimeographed literary revue of limited distribution put out by the poet Frank Scott. No matter. She began by resigning from the newspaper and letting it be known that she was moving abroad. She was told, "You're crazy. You've never written anything. At least stay here for the time being, and see!" Out of the question. "I couldn't set myself up in Montreal in a room, and live penniless in a city where people knew me. To live without hot water and with no television? They really would have thought I was crazy!" She'd had to give six months notice at the Standard. She used the time to try her luck in New York. From a wicker basket where she'd deposited her manuscripts, she pulled out a story and typed it up. American magazines published short stories, and she'd made a long list of them, with the most prestigious right at the top: the New Yorker. She tried it, not for an instant thinking she had a chance. The mail came back: "This story is too Canadian for us, but if you have something else..." Did she! And the next one was accepted. Suddenly, at the age of 27, Mavis Gallant was admitted into the charmed circle, that of the New York intelligentsia, and there she would remain. "In over thirty years," she says, "they've rejected five stories, and have printed more than eighty. I've changed, I've evolved, but they've followed me."

An acceptance from the *New Yorker* was certainly worth the trip. And so Mavis Gallant turned up in person at the famous offices, where without further ado she was presented with a cheque for $600 dollars! One can imagine the impact of such a sum at the time. "I never dreamed of that. I thought they were going to give me $60." Back in Montreal, even the most skeptical in her circle of friends were impressed; to be published in the New Yorker right off the bat! "I wanted to show people that I wasn't crazy, that I could be a writer. Some got around it by saying it was just beginner's luck, but in most cases it won me a certain respect. But also envy, and something close to hatred; I was a young woman, I'd sent them packing with their pension fund - there was some hostility. I was told, you'll come back with your tail between your legs. To myself I said, we'll see who laughs last."

And so her exile began. In emotional terms, it will have lasted for her almost thirty years. It wasn't until 1979 that she returned for a somewhat extended stay in Canada. She left in 1950, and only set foot on Canadian soil in 1955, then 1963. The experiences were not encouraging. "You still have the same crazy ideas?" she was asked. And from a Canadian diplomat in 1971: "But what are you doing in Paris?"

Her first stop had been London, which was emerging from the war, but still had rationing. "I only stayed a few weeks. The English were sad, tired, ill-humored. And I came from a former colony. They put on American accents to talk to me. I felt like killing them."

The next stop was the right one: Paris. In the course of the next thirty years there would be a few other foreign interludes: Madrid, Italy, the south of France. But Paris would become her adopted city for good. First she lived in a hotel room, then with a *good French family*. She quickly made friends, found the French "anything but boring," the Parisians "no more disagreeable than anyone else." In France they had forgotten the war: "They weren't rebuilding the bridges, they weren't taking care of the communications system, but there was whipped cream." In short, Mavis Gallant found herself a writer, "alone at last," in a country that suited her. And she stayed there. Discreet in the extreme. "Most of my friends are French, or at least European. As they don't read English, many of them don't know my work at all, or even that I'm a writer." Unknown in her native land, unknown in her adopted country. She has lived in the same apartment for twenty years, a kind of refuge overflowing with books and precious objects, where she entertains friends, journalists only rarely, and where, in total peace, she can give herself over to her favorite vice, writing. Remote from time and space. She does the occasional piece of journalism for the newspapers, but she almost never strays far from literature. She remembers having written for her former paper a lengthy profile of Vincent Auriol, French president at the time, and an article on Italy perhaps - but that was long ago. Besides her stories, novels and her play, she will only indulge herself in a bit of criticism. Again, it's the big leagues. When Mavis Gallant talks about a book, it's in a long, reflective article, much revised, highly polished, and for no less than the *New York Review of Books*.

There are two exceptions to her rule. The first was, in 1971, an important introduction for a book, in English, on the Gabrielle Russier affair. A woman who was a victim of society: a schoolteacher in her thirties driven to commit suicide because she was passionately in love with one of her students, a minor at the time. A story typical of a certain type of conservative society, but where Mavis Gallant's own preoccupations are clear to see.

The other exception is a formidable one. For ten years now, she has been working on - and almost completed - a book on the Dreyfus affair. He wasn't a woman, but he was certainly an (isolated) victim of bourgeois French society at the turn of the century: a Jewish officer accused of high treason, convicted in the course of a highly dubious trial, then finally rehabilitated. The affair galvanized France, divided families between the left and the right. It's an affair that seems to go back to the beginnings of time, and on which so much has been written in France. "But all the books are so boring, and it really is the portrait of an age." She says that this will be her first and last ambitious piece of non-fiction. She never imagined that her research into the historical documentation and her interviews with witnesses at one remove would take up so much of her time.

Mavis Gallant in her apartment, between Montparnasse and Saint-Germain-des-Prés. "You know, it's not mine." She makes this clear, in case someone might think she were a property-owner. A rather modest two-room apartment, nothing extravagant, perfectly kept. Friends' paintings on the wall. On a table next to the window, a typewriter - electric. "Many of my French friends only found out by accident that I was a writer," she repeats. And in fact, nothing here gives any hint. It could be anyone's home. Secrecy, always - or discretion at the very least.

What sort of life has she lived here for the last twenty years? I'll never know very much more. The story she gave to *Canadian Fiction Magazine* is dedicated to the painter Jean-Paul Lemieux. "Yes, I met him by chance here in Paris, thirty years ago. I've stayed friends with him and his wife." A pure coincidence, or so it would appear. Ms. Gallant cannot think of a single Quebec or Canadian expatriate artist with whom she has really spent much time. Literary groups? "There have been none since the war." Anglo-American intellectuals? "Oh my God, certainly not!" So, no one in particular: "I'd rather meet a doctor or a right-wing butcher, than writers. Writers are all obsessed with themselves, what can they teach me?" She pauses to think. "You know, most of the time I just write, I stay here. In the evening I see friends, I go to bistros, that's all." Mavis Gallant is not only a full-time writer who lives by her pen, she is the complete writer.

France and Voltaire's "Acres of Snow"

Relations between France and Quebec, as might not be obvious at a glance, are not at all like those between France and the United States, and they stem from an endemic misunderstanding. The French - not all of them, but close enough to it - feel that their affection for Quebec is free of any ulterior motives, while the Québécois - not all, but most of them - on a gut level suspect the French of viewing them as a colony (more developed, of course, than those they maintain in Africa), or as a child abandoned at birth, whom they, the unworthy progenitors, would now shower with gifts - not out of love, but to atone for their past sins.

Twenty years ago - more or less - France was in the midst of discovering Quebec. Put another way, she was emerging from a long period of profound ignorance that had lasted a little over two centuries, ever since Voltaire had applauded Louis XV for surrendering to the British crown those far-off territories of the St. Lawrence Valley that were really no more than "a few acres of snow."

But suddenly something happened, something new (and ephemeral) for France, and something Quebeckers would never have dreamed of: a handful of singers - Gilles Vigneault, Robert Charlebois, Diane Dufresne - became genuine stars, while at the same time a few movies (by Gilles Carle, for the most part) were all the rage among film buffs in the Latin Quarter.

The year 1976 had drawn to an end with a Quebec election, on November 15 - and the surprise victory of René Lévesque's sovereignist Parti Québécois. The entire French media, which the day before had been dismissing the question of Quebec independence in just a few lines and treating it as a phenomenon no less ridiculous than De Gaulle's decade-earlier proclamation of "Vive le Québec libre" (Long live a free Quebec), suddenly converged on this francophone "Belle Province" that seemed bent on secession.

From today's vantage point the times seem prehistoric. Besides, was not France itself still half-way immersed in its post-war period? In those days it was still possible in Paris to have an ancient and fearsome concierge, usually a war widow who was an enthusiastic accomplice of the local police. Whoever spent a night in a hotel had to fill out a form for the authorities, and the next day a huge army of bureaucrats in their kepis went around and collected the thousands of useless documents, to assemble, sort, and store them in mysterious offices where no one, of course, would ever turn up to consult them, because bandits and terrorists had better things to do than to walk the streets with authentic identity papers. Order reigned. Television - 100% public - had only just acquired a third channel, it shut down at 11 P.M., and the TV news was firmly in the hands of the government.

In Paris, where people were still coasting on their memories of May 68, the most popular sport for those under 35 years of age was to chase down apartments that fell under the law of 1948, the famous rent-controlled apartments that sold for a fortune but leased for $50 a month or less. The last word was to find an apartment whose rent was uncontrolled and expensive, but which conformed to the criteria of the "law of '48." A legal process that went by the name of "surface corrigée" (amended status), could eventually obtain a court order for a monthly reduction of 90% of the rent - along with, of course, the reimbursement of the excess rent collected by the owner prior to the judgment.

France was another world where, in Paris at least, it could take up to four years to get your telephone connected. An overseas call was much simpler. That only took from one to three hours, but without your ever knowing in advance when the operator would deign to call you back, so that you had to stand by, next to your phone, and above all not touch the receiver. Among the people you knew in Paris - other than the bourgeois families who had not moved for ages - almost no one had a telephone. On the other hand, the postman brought your mail three times a day, and a letter mailed in the morning sometimes arrived the same evening. Even more impressive was the extravagant and poetic Parisian system of "pneumatiques," now in its last days, with its thousands of kilometers of compressed-air tubes linking all the post offices and permitting delivery of a letter in two or three hours. At that time, there weren't even 500,000 unemployed in the country - which amounted to none at all, really. The mainstream culture was left-leaning, and songs were still poetry set to music. France in those years was much closer to that of the immediate post-war and to a virtually static history of 50 or 100 years, than it was to the France of the 1990s, with its cellular telephones, the Internet, and mass tourism.

For someone arriving from Montreal there was still a faint air of exoticism and adventure in the streets. Aside from the staff of the Canadian Embassy, the Quebec Delegation, and the (numerous) university students on scholarship doing their doctorates, the Québécois in Paris were few and far between, and lived very modestly. There were the survivors of the 1950s: the painter Fernand Leduc, or Gérald Robitaille, who had once been Henry Miller's secretary, and who taught English at Orsay. The actor Gabriel Gascon, despite being well-connected (with Mnouchkine, Gabriel Garran, and others), finally had to throw in the towel and return to Montreal to earn a decent living. Outside of the sacrosanct headquarters of Radio-Canada, there were two or three Québécois journalists, at most. You had the charming feeling, still, that you were in a foreign land.

Today, those who frequent Paris come several times a year,. It's as easy as going back and forth between Montreal and Quebec City. The Paris-Montreal route is one of the least expensive and highest-frequency charter destinations on the market. There is the Internet and modems, of course, and the telephone rates, even the official ones of France-Télécom (which fight a constant battle with low-cost suppliers such as Call-Back), are a quarter the price they were twenty years ago. The sense of distance has practically disappeared, as has the very real sensation of long ago, of departing Montreal, going to foreign shores, and coming back home.

From their side of the Atlantic, the French understanding of Quebec - or of Canada, for both words are used - rather than deepening or becoming more nuanced, has largely been trivialized. There are three main reasons for this: the massive exportation of a number of mass-market cultural "products," starting with pop music; frequent subsidized exchanges organized by the Franco-Québécois Youth Office; and more recently, the explosion of French tourism in Quebec.

Twenty years ago Quebec was still an exotic place, typified by distinctive personalities such as Robert Charlebois and Gilles Vigneault, or by films in which the local idiom and accent had spectators doubled over with laughter. Today - in the field of pop music especially, but that counts, after all - both the French public and the artists' show-business colleagues have the greatest respect for Luc Plamondon, Roch Voisine and Céline Dion. There is no longer anything "exotic" about these people, and they compare well to their French equivalents. Québécois "show-biz," that was first ignored, then condescended to, has become a full-fledged partner or competitor. Gilbert Rozon (whose group is responsible for the wildly successful Just for Laughs comedy festival in Montreal) and his Paris ventures are a good illustration of that, as is, in more restricted theatrical circles, the high-flying European career of Robert Lepage. Through them, and the film *The Decline of the American Empire*, Quebec has emerged as a credible modern society. We might also mention corporations like Bombardier and Québécor, whose names are now part of the familiar economic landscape.

Twenty years ago people would still, on meeting you, talk only of Félix Leclerc, his folk ballads, and his plaintive *Ma Cabane au Canada* (My Canadian Cabin). Some might have heard of *"Charleboué"* (Robert Charlebois). Today it's hard to find a Frenchman who has not been to Quebec, whether on a university exchange trip or on business, or on a comparatively cheap exotic vacation, or who is not either applying to emigrate, or thinking about it, or in touch with a relative who has already settled there. This Frenchman might be a journalist or a teacher, a union activist or an artist, a young student or a pensioner.

This massive drawing together has produced great change, but also some optical illusions. The change is that almost all the French, today, know that Quebec exists and where it is, know that it has singers and television programs, a cinema, and yearnings for national independence. The illusion, except of course for those who have actually lived there, is to think they know Quebec.

Relatively informed people will sooner or later get around to saying: "I adore Quebec cinema! I saw a fantastic film called..."

"The Decline of the American Empire?"

"That's it! And I also loved Carole Laure in *Death of a Lumberjack!*"

These same individuals will likely know the name of Réjean Ducharme if they read a lot, and Robert Lepage if they go to the theater.

Most of the French, who know nothing at all about the Quebec sovereignty movement, will have a vague opinion on the subject, but have no understanding of the political background or the details. Among those who are more or less for it, by far the majority are convinced the English "oppress" the Québécois or prevent them from speaking their language, while for others the sovereignty being demanded is primarily cultural, and for others still it's a simple formality, and no big deal. Those who are against it know even less about it, but are opposed to it on anti-nationalist principle. For them it is as absurd as would be the break-up of Belgium: "All that in the time of Maastricht!!!" Just because the French media turned up in droves in Montreal the week before the last referendum, it doesn't mean the French are really interested in the problem or keep themselvesup to date. For most of them, in any case, the rejection of the referendum by 50.3% for the NO side settled the question once and for all.

More and more Québécois come more and more often to France, know the customs, the prices of apartments and hotels, the best places to shop, stay, eat, and travel. Infinitely more of the French now come to Quebec, have friends there, have eaten smoked meat at Schwartz's delicatessen, have even gone skidooing in the Lac Saint-Jean region. But that doesn't mean there are no more transatlantic misunderstandings.

However frequent the exchanges, the balance of power will always be unequal in the French-speaking world between a thinly-populated and peripheral Quebec, and a France that is ten times more important, and central. Quebec will always need France, its literature and its culture, while the opposite is no more true today than it was yesterday. Molière, Balzac, and numerous other writers are vital to Quebec culture, but neither Anne Hébert nor Michel Tremblay are crucial components of French national culture (on the other hand, in business and industry, the Quebec North-American can in certain instances become a useful partner for French corporations - a case in point is the profitable pairing of GEC-Alsthom with Bombardier - who want to establish themselves in the US market.)

There is another grave misunderstanding that may be traced to the great Franco-Québécois coming-together: the mutual illusion that each really understands the other and that they are much alike. It should be said that the Québécois, by definition, address this question more often than the French, who are perplexed by it only now and then. The French are more concerned with their European neighbours. As one French diplomat put it to me, bluntly, "The question of France is central to Quebec, and that of Quebec marginal to France."

As for the Québécois, they may get the feeling, after five or ten trips, that they truly understand France, its customs and its codes of behavior. As a subterranean part of them is ineluctably French, they are sometimes tempted to see themselves as French, or as having much more in common with them than, for instance, with Americans or English Canadians.

It's true that the Québécois - or rather the French Canadians - are unique in North America, in that they have a well-defined common origin: those 5,000 French men and women who arrived from France in the seventeenth century, and who never left. What is more, in great majority they all came from the West of France (hardly anyone from the Lyon, Burgundy, Midi, Provence or Languedoc regions). As a result of this static and for the most part inviolate homogeneity, that endured for centuries, they are very different from the rest of North America, where the founding Protestant Puritans could at best hope to keep themselves afloat on the surface of an immense melting pot, and to some degree found themselves sucked down into it.

But this very homogeneity is what today sets the Québécois apart from the French, who constitute a complex society where countless warring tribes have to some extent drawn together, while others still confront each other more or less openly. If we are to credit the seductive theories of the demographer Emmanuel Todd, the Québécois form a true community animated from the outset by one cast of mind, while French society remains a battleground, civilized for the most part, but not always.

And so despite the apparent and sometimes troubling resemblances, the lingering Frenchness in Quebec and the Americanization and modernization of France, we mustconclude that the Québécois and the French live on completely different planets.

The French have an obvious problem about money and modernity (which still remain dirty and vulgar); their society is made up more of castes and tribes than social classes defined by money alone. The Québécois are foreign to all that, to the point where they have no idea how unbelievably complex and conflictual French society really is, and how almost everybody distrusts just about everyone who is not part of their family.

The average Frenchman, for his part, will never fully grasp that in Quebec society one is favorably disposed, from the outset, toward someone one doesn't know (as long, of course, as he is Québécois). And that in business or public life people tend to say what they think and to be taken at their word by the opposite party. On the other hand, the deep cynicism of French society - where a priori no one believes anybody, and where public statements are only taken seriously by the naïve few - is a deeply-ingrained reality that will always confound those North-American francophones whose ancestral roots are in Poitou-Charentes.

Give them another twenty years and the Québécois will have come to terms with the fact that they will never really understand the French - no more than those Gallo-Roman Europeans are ever likely to comprehend their provincial cousins from the West who have turned into North Americans.

Céline Dion: The Cinderella of Show-Biz

She's the youngest of fourteen children from a family of modest means, an unlikely point of departure for the rocket-ship rise to fame she has enjoyed. A voice like Barbra Streisand's, and on stage the androgynous silhouette, and at times the moves of Michael Jackson. Her album *Colour of my Love* has made her, to all intents and purposes, an American singer. But Céline Dion was born in a small town outside Montreal, and, not yet thirty, she's made it to the top rank of show business worldwide, right up there with a Mariah Carey or Madonna. Céline Dion is living out a fairy tale; could it be the French-Canadian version of Cinderella?

The starry-eyed girl who not all that long ago was cuddling her 14 dolls and dreaming of a wedding gown, who dressed "cheap" and didn't speak a word of English, has now sold more than 20 million albums, most of them with her last two discs: *Colour of my Love* in English and *D'Eux* in French. In the U.S.A. she received the highest possible honour: to sing the inaugural song at the Atlanta Olympics.

Absolute power, in whatever field, transforms you. With Céline Dion the metamorphosis took place - or was consummated - in one fell swoop, around 1995, when the phenomenal European success of *D'Eux* came hard on the heels of her successful American album. Since 1994, her American triumph had been making itself felt, although the star had not quite transcended her shopgirl past. But at the end of 1995, in her dressing room at Bercy, she

246

has suddenly become, with her sophisticated makeup, hairstyle, and costumes, what she truly is: an international star, who fills 15,000 seat halls in Europe and America at will, who provokes hysterical scenes after her shows, and who leads the life of a star, with all the constraints that entails.

In Paris, the hotel where she stays is a closely kept secret. She takes all her meals in her suite and sleeps ten hours a night. She hardly goes out except to be driven to the theatre. A black colossus with an earphone never leaves her side. When on rare occasions she takes it into her head to go shopping at the Galeries Lafayette, it's in mufti and she wears dark glasses.

Aside from that, her only real pre-occupation is to protect her voice. In her dressing room state-of-the-art humidifiers run constantly, and there are lots of green plants. No one, of course, would be advised to light up a cigarette. It's the same in the hotel suites where she stays - and in a polluted city like Paris she remains prudently cloistered all day long. Even if, with her newly-minted aplomb, she allows herself the luxury of a bit of small-talk with friends and visitors after a show (the state of her voice and its attendant ministrations are inexhaustible subjects of conversation), she spends the rest of her time, until the next evening, perfectly mute. It's a practice common among opera singers.

With Céline Dion, vocal chords are a constant concern, ever since she almost lost her voice for several weeks in 1989 and had to be treated by a New York throat specialist, whom she now views as something of a magician. There was another emergency in October 1995 in Paris, right in the middle of a show. The next evening's performance was cancelled at the last minute, on the advice of another high-ranking specialist.

Famous orchestra conductors, opera singers, and show-biz stars are unbearable divas, as everyone knows. Céline Dion, who is in no way outrageous, who on the contrary is very professional in her work, who does not put on airs in front of the technical crew (many of whom are part of her own family), nevertheless, despite herself, has diva-like obsessions. After all, she must protect the golden voice at all costs. Her 1996-97 schedule includes no fewer than 400 mega-shows around the world, close to an Olympic exploit.

This is an incredible dream-come-true for a girl from a modestly endowed family, who is not American, not even Anglo-Saxon. But it's come about so gradually over 15 years, that the little Montrealer seems almost to take it in stride.

The adventure began in 1981, in the office of a downcast Montreal impresario. René Angelil, with his impressive stature, bald head, Eastern mien, was born in 1944 of a Syrian family. His father had left Damas at the age of 34 to settle in Montreal, where he had married a young Christian Syrian. At home they talked Arabic, English and French. Something of a gambler, Angelil, during the 1960s, was part of a group of yé-yé singers, the Baronets, that disbanded at the beginning of the 70s. It was then that Angelil became an impresario. But in 1981 he had just been deserted by his most successful artist, the large-voiced Quebec pop-idol Ginette Reno, and he was close to bankruptcy.

Then one day there appeared in his office a tall, timid, skinny girl, with crooked teeth, brought there by her mother. Céline Dion was not quite 14 years old. He auditioned her on the spot, using a pen for a microphone. On hearing her voice, he became a believer, and he mortgaged his house to produce a first long-playing record. Two years later his protégé was already a superstar in Quebec - she would sing for Pope Jean-Paul II when he came to visit in 1984. Even if her songs, written by various hands (including the lyricist Eddy Marnay) are very uneven, not to say insignificant, the power and richness of her voice is astonishing. In 1984 she caught the attention of THE French variety host Michel Drucker, who invited her onto his show. In 1989 she won the Eurovision Prize - on behalf of the Swiss - and in France, soon had two or three hits. But René Angelil had his eye on the States, and he applied himself with patience and perseverance: TV, galas, intensive English courses, and finally a 10 million dollar contract with Sony Music in 1991.

From that point on, things moved very fast. Concentrating on solid American standards, Céline recorded *Colour of my Love*. It sold 5 million albums. Never mind if the songs chosen were for the most part standards of no great originality, they suited her voice perfectly, and she became, as a result, a real American pop-singer. And above all, as Angelil says, she reached the highest summits of show-biz, on a level with the five or six biggest sellers of records, all of them Anglo-Saxons. Michael Jackson included.

Another turning point, even more important, came in the spring of 1995 when she recorded an album, part-rock, part-arty, written and composed entirely by Jean-Jacques Goldman, a French singer who gave her the first really beautiful songs of her career. Until then she had cautiously hewed to French standards, including the big hits from the rock opera, Starmania. The single *Pour que tu m'aimes encore* sold a million copies in France. The album *D'eux* broke all records in France, all through Europe, and in Canada. It was such a triumph that under the title *Céline Dion, The French Album*, it sold 150,000 in the United States. That summer, Goldman's songs were heard from Italy to Sweden, and from England to Spain. All of Europe knew the name Céline Dion.

In October 1994, a few evenings (triumphant, let it be said) at the Olympia, the venerable temple of Parisian show-biz, had seemed success enough. That was before Goldman. Her repertoire then was unimaginative, and her persona - a bit androgynous, garbed in elegant kitsch - was equally run-of-the-mill. Just a short year later came the near-riot at Bercy Stadium (16,000 seats), where muscle-bound security guards and black marketeers had already taken up their posts by mid-afternoon. She arrived discreetly in a black limousine, accompanied by her bodyguard and her "Godfather" Angelil, calm as ever, and now her husband of eight months, following a princely marriage at Montreal's Notre-Dame cathedral, complete with a carriage and celebrities of all stripes in attendance. This was the fairy tale's grand finale. Or rather, the end of the first volume. We await the serial's next installment. Made in the USA, of course.

The La Fayette Syndrome

For Americans - especially Americans who are francophile, and therefore cultivated - there are these little irritants about France. For example: French intellectuals consider Jerry Lewis to be a great man. They even think Marilyn Monroe was not only a succulent blonde who sparkled quite nicely in comedies, but an actress of genius. Ask French intellectuals who was the greatest (or least insignificant) American president since F.D. Roosevelt, and they'll tell you right off: Richard Nixon! It's a constant conundrum for subscribers to *The New Yorker* or *The New Republic*: how to explain the appeal to French men and women, who are both cultured and politically aware, of this man with the vulgar demeanor and no less vulgar private conversation, afflicted with an abominable five o'clock shadow, and not very scrupulous, to boot - how to explain the appeal of his style of government? For the most prestigious of French observers, Nixon was the only Chief of State in the last fifty years who was spared the classic American naiveté; in matters of government, and in foreign policy especially, he could boast an admirably European cynicism. And for someone whom many New York intellectuals considered a hooligan, he often made astonishing choices, such as that of a German-born Jewish professor, Henry Kissinger, as National Security advisor and Secretary of State. Nixon, whatever one might say, put an end to the Vietnam War under conditions that were not too disastrous, no mean achievement for a man elected primarily by the conservative right. Nixon reestablished relations with China, which was also not what one might have expected. Better still, from the French point of view: he had the flair to consult André Malraux before meeting Mao! Was that due to the fact - not overlooked in Paris - that this was the only administration during which, at the White House, one drank fine Bordeaux wines every day? The same Frenchmen are not far from believing that, if such a big deal was made of that unfortunate Watergate affair - which, they'll say, didn't amount to a hill of beans - it's perhaps because Nixon was too francophile, a Gaullist, a European, too good in short, to appeal to most Americans. Everyone knows that De Gaulle had the greatest respect for Nixon, while he viewed John F. Kennedy as a "kid." So there you go!

The explanation for all this can be simply put: the French are absolutely certain that they know better than the Americans what is good and worthwhile in America, and even what is best for the Americans themselves. From there to talk of a superiority complex (which, all the psychologists will tell you, only masks an inferiority complex), is but one short step, which we can take without hesitation. The feelings of France vis-à-vis the United States are deeply complex and ambiguous. And they are returned in kind (The same cannot be said about France's relationship with Great Britain, her perennial rival in the Old World).

Most great nations have an intimate or incestuous relationship with the United States that stems quite naturally from the waves of immigrants that founded and developed the country. Americans have the sense, or the illusion, that they're not totally foreign to Poland, or Italy, or Russia, because they have their own Poles, Italians, Russians. And inversely, the same Italians, Poles or Russians, are not really foreigners when they set foot in the United States; they find there a bit of their own land. Before them, there were the Germans, the Scandinavians, the Dutch. Then there were the Japanese or the Chinese. The United States is made up of little bits of countries from all around the world.

The British, in this business, are a special case. Even if their distant progeny sent them packing, economically and politically, a good two centuries ago - not as decisively as when Brazil dropped the Portuguese, but almost - they continue to see themselves as progenitors, creators. They are not the immigrants who have made the United States what it is, but they are the country's creators, and nothing can change that. In Europe, the English continue to be odd man out vis-à-vis "the continent," not only because they are insular, but because they remain confident of their "privileged ties" to the Americans. It's an illusion the Americans are quite prepared to cultivate, more through small signs of deference and complicity than any genuinely equal partnership; the Americans will never, or at least as rarely as possible, put the British in an embarrassing situation on the international scene, and despite the balance of power in its favour, will always avoid humiliating them publicly. To the end of time the British will be saying: we know the United States because we made them. And to the end of time they will be allowed to get away with it. That the offspring sometimes shows bad manners or is not as grateful as he should be, doesn't change the nature of America's roots.

The French, of course, do not really claim paternity where the United States is concerned. Not quite. And yet...

One the one hand, it's true that they don't fit the mold. Americans can't claim that because they have "their own French," they know the French well. There has never been massive French immigration to the United States, because France has never been a country of economic emigration. There were the Huguenots in the seventeenth century, but that was very sporadic, and there were adventurers or buccaneers from time to time. But nothing to compare with the Italian or Irish population movements. There is not this deep familiarity created by immigration. Americans have never known ocean liners filled to the brim with poor Frenchmen knocking at their door, but they have seen all the others. From that point of view, the Frenchman remains a foreigner. But he, unlike the Greeks, the Norwegians, etc., has no half-way house in America to help him get a stronger feel for it. The interpenetration, the incest, just never happened.

On the other hand, France cannot help claiming for itself a unique role in American history. If the US today represents the word's dominant empire, it was preceded in that role, yes, by Great

Britain, who held it from the beginning of the nineteenth century to the first half of the twentieth, but also by France, who reigned supreme from the end of the seventeenth century until the Congress of Vienna in 1815. Neither Great Britain nor France have really become reconciled to the idea that they are not the great universal nations they once were, and in one way or the other, they consider themselves the only true peers of the new world leader, with whom they fully expect to talk on equal terms.

Was not the "real" United States of America borne to the baptismal font by France herself, through the good offices of destiny in the person of La Fayette, and was not the spirit of the Great Revolution of 1789 present when France's Royal Navy came to the aid of the Boston republicans? In short, even if America's founding population originated in England, is not its political heritage the offspring of Enlightenment France? At the close of the twentieth century, consciously or not, the French - whether diplomats, scholars or industrialists - tend to send their WASP opposites the following telepathic message: "Please be so kind as not to treat me like the others, because, unlike them, I have never been your handmaiden nor your servant! Besides, if my ancestor La Fayette had not been around, you would perhaps, who knows, still be a miserable British colony." Of course the message is never made explicit, not even in the minds of the French. But it lurks, nevertheless, somewhere in the subconscious. *Don't forget who made you a republic!*

For the average American, the English must seem just as arrogant and snobbish as the French often do to the Québécois. Great Britain flaunts its ancient history, its culture, its language, which, right or wrong, it considers infinitely more refined. But this British arrogance, whether collective or individual, still has something familial about it. It's the paternalism of the ancestor and of the progenitor, a nepotistic shortcoming that children everywhere tolerate in their parents.

The Frenchman who runs a little restaurant in New York on the other hand, or who, on the other side of the Atlantic, serves (unceremoniously) an American tourist in his Paris bistro or his modest *bar-tabac*, is something worse: he is both arrogant and impenetrable. The American certainly has a few preconceptions where the Gaul is concerned: moustaches, beret, baguette, wine bottle and *crêpes bretonnes* - but deep in his heart he knows he can't figure him out. In Italy there is the comfortable illusion that there is real contact, that he's not out of his depth. After all, "The Italians, we know them, we have our own Italians." Of course, that's more often than not pure fantasy - there's a bit of a gap between an Italian labourer in New Jersey and a Florentine art critic - but it's reassuring all the same. In France he can never say: "They're sometimes perverse, but we don't care, because we also have real Frenchmen back where we come from." The Frenchman (usually Parisian) who allows himself to be at least as arrogant as the British, does not have the extenuating virtue of being a distant relative, nor is he a friend. He's a perfect stranger. And that's annoying. The same generic American can console himself by noting that, unlike the Pole who, thanks to his own wave of immigration, can immediately learn, even if it's at a rudimentary level, the signs and the codes that will tell him where he is - especially in Chicago - the Frenchman in the United States is like a fish out of water. He believes, he claims he has figured it out - "It's the land of freedom and wide-open spaces; Americans are big children" - but of all Europeans, he is the most at a loss in dealing with the real America, where other peoples can at least connect with a small authentic part of themselves and their history.

The Frenchman's haughty independence vis-à-vis the New World, even if it greatly irritates American journalists, diplomats, and government officials, does guarantee him a certain aura of mystery (at least in the eyes of those Americans - cultivated, of course - who deign to inform themselves of his existence), and that's always a comfort: the Gaul is not for turning, even into US dollars, so it is said. At the same time he remains, to a degree, incurably ignorant of that continent that dominates the world, and this has its drawbacks. When the Frenchman claims to understand the United States (and in the land of Descartes it's unthinkable not to claim understanding of any important phenomenon), and when, above all, he sets out to explain it, the results are bound to be disastrous.

AND GOD CREATED THE FRENCH

For the New York intellectual who knows Paris, the Frenchman is above all a bizarre individual who religiously follows episodes of Dallas from the 1980s, still worships Jerry Lewis, and thinks that Edgar Allan Poe is the American nation's greatest poet. If this same Frenchman so often gets hold of the wrong end of the stick where Americans are concerned, it's for the same reason he can convince himself that he is viewing them with perfect objectivity: the incest never transpired.

In short, and in long, what we have here is a profound mutual misunderstanding; it's a rock-solid foundation that ensures a great future together.

VI.
Enduring Enigmas

Enduring Enigmas

The Little Everything and the Big Almost Nothing

This was toward the end of the 1970s at La Coupole, which was then a very trendy café indeed. At a table in the "American" bar, the subject of conversation shifted to a matter of supreme importance: who had the best scheme for finding a beautiful well-located Paris apartment, with the lowest possible rent?[1]

Present was a young woman, rather nice looking, who had already lived in Paris, returned on a regular basis, and knew it well; she worked in fashion and photography. "Oh! I live in the provinces," she replied, when asked about herself. Which was something like saying: *I come from that no man's land beyond the "ring" road around Paris, and I know it's of absolutely no interest.* Her way of being "with it" was to make it clear to all concerned that she was aware of her *provincial* status, like unto a state of non-being. As it happens she came from Royan, but she never did dare speak its name.

How many times in Paris did I not hear the same declaration: "Oh! I - (a vague gesture, to indicate: it's of no interest) I live in the provinces!" The confession would for the most part be made in a modest or resigned register, although occasionally it came out

---

1 The other big subject of conversation: who had the best scheme for not paying parking fines?

rather aggressively, as if to say, "Yes, I live in the provinces, and so what? I know you take me for a hick, and I don't give a damn!"

Which is to protest a bit much.

Many of the French that you meet - native born - attempt to deny or downplay this unvoiced antagonism. But their efforts are futile. Somewhere in his subconscious, the Parisian (one who lives in Paris, whether born there or not) looks on the provincial with disdain or condescension (unless he himself is a provincial unhappy in Paris, yearning only to return from whence he came). And somewhere, also, the provincial is powerless to rid himself of the suppressed animosity he feels toward the Parisian who makes him feel inferior. You can't compare this latent, country-wide hostility to the long-standing antipathies in Yugoslavia that reawakened after the fall of the Communists, but it is undeniably well-entrenched.

Of course, in all Western countries - to speak only of them - there is this tension between the city and the countryside, between small and big cities. But when there are two, three or six large metropolises in a country, each with its own character, the opposition between the centre and the periphery is somewhat defused. However, in France there are only two boxers in the ring; Paris in one corner, and in the other a huge anonymous mass referred to only in negative terms, as *la province*. The provinces are everything that is not at the true centre. When it was decided that France's telephone system had, once again, to be split into two zones to make room for more numbers, the dividing line was not between the North and the South, or the East and the West, but between the Parisian enclave and the huge almost-nothing that is the rest of France. To telephone from Chartres to Montmartre (100 kilometers), you first punch in 16 (just as you now dial 00 for a foreign country), then nine digits. On the other hand, you can phone from Nice to Brest with only eight digits, as though it were a local call. For televised games or telethons, there is usually a number for the provinces and another for the Paris region. For some games, there will be an announcement: "Today it's *the provinces* that are playing." Of course, everyone knows that *la province* is made up of many different "provinces," with their own histories and, often, rivalries. And they even have names. But seen from Paris these identities all merge into one amorphous no-man's-land. This does enable the provinces to shelve, temporarily, their countless ancestral quarrels, and form a common front against the capital.

Many in France, as I said, tend to downplay the seriousness of the conflict. At the beginning of the 1980s I was having lunch with M***, an editor at the newspaper *Libération*, in a cafeteria near the paper. At a certain point a young fellow came up to have a word with him, and then left.

"That's our correspondent in... (a provincial city)," said M***.

"He must be dying to get taken on in Paris!"

"Not on your life! He's got it made down there, he has power, he's somebody!"

Certainly, if you have to live in Lyon or Grenoble, it's better to be the powerful correspondent for *Libé* than to work for the gas company, and perhaps the correspondent in question felt he was so well set up that he had no desire to move. But I can't help wondering how M*** would have reacted - with his oh-so-Parisian career - if he'd been sent back to his home town to be the local correspondent for *Libération*, or bureau chief for a regional paper!

I even heard the noted philosopher and autodidact Jacques Martin address this latent conflict on the radio one Sunday afternoon, while everyone was digesting the sabbath meal. He only raised the issue the better to dismiss it, for his concern every God-given Sunday is to damp down all those hot-spots of civil war that might have flared up during the week. "They say that people in Paris look down on the provinces. It's false, and they are wrong. Everyone in Paris has either come here fairly recently from else-where, or was born in Paris, which is just another province. But Paris belongs to all the citizens of France."

These forceful and reassuring words are not all that far from the truth. All that is missing is this: Paris does indeed belong to a mass of people who were not born there, but they all, in their field, wield supreme power, or seek to do so. The Parisian most hated by the provincial, consciously or not, is not the resident of Montreuil or the twentieth arrondissement, whose cynicism and air of having seen it all is, admittedly, most irritating. The really detestable

Parisian is the one obsessed with power, whether it be in hairdressing, publishing, industry, the civil service, fashion, the art market, television, or retailing. He's the one who has made it and lets you know it, who thinks he's made it and doesn't let you forget it, who is prepared to do anything to make it and thinks of nothing else. But it's also often true that people in positions of power in Paris not only come from the provinces, but boast about it. The complete Parisian needs his provincial roots (which to him are sacred). Of course an old Parisian family, well-established and solid, is nothing to sneer at. But note that Philippe Sollers is quick to identify himself with Bordeaux, Poivre d'Arvor and Jean-Edern Hallier with Brittany, Jean-Michel Jarre with Lyon, and Mitterrand with all of the French hinterland. On the other hand Régis Debray and Bernard-Henri Lévy never make much of their Parisian origins, which confer no particular distinction or seal of approval. The true Parisian is someone who can look you straight in the eye, and say: "I hate Parisianism. I only believe in my roots."

* * *

I find the relationship between Paris and the provinces a mystery that, rather than resolving itself as the years go by, just becomes deeper.

I finally understand, more or less, what the history books say and what French friends trying to teach me about their country have been telling me for a long time: the saga of Parisian centralism harks back uninterrupted to the ninth century A.D., and that all the great men and key events in French history have contributed to it. Louis XI, Henri IV, Richelieu, Louis XIV, the French Revolution (Jacobin version), Bonaparte, Jules Ferry, De Gaulle, and I'm sure there are more. Everything has always worked in favor of centralism; the obsession with national unity and the dread of regional peculiarities has done the rest. All that seems logical and understandable.

What I find mysterious is not so much this heritage, but its immutability and the fact that all the French find it perfectly normal, as if to say: that's the way it's always been, and it's not about to change.

Aside from Great Britain, nowhere in Europe is centralization as absolute as in France. An Italian journalist can make a brilliant career in Milan or even Turin. In Spain, Barcelona keeps pace with Madrid in almost every area, be it political, economic or cultural. Germany has three, four, five capitals.

France, amazingly, is unique in that no *national* enterprise may be imagined or undertaken outside Paris. By the same token, everything done in the provinces is destined to remain local or regional (whether in politics, banking, industry, journalism or publishing) - unless it is a satellite-activity guided by remote control from the capital, such as the decentralized theatre, whose productions are for the most part directed by eminences from Paris. One can, in certain fields, be a celebrity while living in the provinces; but it is Paris that has sanctified this celebrity.

This is most obvious in the world of the press, where any daily published in Paris is considered national, whereas very important papers such as *Ouest-France* (with the largest circulation in the country, 700,000) or *Les Dernières Nouvelles d'Alsace*, will always be looked on as regional - prosperous and profitable certainly, but relegated to a subsidiary role. Their opinions are of no interest to the capital, and many push their masochism so far as to pay Parisian writers to send them certified dispatches on what is transpiring in the real world.

Taking a quick look around, I see three exceptions to this rule. Or rather two and a half. The first is Michelin, the extremely successful multinational that first saw the light of day in Clermont-Ferrand and stayed there even when it was no longer a regional enterprise. The second is the establishment in Toulouse of a true European centre for the aeronautics industry. That may seem banal but it is in fact unusual, and these are the only instances where a career may be made in France outside the capital. (Even in sectors that are inherently decentralized, such as medicine and universities, it's clear that most of the stars and top guns are based in Paris).

The half-exception, a modest one but even more revolutionary, is the publishing company Actes-Sud in Arles, which was founded, it is true, by a Belgian with Parisian connections, whose roots were not entirely restricted to the south of France. His publishing house, which is very well regarded in Paris, just happens to have its press office there, and is more like a Parisian business that has chosen to locate in the provinces on a whim. But it's still a worthy effort, unprecedented in this quintessentially Parisian area of activity, and to think that no ministerial directive or blackmail by government grant forced Hubert Nyssen to set up shop in Arles! Unheard of!

Good Parisian society goes through the motions, in the media and the salons, of showing the greatest respect for what's going on in the provinces. "Things are on the move!" "Now there are *oodles* of entrepreneurs and dynamic, creative people!" "From here on in, that's where it's going to be happening!"

The truth is, no one with ambition wants to stay there or go there (except on vacation) and in almost every field you can think of, Paris is the one and only goal: "Onward, to Paris!" is still a stirring cry. By the same token, to be relegated to the provinces remains a ghastly fate unless it be for a short time only, a fleeting phase in a well-designed career plan.

In the provinces you can find quality of life, comfort, a good environment in which to raise a family; there is money and there are sometimes even fortunes to be made. Everything is there, except what counts: real power. The mayor of a big city is a powerful man, but this power leads nowhere unless it is paired with a national career to which it contributes. A good mayor is someone who is also a well-established member of the National Assembly who has real political influence within a major political party, and who in time will get his hands on a desirable ministry. The local political organizations and their electorate almost always choose, not local figures committed to their community, but those who are based in Paris. They do so out of respect for real power, and as a tactical move, on the assumption that a powerful representative in Paris will bring them more benefits, even if they only see him three hours a week on the fly. For that matter why go half-way, why not do like Bordeaux, and vote in the sitting Prime Minister! Ah, if only there weren't that rule (or is it only a custom?) that prevents the President of the Republic from being first magistrate of a commune! Wouldn't he be the best possible choice to lobby the powers-that-be on behalf of electors lost deep in the provinces?

Sometimes I imagine that things had evolved otherwise. That Lyon had become an important financial center for Europe, where you could find the head office of at least one great French bank. That Marseille were the equal of Barcelona. That Bordeaux or Toulouse would have one great national newspaper of record. That one great publishing house and the most prestigious university in the country would be flourishing outside of Paris.

But it's probably easier to imagine chickens having teeth than any inversion of the relationship between Paris and the provinces in France, for the simple reason that the French themselves see the situation as normal, predestined and irreversible.

One of the best illustrations of this is a story that appeared in *L'Expansion* in 1994. It concerned the moving of the École Nationale d'Administration (the National Management School) to Strasbourg. The decision had been made in 1991 by the impetuous Édith Cresson who, wanting to shake things up, had decided to strike at the heart of Parisian power and republican meritocracy. The ENA, whose graduates make up half the ministerial staffs, was to be banished from Paris, relocated in the provinces. This provoked a huge outcry, and even a street demonstration on the part of the elite-to-be.

Three years later, a miracle! The revolution's promises have been kept, and the ENA's headquarters are to be transferred to the Commanderie Saint-Jean, a stone's throw from the German border. The cost: 147 million francs for construction, plus an annual increase in the operating budget of 6 million francs. There's just one small catch. The expenses are designed, essentially, to hide the fact that even if ENA's address has changed, future students will not have to leave Paris, other than for the odd Alsatian escapade. Out of 26 months at school they'll be spending seven in Strasbourg. That comes down to some boring return trips on the train and a few nights in a hotel. The ENA is now in Strasbourg without ever having left Paris. What does it matter if it's all a very expensive conjuring act? The French state has shown the world how much it cares about decentralization and regional development. And in so doing it has put into practice the time-honoured teaching of Prince Salina in Lampedusa's *The Leopard*: "We must change everything so that nothing will change."

When the South Takes Over the North

The other pivotal mystery to which I am drawn concerns the geographical location of France. If it cannot, alas, be everywhere at once, is it in the north or the south?

I agree that every country has its north and its south, that Italy has an Austro-Swiss north, and Germany a southern Bavaria that's Catholic beyond belief. South America goes so far as to boast, in Argentina and Chili, a north that flourishes in the south. Everything is relative in this world.

But in Europe, the distinction between south and north is also extremely precise. By general agreement, countries have been placed on one side or the other of an imaginary line, depending on whether or not they border on that utterly southern sea which is the Mediterranean.[2] The north includes Great Britain, Germany, Poland, Belgium and even Austria and Switzerland. In the south are Spain, Portugal and Italy. All this is indisputable. And France is part of the second group.

But there is a problem here, and there is something murky and ambiguous in the way France is viewed by others. American travellers, for example, place it in the south, confuse Paris with

---

2   This line of demarcation is so critical that is cuts the peaceful department of Corrèze in two: at Brive, where the climate and the speech patterns are Mediterranean, no one wants to have anything to do with the northerners of Tulle and Ussel. The creation of a new department, a project dear to the heart of Brive's former strongman, Jean Charbonnel, is still a very lively issue.

Rome or Nice, and are always astonished to discover that its grey and rainy climate resembles that of London. The Germans and the British, more careful observers, concede that France is a special case but still see it as part of the Mediterranean group.

The Italians also have a troubled view of France. The French, in their opinion, are Latins like themselves, but not quite normal. They are always ill-humored, and tend to be full of themselves. They are Latins with swelled heads, but for no good reason. "Besides," Umberto Eco confessed to me, "when we Italians think of the north, it's Germany that comes to mind." In other words, France can't be taken very seriously as a northern country. On the other hand, even if he declares himself southern, a Frenchman often betrays the heaviness of spirit that is associated with nordic mists. An Italian intellectual who lived in Paris, on spotting a heavy-set French male complete with moustache, exclaimed, "He's so Gallic!" Translation: he can't be Mediterranean. Trying to be everything at once, does France end up being nothing specific? Italians would be inclined to say so, but only when they're in a bad mood, which is rare.

Let's settle for a more neutral observation: in France two elements as contrary as fire and water co-exist, as though the country were half German and half Italian.

Its history, demography and geography all point toward France being a northern country. Its national unity was forged around Paris, far to the north, at the same latitude as Frankfurt or Krakow. For over a thousand years the country's political and economic life has been controlled by the north. As the linguist Henriette Walter explains in her appealing book *Le Français Dans Tous les Sens* (French in Every Sense), the principal founders of the country were the Franks, a Germanic tribe that moved in, settled north of the Loire, and adopted Latin. But *their* Latin was spoken in the German manner, that is, so strongly accented that eventually the Latin endings disappeared. This was the *langue d'oïl*, to be distinguished from the *langues d'oc*, which, in various forms, conserved these endings, as did other Latin languages such as Italian, Spanish, and so on. To this day, pronunciations in the south of France are colored by vestiges of these Latin endings. But

French as it is spoken and taught sounds at least as Nordic as it does Latin. The *langue d'oïl* that prevailed is a northern language. Geographically speaking, the strictly Mediterranean part of France is relatively marginal, representing only two regions out of twenty-two. Certainly, there are a number of intermediate zones that are difficult to slot once and for all on one side or the other: Auvergne, Aquitaine, Rhône-Alpes, etc. On the other hand, from Brittany through to Alsace-Lorraine, and in the Paris Basin, we are in the heart of northern Europe.

And so all indications are that France ought to belong to the same club as Great Britain and Germany.

But the exact opposite has happened. The Mediterranean spirit has, if I may say so, totally colonized the north, and imposed its rules and its codes on a population to which they were once quite foreign. It has even conquered the capital and the world of politics. It has often been pointed out that Paris is governed by the laws of the clan and the Mediterranean.

Just think for a moment of the biblical simplicity of political life in Germany or Great Britain; there one finds an unwavering predilection for stability and consensus. That England's two-party system has endured for so long cannot entirely be attributed to its first-past-the-post voting procedure. Germany's electoral system is largely proportional, but ever since the war it has sustained a perfectly stable political life organized around three large political parties. They were joined eventually by the Greens, but these are sober and responsible Greens, ready to play their part as a social-democratic government party. In England, political crises are rare. By the time a palace revolution brought down Margaret Thatcher in 1991, she had reigned supreme for ten years. And in Germany, even the fall of the Berlin Wall and the immense undertaking of reunification have not managed to destabilize political or economic life.[3]

---

3   There are bands of young Neo-Nazis, especially in the East, but the extreme right doesn't draw even one percent of the votes at legislative elections.

Just to mention these two Nordic examples makes it very clear: French political life is essentially Mediterranean, as the polemicist Jean-François Revel has often claimed, especially where its scandals are concerned. It is even rather Italian. What could be closer to the Italian model than the functioning of the Fourth Republic, with its constant crises, its parade of governments, the repeated foundering of its alliances, followed by the same old deals being struck? There are still respected observers in France ready to defend the Fourth Republic, on the grounds that it at least allowed a variety of views to be heard (and to thrive). Had it not been for the Algerian tragedy, the political class would even now be savoring the pleasures of government by assembly; the authoritarian northerner De Gaulle would never have been returned to power, and the French would never have tolerated such a restrictive constitution, with its majority ballot that was anathema in political circles and to a large part of the electorate.

The French propensity for internecine quarrels and perpetual division has been attributed to the country's Gallic heritage (doubtless to underline the fact that this is a national trait, unique in the world). One might, however, see it simply as a variant of the Mediterranean model, dominated as it is by its countless clans and their differences: left against right, Catholics against the laity, south against north, merchants against bureaucrats, village against village, and so on. Despite the constitutional corset imposed by De Gaulle, French politics is still shot through with constant turbulence. A government's tenure has less in common with a quietly flowing river than with a Renaissance drama; its motto is ever "Dear God, protect me from my friends, I'll take care of my enemies." Shifts from right- to left-wing governments are experienced as national crises. Three and a half major parties dominate the political landscape:[4] of these, the Communist Party and the right-wing RPR (Rassemblement pour la République) are

---

4   But during the presidential elections for 1995, their four candidates barely totalled 50 percent of the vote on the first ballot, half the electorate opting for marginal candidates.

relatively homogeneous, but the UDF (Union pour la Démocratie Française) and the Socialist Party are hotbeds of conspiracy and betrayal. There are ten Orleanist or centrist factions on the right, and another ten clans within the Socialist Party. French political life is an amazing theatrical spectacle where, as the Florentine master of intrigue François Mitterrand once said, "knives are always seeking backs." More prosaically, Bernard Tapie has been quoted as saying that the ABCs of politics in Marseilles consist in firing on one's own troops. Although the attempt is made in Parisian political circles to disassociate oneself from such practices, in fact things go on in much the same way. How to explain to a simple North American (or even Scandinavian) that in 1981 the Communist Party's first priority was to prevent Mitterrand and the left from winning the presidential election, while Chirac's primary goal was to guarantee the defeat of Giscard d'Estaing? When you tell the story around the dinner table in northern countries with their Anglo-Saxon-Protestant traditions, people think you are exaggerating.

Everything transpires as though France - and above all Paris, which is the capital and a microcosm - had two contradictory souls. There is the dominant one, the Mediterranean, and the secondary one, with its northern ties. Sometimes the latter temporarily gets the upper hand - and De Gaulle returns to power. But the two souls never meld to make one whole; Paris remains a field of permanent combat. In an interview published in *Le Monde* on August 25, 1995, the Mexican man-of-the-world Carlos Fuentes gave his Hispanicist view of this age-long duel: "for us Latin-Americans, France has always been a point of equilibrium between the reactionary Hispanic south of the Inquisition, and the cold and materialist north." We can find instances of this duality on all sides, or simply remind ourselves that "a Frenchman is an Italian in a bad mood."

I will resist embarking on an extended discussion of amorous behavior and the relations between men and women. Here French society offers what at first glance seems a very Italian spectacle, where provocativeness and seductive play occupy centre stage. At the same time, Fuentes' nordic "materialism" neutralizes the

LOUIS-BERNARD ROBITAILLE

conservatism (or conformism) native to Italy and the Mediterranean. The explosive Parisian cocktail that results brings with it a
devilish boldness unknown in northern countries, and a moral
liberalism impossible to find in the south. Is this an antechamber
of Paradise buffeted by contrary winds, or the point of contact
between two zones that are irreconcilable?

Pockets of Resistance — Schifres' Law —

A True Question Whose Application Cannot Be Found

There are days when France finds North America very strange. Or would have good reason to do so.

Anglo-Saxon countries tend to be harsh in their assessment of French justice. I myself have trouble getting used to the fact that in France examining magistrates - with the approval of their superiors - systematically resort to preventive detention in an effort to make a defendant "crack," and to get a confession. I am told: yes, but the prisoners are generally guilty, and in the long run they admit to their crime. But in that case, why not just bring back the rack?

I am convinced that in major criminal cases, the French system is more likely to produce a judicial error than the Anglo-Saxon practice, which is far more favorable to the accused (under normal circumstances). But if we make the effort for a moment to step back from our own cultural history, and to look down from on high at both French and Anglo-Saxon justice, we may very well come to the conclusion that more often than not, all justice systems arrive at different but equally surprising results when faced with similar situations.

On July 22, 1983, at Saint-Canut north of Montreal, a lawyer in her forties was arrested and accused of murdering her co-tenant and lover, Rodolphe. The day before, she had engaged the services of some sturdy men to carry a freezer out of her house and bury it at the back of her garden. Intrigued by the request, but also by the weight of the freezer, the movers talked, and the police showed up on the scene. They found Rodolphe's body, whose death-be-fore-freezing dated from July 13. One arm had been cut off by an electric saw. The lawyer explained that yes, she had wanted to leave Rodolphe, who was a gambler, and they had an argument early on the evening of the 13th. Then the lawyer, who was upset, went off in her car and parked under a street lamp for two hours, on a deserted corner. When she came back she found that Rodolphe had been killed. In a state of panic, she began to carve him up with the electric saw. Then, in desperation, she stuffed him - with one arm lopped off - in the freezer (which she had ordered from a department store on July 6), before having him buried in her garden.

All that was a large order for just one accused. During her first trial, which began in October, it was decided that there was reasonable doubt as to her guilt and she was acquitted of murder. However, since Anglo-Saxon justice is most fastidious, there was a new trial in March 1984, and the lawyer, who was found guilty of "desecrating a corpse," was sentenced to four years in prison. In March 1985 she was freed for good.

Had she known the details of this affair, a certain Simone Weber - or Mamy Nova, as she was called by the prison guards - would have had good reason to complain that she had been treated unfairly. Under similar circumstances she had performed much better, had in any case presented a stronger defence than our lawyer from Quebec, but she had been less well rewarded for her efforts. Simone, who was well into her fifties, also had an incon-venient lover. One day he disappeared. That very evening, neigh-bors heard Simone working noisily in her apartment; a chain saw, after all, makes for a lot of decibels. Then, very late, they saw her carry out several garbage bags. Finally, they heard her cleaning her apartment, as though spring had just arrived in the middle of the night.

The lover's automobile and other clues seemed to rule out the thesis of a simple disappearance. But there was no sign of a body! Or, rather, there was: a torso floating in a pond, cut up by a saw, but impossible to identify. The *corpus delicti* left much to be desired. Nevertheless, Simone Weber was condemned to twenty years in prison. In its timeless wisdom French justice concluded that no sensible person could really entertain any other hypothesis than that of guilt with premeditation. But the spiriting away of the body was so complete that it did raise tiny doubts, and these worked in Simone Weber's favor. She got twenty years, instead of life.

*   *   *

There are unbridgeable gaps in communication between France and the New World.

A priori, a North-American intellectual looks upon France as being refined and civilized. And suddenly he comes up against this damnably troubling bit of data: if France is the promised land of literature, it is also home to seven million dogs, including 700,000 German Shepherds trained to behave in restaurants and taxis. Is this canine mania a sign of nostalgia for a rural France that is being gobbled up? If the dog is there can hunting be far behind, and the CB and the horses, and finally what the French call *le beauf* (an abbreviation of *beau-frère*, or brother-in-law), your narrowly conformist ordinary Frenchman who is thick on the ground in hinterland bistros, but scarce in big city centres.

Ought we to see it as simply an anthropological enigma, or should we look further? If we choose to do so, we have to devote some thought to what François Furet has delicately called "the shortfall in military grandeur in France since 1815." Might the French be ardent hunters but unfit for war? Might they have traded in war for hunting? Whatever the case, where warfare is concerned, the French boast a generous storehouse of traditions and fireside tales, but for a century and a half they've done almost as poorly in the field as the Italians. And you have to at least give the Italians this, that if they have no pretensions on the battlefield, they can fall back from time to time on great performances in the Olympics. Italy, frivolous and carefree as it may seem, consistently comes in fourth or fifth in the Olympic Games, just behind the giants: Russia, the United States, Germany, and China. And without any fuss. And look how it excels in soccer, when it comes time for the world championships! France - another mystery - always comes up short, whether in summer or winter. It has few big stars, and they're always delicate. When they have to win they choke, fall, suffer a sprain, and in at least one instance, turn up late for the start of the competition. Were it not for the occasional horse-riding and fencing event we would almost never hear the Marseillaise at the Games.

Now France does have champions of its own, even if she almost always seems to fall on her face in soccer or tennis championships. But these are bizarre individuals who pit themselves only against... themselves, and destiny. They row or swim across oceans, or walk an iron tight-rope between the two towers of New York's World Trade Center. Clearly, the French would rather contend with destiny and the forces of nature than indulge in a trivial competition, which makes them nervous.

* * *

A foreigner, be he settled in France or just passing through, has many good reasons to be puzzled. Why is France so unmusical (compared to Germany and Italy, in particular)? How to account for the double flashing of headlights (a national custom) to warn of a police ambush not far off? Poujadism? The spirit of the Resistance in a different guise? The anarchist or the *beauf* expressing himself?

All these matters add up, more or less, to a book - at least I hope so. It doesn't come close, of course, to being THE book on France. But in any case, is such a book not a mirage?

Whenever I show a few pages of what I've written to friends or volunteers, one of them invariably says, "But you're only talking about Paris, and not the provinces!", while another one adds, "You're missing the point if you don't *really* talk about women!"

And so on. I'm overwhelmed both by my own inadequacy and the scope of the task they would like to assign me. A book on the provinces would have to fill several dozen tomes, say 36,000 by the time one was through. Look at what happened to Peter Mayle's modest attempt to take every hackneyed cliché about

Provence and apply them all to a little corner of the Lubéron: this limited enterprise mushroomed into two whole books and three million copies sold around the world. How many volumes would one need just to close in on the subject of women and begin to tackle that problem head-on? Five tomes, ten tomes, a thousand? The women of Paris alone would set the author meandering, lost, through salons, mazes, and assorted boudoirs, before he could even hope to deal with the sad and bored *bourgeoise* from Bordeaux, the beauty from Arles, the ecologist from Alsace, the lady from the Auvergne who once was young, the professional in the doorway at the Porte Saint-Denis. No one lifetime would suffice.

Given this rich and teeming canvas, any normal person would beat a prudent retreat. One can focus on a few details from the painting, a few pieces from the puzzle, venture a few comparisons between this and that. But no sane man can do much more.

There is no shame in that. When we look at the extremely scattered bibliography on the subject of France, there is only one modest conclusion that can be drawn: those closest to the truth are those who have said the least. In this regard, recent years have seen the emergence of a new master: Alain Schifres, who, having done his scales with *Les Parisiens* (The Parisians), has now produced his masterpiece, *Les Hexagons* (the hexagon being shorthand, of course, for France).

Between the receding past and the modern world that is approaching still, between Louis XI and Charles the Bold, between the beer drinkers of the north and the wine drinkers of the south, Schifres, in a stroke of genius, has found the common denominator, as empty as it is irrefutable: *Hexagonia*, a geometric territory unique in the world, and inhabited by *Hexagons*. They are a hominid species constantly torn between contraries, and Schifres places them somewhere between *the man of the colonies* and *the man of Maastricht*, between the Basque beret and the smart card.

Having set his stage in masterful fashion, Schifres can find room on it for the infinitely small: the (kilometric) milepost that in the Republic, has replaced the Breton wayside cross; the standard paper size of 21 x 29.7 centimetres, that has paradoxically come to prevail in a profoundly Cartesian country. This enables him to deduce and to proclaim, in passing, this second law: Hexagonia is intrinsically dialectical, without knowing it. Everything has its flip side and its opposite, and all contraries come in pairs. "We foster mental symmetry. We love the metaphor of a dual France. Unlike those countries where there is only one instance of a few things, we have two varieties of just about everything." In France, as in the good old days of Mao, the One divides without exception into two opposites: the south and the north, cooking with butter and cooking with oil, the worker and the peasant, the Montagnard and the Girondist, the innate and the acquired, the literary type and the math whiz. Whatever the subject of national concern: the words of the Marseillaise, spelling reform, a knock-out or a draw shot in pétanque, France invariably and spontaneously splits into two opposing camps of relatively equal size. Each Hexagon is himself inwardly divided by a sort of frontier across which opposites confront each other: behind the anarchist lurks the advocate of order, and the Republican likes to be governed by monarchical figures. Although at first glance he looks wild and woolly, even the Marquis de Sade has a penchant for order: "With Sade, hardly do you begin to relax," notes Schifres, "when you have to fall into line, and make a careful arrangement of fat women and nubile girls, incestuous couples and well-endowed footmen. After a while the orgy begins to look like a multi-tiered wedding cake." Long before it was socially fractured, France was inwardly split in the extreme.

Alain Schifres has laid the groundwork for a theory to explain much that remains obscure, but of course it is only a beginning.

Take for example that subject of subjects - and we will conclude with this - food. Why is France, along with China, THE land of gastronomy and fine cuisine, complex, inexhaustible and sumptuous. Because its location and climate are ideal, says a friend from Italy, itself a country whose food on a day-to-day basis is some of the best in the world, without having the same sophistication. Yes, but does gastronomy not flourish primarily in the north of France, and would not then Germany have the same potential? And what of Italy itself?

Seated in his spartan office at *L'Express*, Alain Schifres is not discomfited by my question, which he knows is crucial. One feels that he has given the problem a lot of thought, at least as much as Clausewitz in front of his survey maps and old battle plans. However stripped-down it may be, he has his analytical grid. He also knows, as a French new-philosopher who has been through the wars, that the *real* answer to this question is for the moment beyond our ken. So he will only supplement the notion of geography with this tentative political consideration: "The French monarchy, beginning with Louis XIV, developed a fine court cuisine for political and diplomatic ends. After the French Revolution, all these fine chefs found themselves out on the streets of Paris, and they ended up opening their own restaurants." That was the beginning, I suppose, of a restaurant like the Grand Véfour. Doctor Schifres knows perfectly well that his answer doesn't tell the whole story, and another question comes immediately to mind: why, then, was the French monarchy so attracted to great cuisine, and not the countless German or Italian courts (not to mention, oh horrors! the British!). Any answer to this question will only raise another.

As Bernard-Henri Lévy would say, one day at the very least we must devise a theory to explain why we have failed to produce THE definitive book on France. Unless this is a false question. Or unless, as everything is dialectic, it is a true problem impossible to formulate, so that even when we find what seems to be a true solution, we don't know what to do with it or how to express it because at that very moment we realize that we've lost sight of the damnable question. You can go to the highest authority and consult the most powerful computer of the moment on the matter, and it will be sure to reply, in Microsoft language (our only means of communication at this turn-of-the-millennium): "Cannot open the document 'France.' The application that created this document is in use or cannot be found."

About the author

Louis-Bernard Robitaille has been an intimate observer of Paris and of French society since the mid-sixties, first as a budding author and now, for over twenty years, as correspondent for the Montréal daily newspaper *La Presse* and bi-weekly newsmagazine *L'Actualité*. He has interviewed Catherine Deneuve and Isabelle Adjani, François Mitterrand and Jacques Chirac, newspaper vendors from the Place de la Bastille and five star media moguls, and visited EuroDisneyland three times. He is at home in the bloodthirsty parisian literary jungles where people have been known to kill for a bad review, in the salons of the Upper Crust, and in the working-class bars of the nineteenth *arrondissement*. This is his fourth book, and the first translated into English.